The Liberals and J. Edgar Hoover

William W. Keller

The Liberals
and J. Edgar Hoover

Rise and Fall of a Domestic Intelligence State

Princeton University Press

PRINCETON, NEW JERSEY

Copyright © 1989 by Princeton University Press
Published by Princeton University Press
41 William Street, Princeton, New Jersey 08540
In the United Kingdom: Princeton University Press
Guildford, Surrey

Library of Congress Cataloging-in-Publication Data

Keller, William Walton, 1950–
The liberals and J. Edgar Hoover: rise and fall of a domestic
intelligence state / William Walton Keller II.
p.   cm.
Bibliography: p.
Includes index.
ISBN 0–691–07793–2 (alk. paper)
1. Anti–communist movements—United States—History—
20th century. 2. Liberalism—United States—History—20th
century. 3. Hoover, J. Edgar (John Edgar), 1895–1972.
4. United States—Politics and government—1945–
5. United States. Federal Bureau of Investigation.
6. Internal security—United States—History—20th century.
I. Title.
E743.5.K35 1989
323.1′73—dc19   88–17828
                                                      CIP

This book has been composed in Sabon

Clothbound editions of Princeton University Press books are
printed on acid-free paper, and binding materials are chosen
for strength and durability. Paperbacks, although satisfactory
for personal collections, are not usually suitable for library
rebinding

Printed in the United States of America
by Princeton University Press, Princeton, New Jersey

For LONNA

Contents

Preface

ANY AUTHOR who writes critically about national security is likely to encounter a variety of disparaging comments and occasional admonitions from colleagues, teachers, and professionals within the intelligence community. I was warned that my work would be outside the mainstream of political and historical research, and that I would encounter hostility from potential sources.

My orienting perspective is that we have only begun to cut through the ideological moorings of the national security state, and that there is much to be accomplished by scholars and journalists who can dispassionately evaluate restrictions and diminutions of the rights of persons that are carried out in the name of collective national interests. There is, for example, a great deal of work that needs to be done on the system of classification that so many government agencies have imposed on documentation and distribution of information describing official government business. In a related area, no definite standard or policy defines the legitimate limits of covert intelligence activity, either domestically or in the area of relations with foreign nations. There has always been a need for secrecy in delicate matters of state. But the thoroughgoing institutionalization of official secrecy on a grand scale is an invention of the post–World War II era. Most observers of public policy have accepted it without considering the profound implications that too much official secrecy and national security hold for the future viability of democratic and republican forms of governance.

I was extremely fortunate to have friends and teachers who shared my perspective and supported my work from the outset. Ted Lowi provided constant intellectual resources, adding to the scope and depth of the project at every stage. Martin Shefter was a relentless and good-natured critic. Peter Katzenstein and Sidney Tarrow made many useful suggestions. John Elliff reviewed early drafts of the manuscript. His practical knowledge of domestic security intelligence policy informs this work at many points. Edward Jay Epstein also added important insights. Peter Sharfman and Lou Pauly each offered useful criticisms.

The official historian of the FBI, Susan Rosenfeld Falb, and the staff of the FOIA/PA reading room at the J. Edgar Hoover Building in Washington helped me gain access to important documents. Charles South

ix

and Steven Tilley of the National Archives and Senate historian Dick Baker provided important leads. Page Putnam Miller of the National Coordinating Council of the Historical Sciences was the source of several significant contacts.

The research for this book would not have been possible without the capable assistance of the reference staff of Olin Library at Cornell University. The staff of the Chicago Historical Society searched the Paul Douglas Papers for me and located the passages I needed. The Herbert H. Lehman Suite and Papers of Butler Library at Columbia University is among the best organized and most accessible collections to be found.

The Minnesota State Historical Society and the Hubert Humphrey Family Advisory Committee granted access to the Hubert H. Humphrey Papers, and sent me copies of certain essential letters. I would never have located these letters without the assistance of Mary Curtain, a fellow researcher I met while in St. Paul. Finally, the staff of the Mudd Library at Princeton University helped me to find my way, with pleasure, through the voluminous papers of the American Civil Liberties Union.

I am indeed fortunate to have received the support of a very strong and extended family network. Two deserve special recognition: Dr. Frances Richardson Keller, my first and best teacher, and Captain William W. Keller, for his letters.

Jordan Hollow, Va.

Abbreviations

ADA	Americans for Democratic Action
ACLU	American Civil Liberties Union
AG	attorney general
BNHG	Black Nationalist–Hate Groups Cointelpro
BPP	Black Panther party
CIRM	Communist Influence in Racial Matters
Cointelpro	counterintelligence program
Cominfil	Communist infiltration
CPUSA	Communist Party of the United States of America
DID	Domestic Intelligence Division of the FBI
DOJ	Department of Justice
CORE	Congress of Racial Equality
EDA	Emergency Detention Act of 1950
FBI	Federal Bureau of Investigation
HUAC	House Committee on Un-American Activities
IIC	Interdepartmental Intelligence Conference
IDIU	Interdivisional Intelligence Unit of DOJ
IS	internal security
JEH	J. Edgar Hoover
KKK	Ku Klux Klan
LBJ	Lyndon Baines Johnson
MI5	British military intelligence unit
NAACP	National Association for the Advancement of Colored People
NCDT	National Committee for Domestic Tranquility
NCLCH	National Civil Liberties Clearing House
NSC	National Security Council
PR	Puerto Rican
PSI	paid student informant
SA	special agent
SAC	special agent in charge
SCLC	Southern Christian Leadership Conference
SDS	Students for a Democratic Society
SNCC	Student Nonviolent Coordinating Committee
SI	student informant

STAG	student agitation
SWP	Socialist Workers party
UKA	United Klans of America, Inc.
Videm	Vietnam demonstration
WH	White House

A Note on Sources

THE REPORTS of the Senate Committee to Study Governmental Operations with Respect to Intelligence Activities are cited simply as *Church*, followed by the relevant book or volume and page numbers. In addition, the Hubert H. Humphrey Papers at the Minnesota Historical Society in St. Paul are cited as HHH; the Herbert H. Lehman Suite and Papers in the Butler Library at Columbia University, as HHL; and the papers of the American Civil Liberties Union in the Mudd Library at Princeton University, as ACLU. Unless otherwise indicated, all FBI documents cited are on file in the FOIA/PA reading room in the J. Edgar Hoover Building in Washington, D.C. Many FBI documents are also available on microfilm from Scholarly Resources, Inc.

The Liberals and J. Edgar Hoover

It is absolutely essential for every political association to appeal to the naked violence of coercive means in the face of outsiders as well as in the face of internal enemies.

—Max Weber

CHAPTER ONE

Domestic Security in a Modern Liberal State

THERE IS a tendency to view the application of internal security measures in a liberal polity as aberrant episodes in an otherwise open and democratic process. From this perspective, the Alien and Sedition Acts of 1798 constituted an early misunderstanding of the role of public opposition and of orderly rotation of elites in a fledgling republic.[1] President Abraham Lincoln suspended the writ of habeas corpus in April 1861 "to maintain public order and suppress open treason" because Congress was not in session and could not act.[2] A misplaced reaction to the Bolshevik revolution by an overzealous attorney general explains the Palmer raids of 1919. Mass internment of Japanese-Americans in 1942 was the product of global war and extreme national emergency. Senator Joseph McCarthy merely caught and rode a wave of public hysteria against the subversive influence of Communists in government. And in the 1960s, the FBI expanded its domestic intelligence programs to investigate and disrupt extreme elements associated with the civil rights and antiwar movements in a period of extraordinary public disorder.

But these events also suggest a broader pattern in which the liberal state attempts to deal with the tensions and limits implicit in liberalism itself. Louis Hartz was near the mark when he suggested that American society contains a "deep and unwritten tyrannical compulsion . . . to impose Locke everywhere."[3] He assumes that state-led repression is not central to this process. But his analysis lacks the hindsight provided by three decades of ideological confrontation of liberalism and communism. It is not so much that liberal society generates public opinion against non-conformity of all stripes, as Hartz thought; rather, the American state has erected internal defenses against those individuals,

1. James Morton Smith, *Freedom's Fetters: The Alien and Sedition Laws and American Civil Liberties* (Ithaca: Cornell University Press, 1965), p. x.

2. Clinton L. Rossiter, *Constitutional Dictatorship: Crisis Government in the Modern Democracies* (Princeton: Princeton University Press, 1948), pp. 227–28.

3. Louis Hartz, *The Liberal Tradition in America* (New York: Harcourt Brace Jovanovich, 1955), pp. 12–13.

organizations, movements, and ideologies that appear to challenge or pose a potential threat to its continued sovereignty.

In liberal governments, force and repression are pushed out of the mainstream of the political culture. They are not regarded as integral features of the American regime.[4] They have, instead, been relegated to the margins of political life, to a secret discourse involving intelligence agencies and executives that takes place in the twilight area of national security policy.[5] Reluctance to apply criminal sanctions against subversive persons and ideologies was reflected in the actions of the Warren Court in the 1950s, which reconstructed internal security law from a "staunchly libertarian perspective."[6]

As early as 1956, for example, the Court eviscerated the registration provisions of the Internal Security Act of 1950 by throwing out the government's case against the Communist party.[7] That same year it invalidated forty-two state sedition laws on procedural grounds,[8] and in the next term it rendered the Smith Act unenforceable at the national level.[9] But 1956 was also the year in which the FBI implemented its first domestic counterintelligence program, or Cointelpro, that was designed to disorganize and disrupt the activities of the Communist party in a way that circumvented the legal system.

4.   In contrast, the fascist or antiliberal state draws repression to the center of its politics. On June 12, 1986, for example, the government of South Africa issued an emergency decree that gave "all the nation's security forces—the police, army, prison wardens and railways police—sweeping powers that take them beyond the control of the courts" (*New York Times*, June 13, 1986, p. A12). If a security officer determines that an individual or group poses a threat to the peace, he "may apply or order the application of such force as he under the circumstances may deem necessary in order to ward off or prevent the suspected danger" (ibid.).

5.   The magnitude of state security interests is reflected in the combined domestic and foreign intelligence budget, which tripled over a ten-year period to reach approximately $25 billion in 1986 (Leslie H. Gelb, *New York Times*, July 7, 1986, p. 1).

6.   Alfred H. Kelly et al., *The American Constitution: Its Origins and Development*, 6th ed. (New York: W. W. Norton, 1983), p. 595.

7.   *Communist Party* v. *Subversive Activities Control Board*, 351 U.S. 115 (1956), in Kelly et al., *The American Constitution*, p. 597.

8.   *Pennsylvania* v. *Nelson*, 350 U.S. 497 (1956), in Kelly et al., *The American Constitution*, pp. 596–97.

9.   *Yates* v. *United States*, 354 U.S. 298 (1957). "The requirement of the *Yates* opinion that the government show a nexus of specific acts of advocacy of revolution brought an abrupt end to the main body of Smith Act prosecutions then under way" (Kelly et al., *The American Constitution*, p. 596).

To FBI officials, the social disorder and revolutionary ideologies of the 1960s posed perhaps the most serious threat of subversion in the post–Civil War era. When challenged by a potential internal security emergency, in the form of widespread protest against the government's authority to conduct war in Vietnam and to put an end to Jim Crow in the South, the FBI responded aggressively and independently to maintain the security interests of the state. It is no paradox that the bureau moved with equal force to disrupt the Black Panther party and the southern branches of the Ku Klux Klan in the middle 1960s. Both organizations asserted a right to what Weber called the "legitimate use of violence"[10] in pursuit of their goals, posing a direct challenge to the American state.[11]

Understanding FBI domestic intelligence activities of the 1950s and 1960s requires a state-centered perspective. The bureau was not much influenced by social forces or pressure groups. It was, instead, captured and animated by state interests, including the need to eliminate Nazi saboteurs during the war and, later, to rid the government of Communist agents. In the main, FBI authority over domestic security was not fragmented by the constitutional system of divided sovereignty or checks and balances. Director J. Edgar Hoover learned early on to follow a prudent course between the Scylla and Charybdis of congressional oversight and judicial intervention. As the principal domestic intelligence agency of the United States, the bureau was neither decentralized in its internal structure nor easily permeated by outside forces. FBI administrators themselves adopted a statist point of view, evaluating social disorder and ideologies of the Left and Right in terms of the degree to which each—in their opinion—posed a threat to the state.

These attributes of the FBI suggest not American society and its po-

10. "It is absolutely essential for every political association to appeal to the naked violence of coercive means in the face of outsiders as well as in the face of internal enemies. It is only this very appeal to violence that constitutes a political association in our terminology. The state is an association that claims the monopoly of the *legitimate use of violence*, and cannot be defined in any other manner" (H. H. Gerth and C. Wright Mills, eds., *From Max Weber: Essays in Sociology* [New York: Oxford University Press, 1980], p. 334).

11. For example, in his "Executive Mandate No. 1," Black Panther party leader Huey Newton wrote: "The Black Panther Party for Self-Defense believes that the time has come for Black people to arm themselves against this terror before it is too late. . . . We believe that the Black communities of America must rise up as one man to halt the progression of a trend that leads inevitably to their total destruction" (Huey P. Newton, *To Die for the People* [New York: Vintage Books, 1972], p. 13).

litical organization but, rather, the liberal state, particularly the ways in which such a state defends itself against the consequences of its own liberalism. The very term *liberal state*, itself an oxymoron, implies a philosophical discontinuity at the center of the polity. The tension between society and state is manifested when the security interests of the state conflict with political and constitutional rights of groups and individuals who assert an adversarial ideology or who organize to resist large-scale policies such as the war in Vietnam and the extension of civil rights to blacks in the South.

This conflict is acted out in the United States when Congress outlaws a political party, as it did through the Communist Control Act of 1954, or when the FBI systematically disrupts the organized activities of Klansmen and antiwar groups. The liberal political community has tolerated suppression of the far Left and has sanctioned the application of authoritarian methods to neutralize violent and organized opposition to its civil rights policies. In confronting ideological adversaries, the democratic government demonstrates its willingness to invoke the authority of the state. The tentativeness and fragmentation of the American political system end where a compelling security interest begins.

Liberal political figures promoted and nurtured a domestic intelligence apparatus in the United States beginning with the Roosevelt administration in 1936.[12] By 1950, liberals sought to convert the issue of communism in government from a political liability to a routine process of administration located within the FBI. This strategy weakened McCarthyism as an electoral factor and disabled communism as a political force in the United States. In one stroke, liberals defined the ideological tolerance of American politics and established themselves firmly at the vital center. They understood, moreover, the need for the state to arm itself with a central police organization powerful enough to ensure the internal security of the nation. The emergence of a universal consensus against communism tended to stifle debate about the role and function of the agency of internal security in a constitutional republic.

Two central arguments serve to orient this book: (1) in the two decades following 1950, the FBI transformed itself from a bureau of internal security with delimited functions into an agency resembling more a political police and an independent security state within the state;

12.   This is the year President Franklin D. Roosevelt established the permanent domestic intelligence structure. This development is discussed at length in chapter 2.

and (2) the consistent support of a liberal constituency was a necessary condition to this transformation. Accordingly, this book assesses the contribution that the liberal political community made to the FBI in the 1950s and 1960s, including the variations in its support for the agency over time. And, second, it describes and analyzes changes in the organization, authority, programs, and security role of the bureau in the post–World War II period.

The Role of the FBI

The specific domestic security arrangements that a nation adopts are highly conditioned by the nature of the state in question. As a matter of policy and political tradition, the modern democratic state tends to limit rigorously the range of techniques available to security police and other intelligence officials; for example, acts of torture and assassination—such as those carried out in 1985 by right-wing death squads in El Salvador and the Tontons Macoutes in Haiti[13]—have no counterpart among methods employed by the United States domestic intelligence community.[14] The latitude within which intelligence officials and programs operate depends upon the willingness of various elements of the government and the political elites to delegate internal security policymaking to a central domestic intelligence agency. If the courts and the legislature insist on minute scrutiny of security operations and exercise legislative and judicial controls, the options and activities of the agency will accordingly be constrained.

Even when the more extreme methods and practices are ruled out, there is still a definite tension between the security measures the state imposes on the society and the core attributes of a modern liberal polity, such as the right to due process of law and freedom of political association. In an internal security emergency, or even in the shadow of the threat of such a contingency, it is natural and probably inevitable that various exceptions to established constitutional norms and legal process will be implemented. In the American setting, such exceptions have taken the form of outlawing certain ideologies and political affiliations. They have generated summary incarceration of large numbers of persons based on national origin or racial characteristics. They

13. For Tontons Macoutes see *New York Times*, February 5, 1986, and for death squads see *New York Times*, March 4, 1985.

14. In addition, forced servitude or imprisonment without due process could not easily be undertaken by an agency of internal security in the United States. When such practices came to light they would not sustain constitutional challenges within the justice system.

have included infiltration and disruption of domestic organizations thought to pose a threat to the national security. But there is a theoretical point at which the exceptions overwhelm the rule to challenge the basic principles and legal structures upon which liberalism is founded. And it is at this juncture that the democractic polity would begin to shift slowly and perhaps imperceptibly toward some other form of the state that might be less tolerant of individual freedom and political expression.

The role of the domestic security apparatus is not static, even within the deliberate limits imposed upon it in the context of constitutional, republican government. In the United States, it varies both with the specific historical and political circumstances in which security policy is forged and with the administrative and legal arrangements under which domestic intelligence programs are conceived and implemented. The cold war confrontation of liberalism and communism increased the likelihood that internal security policy would be cast in ideological terms in the 1950s and that the FBI would intercede to disable the Communist party. The FBI was able to develop large-scale programs to neutralize the party because it was granted a high degree of legal and administrative autonomy in this sphere.

In the United States, the nature of the threat has probably been less important to the determination of internal security policy than the overall consensus among political elites concerning the magnitude of the internal threat and the degree of autonomy and insularity with which the FBI was permitted to operate. Again, the fate of the Communist party in the United States is instructive. By most accounts, the party was early and easily infiltrated and thoroughly neutralized by FBI agents and informants. Many supporters and members of the party had been alienated by Khrushchev's acknowledgment in 1956 of Stalin's atrocities, by the Soviet invasion of Hungary, and by revelations of anti-Semitism in the Soviet Union.[15] Yet the threat of American communism remained a principal rationale for expanding domestic security intelligence programs in the fields of civil rights and antiwar protest well into the 1970s.[16]

15.   David A. Shannon, *The Decline of American Communism* (Chatham, N.J.: The Chatham Bookseller, 1971), pp. 272, 284, 314–16. See also Joseph R. Starobin, *American Communism in Crisis, 1943–1957* (Cambridge, Mass.: Harvard University Press, 1972), pp. 225–30. For Khrushchev's famous "secret" speech, see Thomas P. Whitney, ed., *Khrushchev Speaks* (Ann Arbor: University of Michigan Press, 1963), p. 207ff.

16.   Church, bk. 3, pp. 480–81.

The act of protecting a nation's internal security is preventive in nature. If a nuclear installation is sabotaged or a political leader is assassinated, security has been breached and the security agency has failed. The differences between criminal and intelligence investigations help to illustrate this point. Unlike criminal investigations, intelligence investigations do not depend on a standard of probable cause and are not conducted pursuant to specific legislation. Historically, domestic intelligence activity has not been subject to due process, rules of evidence, and other such requirements of the law and the courts, largely because of its role in protecting the national security. There is, accordingly, a natural tendency to exempt the internal security arena from accepted constitutional practice and legal precedents.

In 1939, for example, the Supreme Court first imposed restrictions on wiretapping in the *Nardone* and *Weiss* cases.[17] But shortly thereafter, President Franklin D. Roosevelt moved to establish internal security exceptions. Although he acknowledged the Court's recent decisions limiting wiretapping, the president was "convinced that the Supreme Court never intended any dictum . . . to apply to grave matters involving the defense of the nation." And on that basis he authorized Attorney General Robert Jackson to "secure information by listening devices . . . of persons suspected of subversive activities." After all, he reasoned, "it is too late to do anything about it after sabotage, assassinations and 'fifth column' activities are completed."[18] There is, accordingly, a tendency for domestic intelligence officials to cast a wide net, to err on the side of thoroughness rather than to explain after the fact a failure to detect a particular terrorist or political assassin.[19]

Internal security operations are sensitive both to increased levels of international tension and to periods of public disorder at home, and

17.   *Nardone* v. *United States*, 308 U.S. 338 (1939), and *Weiss* v. *United States*, 308 U.S. 321 (1939).

18.   President Roosevelt to Attorney General Jackson, May 21, 1940, Stephen J. Spingarn Papers, Truman Library, quoted in Athan G. Theoharis and Elizabeth Meyer, "The 'National Security' Justification for Electronic Eavesdropping: An Elusive Exception," *Wayne Law Review* 14 (1968): 759.

19.   This was precisely the situation that FBI officials faced in the aftermath of the assassination of President John F. Kennedy. The bureau sustained severe criticism from the Warren Commission for not sharing information on Lee Harvey Oswald with the Secret Service and for failing to detect that he was in the Dallas area during a presidential visit. For years after, intelligence officials cited the findings of the Warren Commission as authority for expanding domestic intelligence programs (*New York Times*, June 28, 1970, p. 1).

intelligence officials have often assumed a conspiratorial connection between the two.[20] In the event of the former, the agency may, for example, redouble its efforts to detect and arrest Soviet and other hostile spies and agents, and it may track the movements of citizens abroad to determine if they are engaged in activities on behalf of foreign powers.[21] In times of extreme social unrest the agency may lay plans to investigate dissidents and protestors. It may attempt to regulate social protest or to socialize radical or deviant elements of the society. It may even implement programs to disrupt and neutralize individuals and groups selected according to political or ideological criteria.

Because of its centrality to the interests of the state and the secrecy with which it operates, the agency of internal security is particularly subject to political manipulation. Its administrators enjoy a privileged relationship with central decision makers. In time of war, the agency protects not only the political leadership but also critical resources such as transportation networks, energy producers, and information systems upon which a war effort depends. In time of peace, the agency may gather information on the adversaries of the regime in power or merely provide a constant flow of political intelligence to policymakers. As Otto Kirchheimer has observed, so intimate is the relationship between the agency of internal security and the state that "one might nearly be tempted to define a revolution by the willingness of a regime to open the archives of its predecessor's political police."[22]

As the United States engaged in the politics of cold war in the 1950s and public disorder in the 1960s, administrators at the FBI implemented dozens of domestic intelligence programs intended to secure the state against what they thought were subversive groups and individuals. These programs varied substantially in the degree of autonomy with which their goals were formulated and the degree to which they were insulated from other governmental and societal forces. They can be divided into three categories: (1) investigation of Communist-infiltrated groups, extremist groups, and civil disturbances; (2) inten-

20.   J. Edgar Hoover often argued before Congress and in the media that an international conspiracy of Communists influenced and sometimes led the civil rights and antiwar movements of the 1960s. For example, see *U.S. News & World Report*, May 4, 1964, p. 33, and *New York Times*, April 22, 1964, p. 30.

21.   The FBI, for instance, cooperated with the Passport Office of the State Department to monitor the activities of selected Americans who traveled abroad in the 1960s (*New Republic*, April 9, 1966, pp. 9–10).

22.   Otto Kirchheimer, *Political Justice: The Use of Legal Procedure for Political Ends* (Princeton: Princeton University Press, 1961), p. 204.

sive investigation of classes of persons who would be detained in an internal security emergency, including infiltration of Communist, extremist, and militant groups; and (3) designation of individuals and groups for intensive investigation and counterintelligence action to disrupt their activities and neutralize them politically. The severity of intelligence methods increases progressively.

The State and Its Security: Three Models

The significant circumstance is not that the FBI encountered its Waterloo in 1975 at the hands of a group of liberal senators,[23] but that it was able to maintain a contrary course against liberal and libertarian currents for fifteen years after the middle 1950s. Indeed, the FBI retained the support of the liberal political community throughout the 1960s, despite the fact that the bureau operated in opposition to liberal doctrine as enunciated by the courts. In part, the FBI developed counterintelligence programs (or Cointelpros) to disrupt domestic groups because the Supreme Court had made it difficult to proceed against Communists under the Smith and McCarran acts.[24]

This tenacity is most remarkable because the domestic security intelligence programs that the FBI implemented after 1964 were intended to break the back of social protest. They were designed in a way that circumvented due process requirements in an era when administration of criminal procedure was liberalized and civil rights were enhanced by Congress and the courts. Liberals knew that the FBI had infiltrated the Communist party in the 1950s, using specially trained agents to undermine its effectiveness as a political organization. In 1963, they urged the FBI to apply the same tactics against the Ku Klux Klan in the South. Liberals reasoned that Klansmen and Communists were not en-

23.   On January 21, 1975, the United States Senate passed S. Res. 21 "to establish a select committee of the Senate to conduct an investigation and study with respect to intelligence activities carried out by or on behalf of the Federal Government" (Church, bk. 2, p. 343). Chaired by Senator Frank Church, the Select Committee to Study Governmental Operations with Respect to Intelligence Activities held hearings, printed secret intelligence documents, and produced reports throughout 1975 and 1976.

24.   "In the years after 1956 [the year it was formally initiated], the purpose of the Communist Party Cointelpro changed somewhat. Supreme Court decisions substantially curbed criminal prosecution of Communists. Subsequently, the FBI 'rationale' for Cointelpro was that it had become 'impossible to prosecute Communist Party members' and some alternative was needed 'to contain the threat' " (Deposition of Supervisor, Internal Security Section, FBI Intelligence Division, October 16, 1975, pp. 10, 14, in Church, bk. 2, p. 67).

titled to legal protections because both groups sought to deny the rights of others through organized violence.

This subterfuge set up opposing trends within different sectors of government. At a time when the Warren Court undertook dynamic reforms in the administration of justice, extending Fourth, Fifth, and Sixth Amendment requirements to limit the power of the states, the FBI sought to reach subversives and extremists at the local level through covert operations. As the cop on the beat learned the intricacies of new warrant and pretrial procedures and read *Miranda* rights to suspects, the FBI agent and the informants he managed applied coercive powers of the national state to citizens and groups without reference to the legal system or to established constitutional principles.

Such divergence increased as public disorder deepened throughout the 1960s. While government generally exhibited extraordinary tolerance toward the protest movement against the war in Vietnam, the FBI engaged in dirty tricks intended to confuse antiwar groups and discredit their leadership. In 1968, for example, the bureau established the New Left Cointelpro, a covert program that sought to disrupt the activities of many antiwar groups and their leadership.[25] While the Kennedy and Johnson administrations effectively used the vast powers of the executive in support of integration and voting rights, the FBI conducted hostile intelligence investigations of prominent civil rights leaders and harassed their organizations.[26] The bureau's Black Nationalist–Hate Groups Cointelpro specifically targeted Martin Luther King and his Southern Christian Leadership Conference (SCLC) after March 1968.[27]

In part, the bureau was able to operate at variance with the courts and higher executive and congressional authority because of the nebulous legal structure upon which its internal security activities rested. No statute specifically authorized domestic security intelligence investigations.[28] Instead, for forty years following 1936, the FBI conducted

25.   Ibid., bk. 3, p. 23.

26.   David J. Garrow, *Bearing the Cross: Martin Luther King, Jr., and the Southern Christian Leadership Conference* (New York: William Morrow, 1976).

27.   Director, FBI (100-448006), to SAC, Albany, "Counterintelligence Program/ Black Nationalist–Hate Groups/Racial Intelligence," March 4, 1968, p. 3.

28.   The FBI relied, instead, on the general language of 28 U.S.C. 533: "Investigative and other officials; appointment[:] The Attorney General may appoint officials—(1) to detect and prosecute crimes against the United States . . . (3) to conduct such other investigations regarding official matters under the control of the Department of Justice and the Department of State as may be directed by the Attorney General" (quoted in Controller General of the United States, *FBI*

intelligence programs "within the broad framework of Presidential statements and directives, statutes, Executive orders, and Attorney General directives . . . [that were] generally ambiguous."[29] But perhaps more important, FBI operations became increasingly autonomous and insulated from the Congress, the courts, other units of government, and societal actors generally. In the 1960s, liberals continued to support the FBI because they were largely unaware of the nature and scope of most FBI internal security activity.

These circumstances suggest that security arrangements in the democratic polity are volatile or elastic at best and that a single conception of the nature and role of the FBI in American politics cannot account for changes in the security apparatus over time. Accordingly, three models of the FBI—as (1) a bureau of domestic intelligence, (2) a political police, and (3) an independent security state within the state—inform this book. Each captures a part of the significance and a part of the reality of domestic intelligence activity in the 1950s and 1960s, which finally progressed beyond the zone of liberal tolerance. Together these models can be used to describe and calibrate broad variation in the empirical data concerning FBI operations. In addition, they provide an analytical frame of reference to evaluate the claim that in the two decades following 1950 the FBI became increasingly autonomous, insulating its security operations from governmental and societal actors alike, and employing more aggressive modes of domestic intelligence activity.

The animating principle of the first model, that of a bureau of domestic intelligence, is to meet but not exceed a minimum standard of domestic intelligence activity sufficient to maintain the security interests of the state. Within this conception, all intelligence activities are consistent with established constitutional norms and other requirements of the legal system. Like other agencies, a bureau of domestic intelligence draws limited and specified powers from a charter or authorizing legislation. To the extent possible, intelligence policy remains

---

Domestic Intelligence Operations—Their Purpose and Scope: Issues That Need to Be Resolved, Report to the House Committee on the Judiciary [Washington, D.C.: General Accounting Office, February 24, 1976], p. 189).

29. Ibid., p. 16. After a thoroughgoing review, the General Accounting Office concluded in 1976: "As to the authority now asserted [by the FBI] to conduct domestic intelligence investigations based on 28 U.S.C. 533 and various Executive orders, however, we cannot say that it does not exist. The problem with the FBI's authority even under these delegations remains: it is not clearly spelled out, but must be distilled through an interpretive process that leaves it vulnerable to continuous questioning and debate" (ibid., p. 26).

a matter of public record. Such a bureau does not conduct aggressive or disruptive intelligence operations against citizens or domestic groups. Its primary function is to gather information related to criminal prosecution of persons and groups that pose a threat to internal security. It is responsive to the legislative process, to higher executive authority, and to the decisions of the courts interpreting a body of security law. This model probably comes closest to what liberal political leaders had in mind when they first embraced the FBI in the late 1930s and early 1940s.

The Senate, the General Accounting Office, and domestic intelligence professionals seriously contemplated such a model in the late 1970s.[30] After a widely publicized investigation and housecleaning of domestic security policies and operations, the Church Committee concluded that intelligence activities within the United States had undermined basic constitutional rights of American citizens and that the constitutional system of checks and balances against abuse of state power had been disabled.[31] The committee established three principles to control domestic intelligence: (1) intelligence activity that "directly infringes the rights of free speech and association must be prohibited"; (2) security operations that exert an indirect or "collateral" effect on these rights must be consistent with constitutional requirements established by the Supreme Court; and (3) in addition to substantive restraints on intelligence activity, procedural safeguards should be instituted "which range from judicial review . . . to formal and high level Executive branch approval, to greater disclosure and more effective Congressional oversight."[32]

A second model, that of a political police, is distinguished from the first because it permits intelligence activities that exceed the minimum standard necessary to protect the security interests of the state. In general it is marked by a greater degree of autonomy from the policymaking process of democratic institutions, and its activities are more insulated from judicial scrutiny and legislative oversight. A political police

30.   For a sophisticated treatment of guidelines for intelligence activities and terrorism, see John T. Elliff, *The Reform of FBI Intelligence Operations* (Princeton: Princeton University Press, 1979), pp. 112–20, 131–32.

31.   The central conclusion of the Senate Select Committee to Study Governmental Operations with Respect to Intelligence Activities was: "*Domestic Intelligence Activity Has Threatened and Undermined The Constitutional Rights of Americans to Free Speech, Association and Privacy. It Has Done So Primarily Because The Constitutional System for Checking Abuse of Power Has Not Been Applied*" (Church, bk. 2, p. 290).

32.   Ibid., p. 293.

is most responsive to the regime in power, to elites that have captured the governance machinery of the state. Accordingly, its powers and responsibilities are not precisely specified by statute. It may draw its authority instead from broad and loosely defined delegations of inherent or implied executive powers. Unlike the first model, the political police may engage in aggressive intelligence action directed against the enemies of ruling elites and gather political intelligence that is neither authorized by nor conducted in relation to specific legislation.

The distinction between criminal and domestic security investigations helps to define the role of a political police. It is more than a difference in emphasis because "the political police's attention centers on the surveillance of the adversaries of the present regime and, if need be, on foiling their plans of subverting it."[33] Although security investigations are not constrained by rules of evidence or established criminal procedure, under a constitutional government "where the political police's action is limited by normal life satisfactions, public opinion, and access to the courts for the government's foes . . . the police keep some measure of similarity with a normal governmental bureaucracy." But a political police differs from other agencies and from the model of a domestic intelligence bureau because its privileged position with respect to governing elites tends to insulate it against review or oversight by other units of government.[34]

A final model, that of an independent security state, is characterized by an absence of outside controls over its activities. It is distinguished from the political police, because its goals and methods may not coincide with those of political elites and central decision makers. Its administrators exercise discretionary authority over its programs and methods. The primary function of the independent security state is to investigate and neutralize ideological enemies of the parent state, as identified by administrators within the agency itself.[35] Because it undertakes aggressive or hostile intelligence activity against persons and groups, and is not authorized by elected officials, it is largely incompatible with constitutional forms and with the basic legal assumptions that underlie the liberal state. If it is funded through a pro forma ap-

33.   Kirchheimer, *Political Justice*, p. 202.

34.   "During the total lifetime of the regime [that they serve] they [the political police] are foolproof against any investigation into their methods, assumptions, and efficiency" (ibid., p. 204).

35.   This is a paradox because when the agency of internal security takes on the qualities of a security state within the state, it has itself become an enemy of liberalism.

propriations process, the specific nature of its programs and their existence would remain unknown to the legislative and judicial branches of the government.[36] It can be said to constitute a security state within the state.

The phrase "state within the state" was used to explain the relationship of the Prussian army to the German state in the decades leading up to World War I. The army was described as a state because it was able to resist constitutional and parliamentary controls. It "claim[ed] the right to define what was, or was not, to the national interest and to dispense with those who did not agree with the definition."[37] In a like manner, the independent security state model claims the right to define legitimate security interests and to neutralize those who disagree. And precisely because it is embedded in a liberal democratic polity, it circumvents legislative and judicial controls that otherwise would force it to submit to constitutional restraints. Unchecked, it would mean the end of the liberal state.

These models of the agency of internal security can be distinguished from one another by their relation to the state and the mode of intelligence activity each undertakes. In the first cell in figure 1.1, the relation of the domestic intelligence bureau to the state is largely ministerial. The bureau gathers domestic security intelligence, which may or may not be acted upon by higher authorities at some future time. The intelligence techniques it employs are passive because they do not interfere with the activities of subjects under investigation.[38] Such techniques might include compiling data from government computer banks on a group or individual, or collecting public source materials such as newspaper clippings, articles, speeches, membership lists, and information on employment and funding sources.

The fourth cell remains empty and is unstable because there is a tendency for an agency of internal security to act on information as its discretion increases. Cell 4 represents the model of security that many

36.   Its activities are so highly insulated that even the executive branch may be unaware of the nature of its methods, programs, and policies.

37.   Gordon A. Craig, *The Politics of the Prussian Army, 1640–1945* (Oxford: Clarendon Press, 1955), pp. xix, 252.

38.   The range of intelligence techniques is extremely wide, and even the FBI could not make hard-and-fast distinctions: "The word 'counterintelligence' had no fixed meaning even before the [Cointelpro] programs were terminated [in 1971]. The Bureau witnesses [who appeared before the Church Committee] agreed that there is a large grey area between 'counterintelligence' and 'aggressive investigation,' and that headquarters supervisors sometimes had difficulty in deciding which caption should go on certain proposals" (Church, bk. 3, p. 12).

Fig. 1.1

Three Models of Internal Security in a Liberal State

Relation to the State

		Ministerial	Discretionary
	Passive Intelligence	**1** Domestic Intelligence Bureau	**4** Unstable/ Transitional
Mode of Intelligence Activity	Aggressive/ Counterintelligence	**2** Political Police	**3** Independent Security State

liberals of the 1950s had in mind when they delegated authority to the FBI to safeguard the nation's internal security against Communists, subversives, and extremists without providing mechanisms for oversight and accountability. But almost from the outset, the bureau's aggressive intelligence techniques directed against members of the Communist party[39] resembled the methods of the models in cells 2 and 3.

Certain intelligence techniques are inherently aggressive or disruptive to the activities of the person or group under investigation. This is often the case, for example, when the government pays informants to infiltrate groups that advocate civil disobedience or otherwise oppose its policies. When the presence of an informant is suspected, as often happens, seeds of distrust and conflict are planted within the group. Because the government is an interested party to the dispute, there is a presumption on the part of its agents that the group in question is acting against the interests of the state. Accordingly, unless the activity of the agency of internal security is circumscribed by procedural, administrative, and legal controls, the agency begins to resemble more closely the model of a political police or an independent security state.

39.   "During its investigation of the Communist Party, USA, the Bureau has sought to capitalize on incidents involving the Party and its leaders in order to foster factionalism, bring the Communist Party (CP) and its leaders into disrepute before the American public and cause confusion and dissatisfaction among rank-and-file members of the CP" (A. H. Belmont to L. V. Boardman, "CP, USA—Counterintelligence Program/Internal Security—C," p. 1, August 28, 1956, in Church, vol. 6, p. 372).

Control over the second model, that of a political police, may be weakened but is still partly in place because security forces are responsible to ruling elites and ultimately to their elective constituencies. A political police may initiate aggressive intelligence techniques that are intended to decrease the effectiveness of a subversive group or political adversary.[40] These might include frequent and abrasive interviews with a person under investigation, warrantless electronic surveillance, contact with employers and associates, invasion of privacy, or trespass. But a political police in a constitutional republic will generally be constrained because the mission of the organization is defined by the leadership of the government in power, and the opponents of the government can challenge the actions of the police in the courts and in public debate.

The agency in cell 3 has sufficient discretion and financial resources to define its own mission and carry out aggressive or counterintelligence programs on the authority of its internal administration. This is, of course, the limiting case, as in the example of the Prussian army. But this security state within the state is incompatible with basic legal principles of liberal government and with the principal democratic institutions. It must therefore attain a very high degree of autonomy and insularity from other sectors of the government, from interested groups, and from the public generally if it is to survive in an otherwise liberal, and therefore hostile, environment.

These models of the agency of internal security are intended to be inclusive in one direction and exclusive in the other. A political police, for instance, could undertake all of the programs and activities of a domestic intelligence bureau, but not vice versa. Similarly, an agency modeled on an independent security state could conduct all of the operations of a political police and a domestic intelligence bureau, but not the reverse. Increasingly coercive and discretionary security programs presuppose and build upon an intelligence base that is developed using model 1 and 2 activities.

Intelligence operations directed against the Ku Klux Klan provide a good illustration. A security agency must gather basic information on the Klan (model 1 activity) before it can send informants to penetrate local klaverns (model 2 activity). Based on a continuous flow of detailed information, it then becomes possible to design and carry out counterintelligence operations (model 3 activity) that disrupt or neu-

40. But note that there are definite limits in a constitutional republic because, as Watergate has demonstrated, even a sitting president of the United States cannot send security teams to investigate the offices of an opposition political party.

tralize the target groups and their leaders. As the ensuing chapters demonstrate, the FBI added programs that indicated the presence of a political police and an independent security state starting in the late 1950s and continuing into the early 1970s.

Autonomy and Insularity

Few attempts to apply a state-centered analysis to American politics have succeeded. This is because most observers insist on treating the American state as a single conceptual entity and do not allow for variation in the form of the state or for pockets of consolidated state power within an otherwise fragmented and weak political structure.[41] Eric Nordlinger, for example, contemplates a homogenous polity in which "the state is made up of and limited to those individuals who are endowed with society-wide decision-making authority."[42] Accordingly, his notion of state autonomy is cast in terms of the aggregate preferences of individual policymakers, which somehow cumulate into "state preferences" that can presumably be imposed on the society. In what is all too reminiscent of fundamentalist pluralism, Nordlinger suggests that state preferences "are usually the product of all sorts of conflict, competition, and pulling and hauling."[43]

In a constitutional republic, where the powers of the government are purposefully divided and legal and institutional structures stand between citizen and sovereign, state authority is minimized and constantly challenged as an article of the liberal faith. State powers recede before constitutionally enshrined rights of individuals. The raison d'être of liberal government is to frustrate the authority of the state, to set one branch against another, creating political space within which individuals and various organized societal interests can maneuver. To apply a state-centered analysis to American politics, it is therefore first necessary to locate or define the state in terms of concentrations of power, that are not mitigated by democratic institutions and legal structures or penetrated by interest groups.

41. In one notable exception, the U.S. Department of Agriculture was characterized as "an island of state strength in an ocean of weakness" (Kenneth Finegold and Theda Skocpol, "State Capacity and Economic Intervention in the Early New Deal," *Political Science Quarterly* 97 (1982), p. 271. See also Stephen Skowronek, *Building a New American State* (Cambridge: Cambridge University Press, 1982).

42. Eric A. Nordlinger, *On the Autonomy of the Democratic State* (Cambridge, Mass.: Harvard University Press, 1981), p. 11.

43. Ibid., p. 15.

It is natural to look to relations among nations and military engagement as arenas in which the state is likely to exhibit concentrated authority. In foreign policy matters, for example, Stephen Krasner has isolated the White House and the State Department as the central repositories of state power and has designated the secretary of state and the president as key state actors. These officials and institutions are distinguished, he suggests, because of "their high degree of insulation from specific societal pressures and a set of formal and informal obligations that charge them with furthering the nation's general interests."[44] For Krasner, the key to the analysis of state power in the United States is to disaggregate the policymaking process and to define the state as a unique set of actors in relation to each of several distinct issue areas.[45]

Although the concept of insularity is central to his work on raw materials investments, Krasner has been justly criticized for failing to develop it as a variable in political analysis.[46] He does not specify precisely the conditions under which insularity is achieved, and he does not indicate its relation to state autonomy or even to authoritative state action.[47] And for this reason, he has failed to recognize the utility of this concept within the framework of domestic policy.[48] The concept of insularity must, accordingly, be refined to make it applicable to the agency of internal security in a liberal polity. In particular, insularity conditions the domestic security activities that can be undertaken in a constitutional republic. It refers to the ability of the agency to carry out programs without interference from societal and state actors that assuredly would exert countervailing force in its absence. A high de-

---

44. Stephen D. Krasner, *Defending the National Interest* (Princeton: Princeton University Press, 1978), p. 11.

45. Ibid., p. 83.

46. Theda Skocpol et al., *Bringing the State Back In* (Cambridge: Cambridge University Press, 1985), p. 13.

47. He does, however, suggest that when the Congress is involved, both insularity and the authority of the state are impaired. See Stephen D. Krasner, "United States Commercial and Monetary Policy: Unravelling the Paradox of External Strength and Internal Weakness," in Peter J. Katzenstein, ed., *Between Power and Plenty* (Madison: University of Wisconsin Press, 1978), p. 57.

48. "Although it has become very fashionable to claim that there is little difference between domestic and international politics, the fact remains that there is no domestic equivalent to war, and there are few analogs to the kind of solidarity appeals that political leaders can make when the state acts in the international system. Politics never really ends, but the claim that it should can only be staked out at the water's edge" (Krasner, *Defending the National Interest*, p. 86).

gree of insularity enables the exercise of concentrated state powers that otherwise would encounter consititutional, legal, or societally based challenges from the press or other interests not easily resisted in the context of liberal government.

The utility of a companion concept, that of autonomy, also depends on the delineation of different parts of the state. Any particular segment of the state is subject to variation in its capacity to formulate policies that, as Theda Skocpol has suggested, "are not simply reflective of the demands or interests of social groups, classes, or society."[49] She argues, further, that the "very *structural potentials* for autonomous state action change over time, as the organizations of coercion and administration undergo transformations, both internally and in their relations to societal groups and to representative parts of government."[50] But with respect to the agency of internal security in a liberal state, extreme autonomy refers to police activity that is not controlled or regulated by statute or by any formal executive or judicial policy instrument. The capacity to implement autonomous policies depends particularly on the degree of insularity with which the programs of the agency are protected from other state and nonstate actors.

There is, accordingly, a very high correlation between the degree of autonomy and insularity for each of the models of internal security described above (see fig. 1.2). For the model of an independent security state, both autonomy of goals and insularity of operations are very high. Although the security policies of ruling elites might coincide with those of the administrators of an independent security state, elites would not know it and could not officially be informed. This is because the act of informing them would, in most cases, oblige them to curtail the operations of the independent security state—precisely because these activities are not compatible with the legal structures and constitutional arrangements that define the liberal polity. For this reason, the programs of the security state within the state must be conducted with the highest degree of insulation, both from societal and from other state actors. Individual citizens could compel disclosure of operations through a judicial process of discovery, or the courts and the legislature could demand to exercise review and oversight prerogatives.[51]

At the other extreme, the domestic intelligence bureau is low as far as both variables are concerned, and, in this respect, resembles a de-

---

49.   Skocpol, *Bringing the State Back In*, p. 9.

50.   Ibid., p. 14; Skocpol's italics.

51.   This is exactly what the U.S. Senate did on January 21, 1975, when it passed S. Res. 21, which created the Church Committee.

Fig. 1.2

Autonomy and Insularity of Internal Security Arrangements

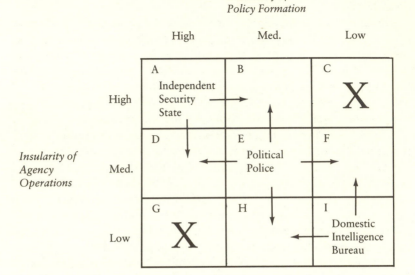

Autonomy of
Policy Formation

partment of labor or of agriculture as much as an agency of internal security. Its goals are formulated within an open policymaking process and exhibit little autonomy because of the influence of various state and nonstate actors. Because the programs of such a bureau are subject to review by the courts, the legislature, and higher executive authority, they can be penetrated by the press and might in rare circumstances become vulnerable to public opinion. They tend to exhibit relatively low insularity against many other state and societal actors as well.[52]

Finally, the political police model, which is situated at the center of the diagram, occupies a middle (if more volatile) range, both as regards autonomy of policy formation and the insularity of its operations. As long as central decision makers act in accordance with the security interests of the state, the supervision of which they usually delegate to the political police, the police and governing elites share the same security goals. But because the authority of the political police arises largely from executive powers, it exercises substantial influence in

---

52.   But even when it is characterized by limited autonomy and its programs are not well insulated, the agency of internal security is not permeated by societal interests in the same way as other domestic agencies of government. This is because the security agency, no matter what form it assumes, is always captured by a single compelling state interest, that is, to protect the security of the liberal state.

forming security policy. In this situation, executive orders and delegations obviate the need to subject security goals to legislative approval or a process of judicial review. Moreover, the programs of the political police are not insulated from political elites and perhaps not even from their political supporters who might share the same interests. But because most aspects of program implementation are secret and therefore more difficult to bring before the courts, the degree of insularity of the political police is decidedly higher than that of a bureau of domestic intelligence.

Although the three models of the agency of internal security are not mutually exclusive, the attributes of a domestic intelligence bureau and an independent security state are largely incompatible.[53] This is indicated in figure 1.2 by an X in cells C and G. The combinations of high autonomy–low insularity and low autonomy–high insularity create inherently unstable or unworkable security conditions. In the former case, the agency's programs would be highly vulnerable to challenges through the courts and review by the legislature. Its policies, when discovered, would be brought into line with democratic process. In the latter situation, the goals of the agency would have to be consistent with accepted constitutional norms and legal practice, and this would tend to circumscribe the programs and methods the agency could undertake.

Within a given polity, the nature of the agency of internal security can shift along the IEA axis of figure 1.2 or toward any of the DBFH hybrids. In the American context, the FBI exhibited definite variation, usually expressed as increases in autonomy and insularity throughout the 1950s and 1960s. At each step along the road, the participation and support of its liberal consituency was a precondition to increases in or maintenance of the autonomy and insularity of FBI domestic security intelligence programming. This book is an effort to assess not only variation in the form of the FBI, but also the circumstances that at first guaranteed—but in the end helped to disengage—the support of the liberal political community.

Status of the FBI

By the late 1940s, liberals were inclined to place their faith in the FBI as the best answer to the problem of internal security. They did so in part because of the public relations genius of its director, J. Edgar Hoo-

---

53.   They are, instead, exclusive in one direction only; that is, an independent security state can undertake all of the activities of a political police and a domestic intelligence bureau, but not vice versa.

ver. As one contemporary political pundit observed, "So effective has been his continuing [publicity] campaign that when Mr. Hoover makes a request of Congress newspaper editors all over the land editorialize in support of his position."[54] By 1950, Hoover's name was a household word, associated with everything that was right about America, and his bureau was a locus of power at the center of national politics. Hoover and the FBI would dominate the formulation and execution of internal security policy in the United States for the next quarter century.

If Hoover stands out as a striking anomaly amid bureau chiefs in American politics, so too does the FBI among other bureaus and divisions of government. Consider, for example, the Forest Service or the Tennessee Valley Authority (TVA). The directors of the Forest Service struggled continuously to enforce central policies on sometimes recalcitrant forest rangers, who were at times too responsive to local pressures and interests. The job of the ranger "demands a relatively high degree of personal autonomy . . . [and] decentralization places a high value on assertion of independence, willingness to make decisions and to act without consulting superior officers."[55] And for at least one extended period in the early 1930s, "the control of Forest Service policy slipped from Washington into the hands of the regional foresters."[56]

The basic modus operandi for the TVA was to work with existing state and local government agencies as well as private associations to carry out the mission of the authority. In this way programming could be conducted from a perspective reflecting "the responsibility of leadership in a democracy to offer the people alternatives for free choice rather than ready-made prescriptions elaborated in the vastness of planning agencies."[57] Although this "grass roots approach" tended to ensure the cooperation of interested groups, both public and private, it also led to the integration of local associations and state planning agencies into the policymaking machinery of the TVA.[58]

For different reasons, both agencies offer stark contrast to the FBI. The TVA was conceived—as a matter of principle—to be captured by societal interests and existing administrative agencies. As such, it is a

---

54.   V. O. Key, *Politics, Parties, and Pressure Groups*, 2d ed. (New York: Thomas Y. Crowell, 1947), p. 711.

55.   Herbert Kaufman, *The Forest Ranger: A Study in Administrative Behavior* (Baltimore: Johns Hopkins University Press, 1967), p. 86.

56.   Ibid., p. 208.

57.   Philip Selznick, "TVA and the Grass Roots," in Francis E. Rourke, ed., *Bureaucratic Power in National Politics*, 2d ed. (Boston: Little, Brown, 1972), p. 40.

58.   Ibid., pp. 41–42.

quintessential example of the stateless liberal polity hiding the machinery of coercion behind the legitimacy of democratic process. The TVA exhibited little or no insularity or autonomy of policy formation precisely because it was designed to integrate local and state organizations into the process of goal definition. But there is no compelling state interest related to conservation decisions comparable to that in the security arena. In the final analysis, it matters little whether it is entrenched interests or newly formed ones that solve the problems in the Tennessee Valley.

The character of the Forest Service also provides a telling comparison with the nature of the FBI. Unlike forest rangers, the special agents of the FBI operated within the hierarchical constraints of a paramilitary organization. Agents were organized into squads, and the chain of command ran from J. Edgar Hoover to the special agent in charge of each regional office to the individual special agent. No agent undertook any action without authorization from headquarters, and, in the case of domestic counterintelligence activity, each operation had to be approved in writing on a case-by-case basis by the director himself. While the ranger was expected to act with some degree of independence and even without consulting superiors, Hoover ruled his special agents with an iron hand. Unlike the forest ranger, who might develop conflicting loyalties to local interests, the special agent's first and only allegiance was to J. Edgar Hoover and his FBI.

Hoover represented a patriarchal authority at the center of a thoroughly modern bureaucratic enterprise.[59] The FBI was an ultimately rational organization whose normative structure "appeal[ed] to the sense of abstract legality, and presuppose[d] technical training" in every aspect of its operations.[60] But at the same time "the legitimacy of the master's orders," even when they ran contrary to rational planning and established legal practice, was "guaranteed by personal subjection." To paraphrase Max Weber, the fact that Hoover was indeed their ruler was always uppermost in the minds of his agents, administrators, and clerks.[61]

---

59.   Hoover was the patriarch of the FBI in Weber's sense of the term: "[Patriarchal domination] is based not on the official's commitment to an impersonal purpose and not on obedience to abstract norms, but on a strict personal loyalty" (Max Weber, *Economy and Society*, ed. Guenther Roth and Claus Wittich [Berkeley and Los Angeles: University of California Press, 1978], p. 1006).

60.   "But under bureaucratic domination these norms are established rationally, appeal to the sense of abstract legality, and presuppose technical training; under partriarchal domination the norms derive from tradition: the belief in the inviolability of that which has existed from time out of mind" (ibid.).

61.   "Under patriarchal domination the legitimacy of the master's orders is guaran-

The FBI director could exact such loyalty because, during the 1950s and 1960s, there was no outside review of his personnel policies. He could hire, transfer, promote, or fire at will, and there was no possibility of appeal.[62] Employees of the FBI were also subject to patriarchal authority outside the bureau; the FBI official manual prescribed codes of conduct for all aspects of an employee's life, including dress, sexual habits, and living conditions. Most unmarried employees, for example, were expected to live in FBI-authorized apartment buildings in close proximity to other FBI workers, all of whom were required to report any infractions of the official code of conduct. The director's authority was potent enough to break down the "bureaucratic separation of the 'private' and 'public' sphere."[63]

In 1950, then, the FBI retained important attributes associated with patriarchal authority, but coupled them with an otherwise thoroughly rationalized bureaucratic structure. Perhaps because it contained these atavistic elements, the FBI was able to resist other major trends of its day in public administration. Hoover's domination of the bureau contrasted sharply with the rise of experts and specialization of function throughout public bureaucracies.[64] While other bureau chiefs embraced a "line of confidence," placing trust in the professional assessments of their technicians, the FBI director tightened the "line of command" over his subordinates.[65]

The bureau also resisted a second tendency, that of centralization of "staff" or "auxiliary" functions such as budgeting, accounting and personnel at increasingly higher levels within the government.[66] In ad-

---

teed by personal subjection. . . . The fact that this concrete master is indeed their ruler is always uppermost in the minds of his subjects" (ibid.).

62. Because of their role in national security, the FBI and the CIA alone were exempted from the authority and regulations of the Civil Service (Victor S. Navasky, *Kennedy Justice* [New York: Atheneum; 1971], p. 16).

63. Weber, *Economy and Society*, pp. 1028–29.

64. Writing contemporaneously, Herbert A. Simon observed: "With the growing importance of the professional and technical specialist, there is a corresponding tendency for the working rules of organization—the rules that define the authority of legitimacy—to place more and more emphasis upon functional status, and less and less upon hierarchy" (Herbert A. Simon et al., *Public Administration* [New York: Alfred A. Knopf, 1950], pp. 200–201).

65. "To a very large extent, especially at the higher hierarchical levels, executive approval of staff recommendations is based almost entirely upon confidence in subordinates. To speak of a 'line of confidence' from top to bottom describes administrative behavior more realistically than to speak of a 'line of command' " (ibid., pp. 533–34).

66. Simon et al., identify centralization as "one of the most characteristic adminis-

dition to its exemption from Civil Service regulations, for example, the FBI was largely able to control its own budgets with little or no outside intervention. With a single exception, the FBI director always received the funds he requested from Congress. Although these requests were framed as the need for additional agents and clerks, the money came in lump sums and could be allocated at the discretion of the director. Even so, the Bureau of the Budget and its successor, the Office of Management and Budget, "rarely exercised meaningful supervision over the FBI's financial desires and there was no other external audit of the Bureau's finances."[67]

The special status of the FBI, derived in particular from its national security mission and relative independence from budgetary and other political controls, tended to place the agency at odds with the American tradition of liberal government. Nevertheless, from the outset of domestic intelligence activities in the late 1930s, the liberal political community displayed trust in the FBI and a willingness to delegate internal security policymaking to its director and his subordinates.[68] The aim was to fashion a central domestic intelligence agency that would meet the threat of Nazi and Communist subversion without itself subverting democratic and constitutional processes. By the year 1950, liberals viewed the FBI as an alternative preferable to the rising tide of McCarthyism. They were consistent both in their support for the agency and in their belief that security policy could be reduced to a matter of administrative efficiency in accordance with the values of a liberal society.

---

trative trends of our age—the tendency to lessen organizational self-containment" (ibid., pp. 272, 280).

67. Sanford J. Ungar, *FBI* (Boston: Little, Brown, 1975), p. 162. In addition, "the FBI has only four legally binding requirements in its appropriations: the number of new and replacement automobiles . . . $10,000 for taxicab hire, a historic item; a $70,000 contingency fund 'to meet unforeseen emergencies of a confidential character' . . . and finally $42,000 as 'compensation for the director' " (Walter Pincus, "The Bureau's Budget: A Source of Power," in Pat Watters and Stephen Gillers, eds., *Investigating the FBI* [New York: Doubleday, 1973], p. 64).

68. The idea of delegation here begins with Lowi's concept of "policy without law," by which he meant delegation of unspecified and broad grants of authority to administrative agencies through vague legislative enactments (Theodore J. Lowi, *The End of Liberalism: The Second Republic of the United States*, 2d ed. [New York: W. W. Norton, 1979], pp. 92–94). In the internal security arena, liberals pushed delegation a step further, conferring undefined authorities and unknown powers on the FBI literally in the absence of law.

CHAPTER TWO

The Liberal Theory of Internal Security

THE LIBERAL position on internal security was most clearly enunciated in the superheated politics of anticommunism in 1950. Liberals
sought to meet the security requirements of the nation and, at the same
time, build an electoral hedge against their opponents in Congress who
had taken the high ground on the issue of Communist subversion. This
chapter examinines a new and strident attack by liberals on communism that emerged in 1950 at the national level, and traces the origins
of the liberal view of internal security to the Roosevelt administration
in the late 1930s. Liberals did not oppose suppression of the Left. They
hoped to establish a hard line against Communists that would be enforced by the FBI. In the process, they contributed to a universal anti-
Communist consensus that placed the FBI beyond the reach of responsible criticism as well as higher executive and constitutional controls.
The political stage was set for an administrative transformation
through which the FBI would come to resemble an agency of internal
security modeled on a political police and an independent security state
within the state.

Hubert Humphrey once explained to a constituent that Americans
for Democratic Action (ADA) was formed in 1947 "as part of a nationwide movement by many liberal-minded men and women to stop the
growth of Communism and to end the influence of Henry Wallace and
his Progressive Party."[1] The ADA did bind together the non-Communist
left in the early years of the cold war and did take active steps against
the Wallace third-party candidacy,[2] but Humphrey's statement is par-

1. Hubert H. Humphrey to Rudy Schiro, October 8, 1954, 23.H.9.10F, Box 551,
    "HH Campaign: ADA," HHH.

2. In the early stages of the campaign, ADA published an attack on Wallace. Former
    attorney general Francis Biddle assessed ADA action before a House committee:
    "I think the best job on the Wallace movement was done by ADA. . . . They did a
    pamphlet . . . that show[ed] the Commie tie-up right down the line" (quoted in
    Kenneth O'Reilly, *Hoover and the UnAmericans* [Philadelphia, Pa.: Temple
    University Press, 1983], p. 177). In addition, the ADA worked closely with the
    Truman campaign to discredit Wallace: "During the campaign the ADA led the
    attack against the Progressives, publishing lists of party petition signers along
    with their alleged Communist-front connections and consistently portraying

ticularly informative because it indicates the degree to which liberals had taken up the fight against communism by the late 1940s.[3]

Humphrey and his circle of supporters had been in the forefront of the drive to organize the Minnesota chapter of the ADA, and Humphrey personally recruited anti-Communist CIO union leaders throughout the state. As a result of his efforts, in August 1947 the union leaders who supported Humphrey formed a committee that systematically signed up rank-and-file union members for the ADA.[4] In a prolonged and bitter struggle to wrest control of Minnesota's Democratic-Farmer-Labor party from Communists and Popular Front liberals, Humphrey built a powerful political coalition among the unions, the ADA membership, and other anti-Communist liberals. This alliance and the creed of anticommunism became catalytic elements in his personal transformation from mayor of Minneapolis to a national leader among American liberals in the space of a few years.

At the political and intellectual core of anti-Communist, or cold war, liberalism was an approach to internal security that supported delegation of authority to a strong central domestic intelligence agency. It was characterized by a commitment to preventive and emergency security measures, a respect for freedom of thought and speech—if not association[5]—and a conception of communism as a monolithic force bent on the destruction of the government of the United States and of Western society generally.

In part, the liberal view of internal security in 1950 originated in emergency procedures instituted by the Roosevelt administration to protect the United States against Nazi spies and saboteurs. In the wake of a rash of espionage cases, high-level charges of Communist infiltration of the State Department, the Communist revolution in China, ac-

---

Henry Wallace as a pathetic pawn of the Communists" (Norman Markowitz, "A View from the Left: From the Popular Front to Cold War Liberalism," in Robert Griffith et al., *The Spector* [New York: New Viewpoints, 1974], p. 114).

3.   Humphrey's strident anticommunism extended beyond the domestic arena: "I do not think we have put sufficient emphasis on the philosophy of a counter attack, of trying to get behind the iron curtain and engaging in guerrilla warfare, whether it be political, economic, or diplomatic. We have not done enough along that line" (Hubert H. Humphrey, *Congressional Record*, February 12, 1951, p. 1248).

4.   John Earl Haynes, *Dubious Alliance: The Making of Minnesota's DFL Party* (Minneapolis: University of Minnesota Press, 1984), p. 155.

5.   By 1954, some liberal leaders were no longer willing to tolerate association with the Communist party. In that year Hubert Humphrey introduced the Communist Control Act, which declared the Communist party an illegal conspiracy and enacted criminal sanctions against its members.

quisition of atomic weapons by the Soviet Union, and direct hostilities in the Korean conflict, liberal thinking in 1950 reverted to a wartime mentality that supported the use of emergency executive powers as a means of dealing with the threat of communism.[6]

The principal elements of the liberal theory of internal security are embodied in the Emergency Detention Act (EDA), designed and introduced by Senators Herbert Lehman, Harley Kilgore, Paul Douglas, Hubert Humphrey, William Benton, Estes Kefauver and others on September 6, 1950.[7] The bill provided for the immediate detention in an emergency of any individual when the attorney general "finds that there is reasonable ground to believe that such person may engage in, or may conspire with others to engage in acts of espionage or of sabotage." This legislation also contained a lengthy discourse on the nature of communism.[8] It was declared to be a "revolutionary political movement whose purpose it is, by treachery, deceit, infiltration . . . espionage, sabotage, [and] terrorism . . . to establish a communist totalitarian dictatorship in all the countries of the world through the medium of a single world-wide Communist political organization." The bill specifically named the Communist party of the United States and indicated that indigenous Communist political organizations were "constituent elements" of a larger Communist whole. It stated that persons who participate "repudiate their allegiance to the United States and in effect transfer their allegiance to the foreign country in which is vested the direction and control of the world Communist movement."[9]

6. On December 16, 1950, President Truman declared a national emergency. "And with the outbreak of the Korean war, Congress in 1950 passed the Defense Production Act, which established once more general presidential control over the economy for war purposes. A new executive proclamation of war emergency followed in December. Thereafter, the president by executive order created the Office of Defense Mobilization and the Office of Price Stabilization for executive regulation of the war economy" (Kelly, *The American Constitution*, p. 575).

7. The measure S. 4130, Title II, "Emergency Detention," eventually was enacted as Title II of the Internal Security Act of 1950, popularly known as the McCarran Act.

8. The findings of Congress on the nature of communism, which prefaced the EDA, were lifted verbatim from the Mundt bill (S. 2311). The Senate liberals and the Truman administration were determined to defeat the Mundt legislation because it contained provisions for registration of Communists and Communist-front organizations that they believed posed a significant threat to freedom of thought, speech, and association.

9. *Senate Bills*, 81st Cong., 2d sess., S. 4130, September 6, 1950, pp. 26, 21, 20. In addition, the bill cited the holding of membership in the Communist party after

This conception of communism was virtually identical with definitions offered by conservatives. But on the issue of registration of Communists and Communist-front organizations, liberals, as might be expected, parted company with their more conservative colleagues. Here, their views resembled more nearly those of FBI director J. Edgar Hoover, who on various occasions praised the liberals and warned against drastic legislative measures aimed at registering or abolishing the Communist party.[10] Liberals cited Hoover's approval and agreement in their arguments against the Mundt-Ferguson and McCarran legislative contributions to the Internal Security Act of 1950.[11]

In 1950, then, the liberal senators sought to meet the threat of sabotage and espionage before it occurred. Although their bill, the EDA, did establish a variety of procedural safeguards for the accused, it circumvented usual constitutional requirements of due process and the writ of habeas corpus.[12] These legislative provisions indicated a contradiction at the heart of liberal thinking concerning the threat posed by Communist ideology and organization in the United States. First, the legislation that liberals proposed in 1950 was not intended to reach or inquire directly into patterns of thought or association in the community. But because it defined communism as a movement of "sabotage" and "terrorism," it required that the Communists be identified in order to foil their conspiracy.[13]

January 1, 1949, as a reasonable ground for detention in an emergency (ibid., pp. 40–41).

10. As early as 1947, Hoover defended liberals against indiscriminate charges: "It is deceptive and detrimental, however, to pin the label of 'Communist' on honest American liberals and progressives merely because of a difference of opinion. Honesty and common decency demand that the clear-cut line of demarcation that exists between liberals and Communists be recognized" (J. Edgar Hoover, "How to Fight Communism," *Newsweek Magazine*, June 9, 1947, p. 31).

11. In a letter to the chairman of the board of the American Civil Liberties Union (ACLU), Senator Estes Kefauver cited Hoover's position: "I could not, however, go along with the registration part [of the McCarran bill] as presently written because I think it is unworkable and would defeat the purpose of better security. This latter opinion is based upon the statements and belief of J. Edgar Hoover and the FBI" (Estes Kefauver to Ernest Angell, September 21, 1950, vol. 22, 1950, "5. Correspondence with Congressional Leaders," ACLU).

12. Among others, these safeguards included establishing a Detention Review Board, preliminary hearings, provision of counsel to the accused, appeal procedures, rules of evidence, judicial review, and right of petition.

13. The question of whether Communist conspiracy did in fact exist in the United States had been laid to rest several months earlier when eleven leaders of the Communist party, including Eugene Dennis, were convicted under the Smith Act on conspiracy charges. Judge Harold R. Medina instructed the jury: "Let

Second, the liberal course was to distinguish rigorously between thought or speech on one hand and violent action on the other. As Senator Paul Douglas explained when arguing in favor of tolerating Communist propaganda, "We are presented with a tremendous problem of democracy, namely, how to prevent sabotage and spying while at the same time to protect not only the democratic rights but the practical necessity for free discussion."[14] But because the EDA defined all Communist parties as "constituent elements" of a political organization whose purpose was "to establish a communist totalitarian dictatorship in all the countries of the world," the distinction between thought and action tended to break down.

The answer that the liberal political community proposed to this "problem of democracy" was J. Edgar Hoover and the FBI.[15] Indeed, a central role for the FBI in security matters emerged as a cornerstone of the liberal approach in the debates surrounding the Internal Security Act in the summer of 1950. Liberals offered the EDA as a responsible alternative to what they saw as a variety of drastic anti-Communist legislative measures proposed by conservative Republican and Democratic senators. In support of the EDA, liberals argued for a strong, centralized FBI—what Arthur Schlesinger, Jr., had called "the best professional counterespionage agency we can get to protect our national

---

me repeat that the crime charged is a conspiracy. The crime charged is not that these defendants personally advocated or taught the duty or necessity of overthrowing and destroying the Government of the United States by force and violence . . . The charge is that these defendants conspired with each other . . . to advocate and to teach the duty or necessity of such overthrow and destruction" (*New York Times*, October 14, 1949, p. 14).

14. *Congressional Record*, September 8, 1950, p. 14405. Senator Herbert H. Lehman demonstrated similar concerns in a speech for a Roosevelt Day Dinner sponsored by the ADA: "Liberty is challenged not only by those who openly declare their allegiance to totalitarianism, but also by some who solemnly swear their devotion to democracy . . . [who] insist that we must suppress free inquiry in order to preserve our institutions and our way of life. I judge this attitude to be heresy of the worst kind. I judge it to be, in fact, the denial of democracy" (Speech, Herbert H. Lehman, January 27, 1950, 23.L.3.8F, "ADA Correspondence-Misc. 1950–51," HHH).

15. One noted liberal, Morris L. Ernst, counsel for the American Civil Liberties Union, wrote: "New political movements, by underhanded methods, seek to bypass the honest competition of ideas. We face an invisible underground where Fascists and Communists work furtively and zealously against our freedom and our ideas. Something *had* to be done about that, and the FBI had to do it" (Morris L. Ernst, "Why I No Longer Fear the FBI," *Reader's Digest*, December 1950, p. 136).

security."[16] Testimony by J. Edgar Hoover figured prominently in liberal arguments favoring the EDA and opposing the registration and deportation sections of the Mundt-Ferguson and McCarran bills.

Hubert Humphrey has provided perhaps the best exposition of the role liberals contemplated for the FBI in the administration of internal security. Above all, internal security matters were to be removed from political, and particularly legislative, arenas. In reference to pending anti-Communist bills, he argued that "this futile legislation . . . has already done serious damage to our counterespionage operations by making it increasingly more difficult for the FBI to follow the activities of the Communist Party."[17] In the place of congressional probes of communism in government, liberal theory advocated additional resources for and professionalization of the nation's principal internal security agency. As Humphrey explained to his colleagues in the Senate: "If the FBI does not have enough trained manpower to do this job [control communism], then, for goodness sake, let us give the FBI the necessary funds for recruiting the manpower it needs. I do not believe there is a Senator or a Member of the House of Representatives who could even catch a Communist, or would know how. This is a job that must be done by experts."[18]

Liberal politicians of this period sought to remove the explosive issue of internal security from the political arena and to install it in the FBI as a routine process of administration. In an early attempt to stem public hysteria associated with Senator Joseph McCarthy's charges of Communist infiltration of the State Department, Senator Herbert H. Lehman of New York wrote, "It would seem to me that the F.B.I. and the other government Security Agencies can be depended upon to protect the Government and the nation generally from infiltration by subversives of any kind."[19] Belief in the efficacy of the FBI would characterize the liberal attitude toward the bureau for many years to come.

16.   Arthur M. Schlesinger, Jr., *The Vital Center: The Politics of Freedom* (Boston: Houghton Mifflin, 1949), p. 129.

17.   *Congressional Record*, September 11, 1950, p. 14462.

18.   In the same speech, Humphrey developed his ideas on administration in the field of internal security: "The security of our country is not something which can be preserved by means of 10-cent pamphlets or grandiose, hit-or-miss legislation. . . . [It] requires careful, detailed, systematic, scientific study by men with a long background of experience in dealing with sabotage, espionage, and subversive activities. . . . by the men who are in the Federal Bureau of Investigation and the men who are in the Department of Justice" (ibid., pp. 14459, 14458).

19.   Herbert H. Lehman to Mrs. Kenneth S. Strayer, January 11, 1951, Senate De-

The liberal contribution to internal security is not well understood or even well represented in the literature that deals with McCarthyism, the FBI, or the cold war period generally. Much of it attempts to explain what McCarthyism was or was not—mass political movement, elite-led hysteria, reaction to a unique set of cold war circumstances, and so on. Many interpretations overlook the fact that McCarthyism —as a movement that found expression in Congress—was a fleeting and transitory phenomenon. It was the liberal approach to internal security that prevailed. Domestic intelligence innovations first established by the Roosevelt administration proved more enduring than McCarthyism precisely because the liberal political community institutionalized internal security policymaking and powers in the FBI.

Over the past decade, a small but detailed literature—drawing on the Freedom of Information Act and the printed proceedings of several committees of Congress in the middle 1970s—has sought to revive the issue of McCarthyism by concentrating on secret programs of the FBI and other intelligence agencies.[20] It attempts to demonstrate that the means and ends of McCarthyism were adopted by FBI bureaucrats and their superiors in the Justice Department and the White House. This literature performs an invaluable service by levering important, formerly inaccessible information into the public domain, but much of it is marred by a tendentious spirit, a fixation on facts and exposé, and a tendency to draw rough-hewn conclusions without sufficient regard for analytical precision and theoretical clarity.

Following the lead of President Roosevelt in 1936, liberals consistently sought to vest internal security powers in the executive. That the

---

partmental Files, Loyalty Investigations, HHL. On the same issue, Hubert Humphrey reiterated his view in characteristically more colorful language: "I submit that if there are communists in the State Department, we have the machinery to find out. I shall always believe that the Federal Bureau of Investigation and its agents are more qualified to find Communists than any United States Senator. . . . If the Department of Justice does not have the manpower it needs in order to do the things which need to be done, I submit that we should vote for the necessary appropriations, instead of trying to get ourselves Junior G-man badges and trying to act as supersleuths, when we are not equipped, either by experience or background, to do so" (*Congressional Record*, February 12, 1951, p. 1259).

20.   For example, see Frank J. Donner, *The Age of Surveillance: The Aims and Methods of America's Political Intelligence System* (New York: Alfred A. Knopf, 1980); Kenneth O'Reilly, "The FBI and the Orgins of McCarthyism," *Historian* 45 (May 1983), pp. 372–93; Athan Theoharis, *Spying on Americans: Political Surveillance from Hoover to the Huston Plan* (Philadelphia, Pa.: Temple University Press, 1978); and David Wise, *The American Police State: The Government against the People* (New York: Random House, 1976).

anti-Communist committees of Congress succeeded for a time in wresting the issue of internal security away from the liberals indicates a failure less of nerve than of strategy.[21] Many liberals could and did oppose the Truman loyalty boards, McCarthy, and the strident anti-Communist committees of Congress.[22] The liberal agenda in 1950, however, was to institutionalize security and investigative powers in the FBI. This involved an expansion of policies first set forth in the heyday of the Roosevelt presidency, before the establishment of the House Committee on Un-American Activities and liberal loss of initiative in the politics of internal security.[23]

Theory and practice in the field of internal security degenerated in the 1950s because liberal leaders made the anti-Communist consensus of the times their own. In part, this accommodation ended a long and acrimonious conflict between anti-Communist and Popular Front liberals concerning their relationship with the Communist party. After 1935, when the Seventh World Congress called for a Popular Front to

21. An aide to Hubert Humphrey indicated the senator's assessment of liberal failures in the security arena: "Hubert has felt for a long time that the liberal movement unnecessarily abandoned 'anti-communism' to the reactionaries. It's his feeling that the result of this abandonment was the fact that the reactionaries were able to grab hold of the issue and not only gain politically but also perpetrate on the American society a whole series of legislative proposals that tended to injure the innocent people as well as the guilty people. At the same time, he had a strong personal feeling that anti-subversive legislation was desirable and necessary" (Max M. Kampelman to Mulford Q. Sibley, September 16, 1954, 23.G.8.4F, Box 641, "Research Files. Internal Security. Communist Control Act of '54 [1]," HHH).

22. Hubert Humphrey stated his position clearly: "I have, for example, consistently opposed Senator McCarthy and I will continue to do so as long as he uses the methods he does to combat Communism. It is these methods that constitute the great danger to American freedoms. Persons are deprived of rights and privileges for belonging to wholly legal groups, and others are subjected to smears and damaged reputations through star-chamber proceedings where no legal protections are available" (Humphrey to John G. Rombeck, September 13, 1954, 23.L.10.3B, Box 104, "Leg.: Communism—HH Amendment to Butler Bill—Outlawing C.P.," HHH).

23. In August 1936, President Roosevelt used executive authority to expand domestic intelligence operations in preparation for war and to centralize them in the FBI. His secret orders "establish[ed] the basic domestic intelligence structure and policies for the federal government," which would not be challenged until the early 1970s. HUAC's predecessor, the Dies Committee, was not established until May 1938. Thereafter it was active in attacking the New Deal and pressing the issue of anticommunism, although it was somewhat muted during World War II (Church, bk. 3, p. 292; Richard M. Freeland, *The Truman Doctrine and the Origins of McCarthyism* [New York: Schocken Books, 1974], p. 118).

combat fascism, American liberals and Communists had made common cause against the rise of Fascist regimes around the world.[24] While many liberals turned on the Popular Front during the short period of the Nazi-Soviet pact in 1939, Hitler's subsequent attack on the Soviet Union brought most of them back into the fold. Indeed, many believed that Stalin had only used the pact as a delaying tactic to ready his forces for war with the Axis powers.[25] But as the cold war heated up in the immediate postwar period, the dominant strain of American liberalism turned resolutely against antidemocratic ideologies on the Left as well as the Right.

Liberal participation in the anti-Communist consensus after 1950 tended to disable rational public debate and legislative oversight of the national security apparatus. It encouraged delegation of broad and ill-defined investigatory and intelligence powers to the agency charged with fighting and containing the Communist menace at home. In the early 1950s, members of the liberal political community envisioned an FBI based on the model of a bureau of domestic intelligence. But because they were not prepared to impose ministerial controls over the FBI, the bureau soon began to resemble more the model of a secret police. The liberal theory of internal security therefore spawned a host of unintended consequences with serious implications for the rights of citizens and democratic government more generally. These failures can be isolated and analyzed in relation to the liberal politics of emergency detention in 1950 and subsequent administrative politics within the FBI.

Politics of Emergency Detention

The liberal thrust to enact emergency detention measures in September of 1950 was largely a futile, if sincere, attempt to gain control of anti-Communist legislation and subject it to liberal principles. The senators hoped to preserve freedom of speech and association in ordinary times through legislation to govern the control of potential saboteurs and spies under emergency conditions. It was, from the outset, an uphill

24. By the end of the 1930s, the American Communist party line "sounded closer to the rhetoric of Woodrow Wilson than to the ideas of Karl Marx, [and] it reflected the Communists' growing eagerness to float placidly in the 'main currents' of [the New Deal and] American life" (Richard H. Pells, *Radical Visions and American Dreams: Culture and Social Thought in the Depression Years* [New York: Harper & Row, 1973], p. 297).

25. Diana Trilling, "A Memorandum on the Hiss Case," *Partisan Review* 17, no. 5 (1950): 491.

battle because events had already propelled conservative and reactionary proposals to the forefront. These included bills to register the Communist party and a variety of immigration measures.

The months preceding the passage of the Internal Security Act were littered with sensational events that tended to ensure that even the most extreme security legislation would receive a warm reception on Capitol Hill. In a theatrical trial in the fall of 1949, eleven leaders of the Communist party, including Eugene Dennis, had been convicted under the Smith Act of conspiracy to teach the violent overthrow of the government of the United States.[26] The following spring, a subcommittee of the Senate Foreign Relations Committee, chaired by Senator Millard Tydings, investigated charges of Communist infiltration of the State Department initiated by Senator Joseph McCarthy at Wheeling, West Virginia, on February 11, 1950.

In March, Harry Gold was charged in connection with the Klaus Fuchs atomic espionage case. Gold's confession led eventually to the arrest of nine Americans, including Julius Rosenberg, on July 11.[27] Justice Department employee Judith Coplin was convicted for passing secret documents to her Russian lover.[28] By April, the Tydings Committee investigation had heated to a boiling point, with McCarthy naming Owen Lattimore as the "top Russian espionage agent."[29] In June, economist William Remington of the Commerce Department was indicted for perjury, a charge growing out of accusations by Elizabeth Bentley.[30] And on June 25, North Korea invaded the south, drawing the United States, for the first time, into direct hostilities with a Communist power. This constellation of events set the stage for drastic internal security legislation from both conservative and liberal quarters and from both sides of the aisle.

Not only were the times favorable to the most radical anti-Communist proposals, but conservative forces had captured the agenda in Congress. In July of 1950, the Republican Policy Committee put the Mundt-Nixon bill to register Communists and Communist-front organizations on its "must list."[31] Ultraconservative Democrats, such as

26.   *New York Times*, October 15, 1949, p. 1.

27.   David Caute, *The Great Fear* (New York: Simon and Schuster, 1978), p. 62.

28.   Richard M. Fried, *Men Against McCarthy* (New York: Columbia University Press, 1976), p. 15.

29.   Robert Griffith, *The Politics of Fear* (Lexington: University of Kentucky Press, 1970), p. 77.

30.   *Washington Post*, June 9, 1950, p. 1.

31.   Griffith, *Politics of Fear*, p. 117.

McCarran and Wood, who chaired powerful committees of Congress, had held hearings and prepared a battery of anti-Communist legislative proposals. Subsequent to the outbreak of the Korean War, these measures gained standing in official Washington. The Mundt-Nixon bill was redrafted as the Mundt-Ferguson-Johnson bill (S. 2311), joining perhaps a dozen well-developed, if ill-conceived, reactionary internal security proposals from both sides of the Capitol.

The White House was determined not to let the Mundt legislation to register Communists come to a vote in the Eighty-first Congress,[32] but it had failed to produce a viable alternative, and pressure for enactment mounted steadily after mid-July.[33] There was considerable consternation and confusion on the part of the White House, pro-administration forces in the Congress, and liberal organizations associated through the National Civil Liberties Clearing House (NCLCH). The administration bill (S. 4061), which finally emerged on August 17, followed suggestions made by President Truman to the Congress in his internal security message of August 8.

The bill reaffirmed the previous legislative intent of Congress by tightening existing anti-espionage laws and expanding the powers of the attorney general to deal with deportable aliens.[34] But the Truman

32.   Senator Lehman was among the administration supporters who took direct action against the Mundt bill: "I am sure that you are familiar with my position on the Mundt-Ferguson Bill, which I think would endanger many of our civil liberties. As you may know, I entered the formal objection which prevented the consideration of the Mundt-Ferguson Bill when it came up on the Senate calendar on August 8th" (Lehman to Jacob S. Potofsky, August 10, 1950, Senate Subject Files, "91. Internal Security Correspondence," HHL).

33.   The ADA advised that "pressure on the Hill for Senate passage of the Mundt-Ferguson-Johnson 'communist control' bill (S. 2311) has skyrocketed within the past few days. Senator Eastland has shown that there is a strong Republican-Southern Democrat coalition intent upon moving to substitute the Mundt Bill for the Hawaiian Statehood Bill. . . . The Chamber of Commerce, American Legion and other organizations are reported to be 'blanketing' the Senate with communications demanding passage of S. 2311" (Violet M. Gunther, ADA to Organizations Cooperating Through the National Civil Liberties Clearing House, July 20, 1950, Senate Subject Files, "93. Internal Security. Administrative Bill [Pro]," HHL).

34.   *Congressional Quarterly Almanac*, 1950, p. 392. A document entitled "Analysis of Internal Security Bill" that accompanied the administration's bill to Congress cited specific improvements to the Smith Act, the Nationality Act, the Immigration Act, and the Foreign Agents Registration Act as well as "The Treason Statute," "The Peacetime Espionage Laws," "Law Relating to Sabotage," and "The Loyalty Program." In a handwritten note covering the analysis of S. 4061, Mary Alice Baldinger of the ACLU accurately characterized the administration bill as "a patch work quilt" (vol. 22, 1950, "7. ACLU Memos and Policy Statements," ACLU).

administration did not provide leadership or even significant support for its allies in the Senate. On August 5, Mary Alice Baldinger of the ACLU reported, "The White House is still working on the Internal Security Bills (HR 4703 and S. 595) [two relatively mild proposals] but, frankly they don't seem to know what they are doing."[35]

By August 10, a coalition of conservative Republicans and southern Democrats in the Senate had consolidated forces behind the chairman of the Judiciary Committee, Pat McCarran, who introduced an omnibus antisubversive bill. The McCarran proposals combined the Mundt-Ferguson-Johnson registration provisions with four other immigration and anti-espionage bills already approved by the Judiciary Committee.[36] At this critical juncture, indecision among most Democrats and the Truman administration appeared to increase. As of August 12, there was still no indication from the White House as to what bills it would support or whether, indeed, there would be a separate administration bill on internal security. Baldinger assessed the situation:

> The Democratic Policy Committee still seems to be completely confused about what is the best course to take. . . . The whole imbroglio seems to be a really shocking example of lack of leadership and direction from the White House. As I told you, the majority of the Administration's staunchest Senatorial supporters did not know Truman's proposals [of August 8] were coming until they came. They arrived on the Hill so late that [Majority Leader] Scott Lucas was put in the position of searching for them as he fended off the Mundt Bill on the calendar call. They came without any direction whatever as to strategy on concrete legislative work, either along the line of a new bill or with definite support for either S. 595 or HR 4703.[37]

35. She continued, "The man who had been working on them [the internal security bills] has gone on vacation, and the people who have them now seem sort of baffled as to how the Administration's problem can be finally worked out. They were calling around yesterday to make another check on the attitude of liberal organizations toward these bills; they were told—I believe in every case—that there was no opposition to them. . . . In other words, the situation is still confused, and so am I, and so is everybody else I know including the Democratic Policy Committee. I would hate to have to bet any money on how this will all eventually be worked out" (M. A. Baldinger to ACLU, August 5, 1950, vol. 22, 1950, "5. Correspondence with Congressional Leaders," ACLU).

36. *Congressional Quarterly Almanac*, 1950, p. 392.

37. Baldinger concluded, "It is difficult to see how any intelligent legislation such as was described in the President's message can possibly be reached under the present conditions. Maybe next week will clear things up a bit" (M. A. Baldinger to

When the administration's bill (S. 4061) finally did arrive on August 17, it was introduced by Warren Magnuson and cosponsored by Senators Lucas, Kilgore, Graham, Meyers, Kefauver, Green, Humphrey, Douglas, and Lehman. By this time, however, the conservative antisubversive proposals had substantial support. The Democratic leaders believed that even if they were successful in substituting the Magnuson bill, any moderate legislation brought to the floor would be amended with the Mundt registration or McCarran omnibus proposals and that these would carry.[38] Relations between the cooperating Democratic senators and the Truman administration deteriorated. "There is a tremendous amount of resentment," Baldinger noted on August 19, "among the top Democratic Senators at the bungling ineptitude with which the White House has handled this whole subject. They feel it will very likely cost some of them their election."[39]

Despite the adverse parliamentary situation, liberal organizations threw their support behind the administration bills. On August 28, the leadership of twenty-two organizations, including the ACLU and ADA, issued a statement denouncing the McCarran, Mundt, and Wood bills and endorsing the administration's alternatives proposed by Magnuson in the Senate and Emanuel Cellar in the House.[40] And on September 1, the ACLU mailed out a bulletin requesting the assistance of its local affiliates and state correspondents in defeating the McCarran bill. This ACLU communication underscored the confused and volatile legislative environment in which the Internal Security Act of 1950 was forged: "The reason we have been unable to send you these bulletins more frequently is that the legislative picture has changed so much even from hour to hour that it was impossible to give a plan of cohesive action to the affiliates."[41]

Herbert Levy, August 12, 1950, vol. 22, 1950, "5. Correspondence with Congressional Leaders," ACLU).

38. "It cannot be predicted until after Monday's meeting [of the Democratic Party caucus] when the anti-subversive legislation will come up, or how. . . . The probability is that S. 4061 will then be amended on the floor with the registration provisions of the Mundt Bill. That is the best we can expect. That will be very bad; and maybe we will wind up with something even worse than that" (M. A. Baldinger to George Soll, August 19, 1950, vol. 22, 1950, "5. Correspondence with Congressional Leaders," ACLU).

39. Ibid.

40. NCLCH release, "Joint Statement on National Security Legislation Now Pending Before Congress," date stamped August 28, 1950, Senate Subject Files, "93. Internal Security. Administrative Bill (Pro)," HHL.

41. Herbert Monte Levy to Local Affiliates and State Correspondents, September 1, 1950, (vol. 22, 1950, "7. ACLU Memos and Policy Statements," ACLU.

It was under these conditions that the liberal bloc in the Senate introduced on September 6 what was apparently an eleventh-hour substitute, the Kilgore bill (S. 4130), which contained tough new emergency detention provisions. That same day the liberal sponsors of the proposal met with President Truman and explained that "they had to make a move of this sort as the only possible way of beating the McCarran bill." Although the president told the senators to press forward with the legislation, he reportedly refused to give it his unequivocal support.[42]

From this point until September 20—when the Senate passed the McCarran Act—the actions, arguments, and motivations of the liberal senators reflect, in condensed form, a politics of consensus that came to dominate the field of domestic security. The logic of this politics, which traced its liberal heritage to the Roosevelt years, set in motion a process through which the responsibility for setting internal security policy was delegated to a centralized domestic intelligence agency. And it was at this juncture that the FBI began to assume some of the characteristics associated with the model of a political police. The highly charged issue of domestic communism was levered out of the congressional arena and transformed into a set of routine administrative procedures under the authority of J. Edgar Hoover and the FBI.

The origins of the Kilgore bill are somewhat shadowy,[43] although it appears that the bill was first drafted by the office of Senator Paul Douglas of Illinois.[44] In his published memoirs, Douglas describes the

42. Quoted in Griffith, *Politics of Fear*, pp. 120–21. Griffith's source for the quotation is "Stephen J. Spingarn, Memorandum for the Files, Sept. 6, 1950, National Defense—Internal Security and Individual Rights, vol. 3, Spingarn Papers."

43. The first official announcement of the emergency detention proposal was a vague press release from the office of Senator Kilgore, which attacked the McCarran legislation and presented a lengthy outline of the emergency detention bill but without naming the bill or citing its number. A quote attributed to Senator Kilgore stated: "The substitute legislation tightens present internal security legislation and provides for the detention in time of emergency of Communists and all other persons who may commit acts of espionage or sabotage" (Press Release, Office of Senator Kilgore [D. W.Va.], September 6, 1950, vol. 22, 1950, "5. Correspondence with Congressional Leaders," ACLU).

44. In a letter written two years after the fact, Senator Lehman attributed the EDA to Douglas: "As I recall, Senator Douglas' staff prepared the preliminary draft of this proposal, although it may have come to Senator Douglas from an outside source of which I am unaware" (Herbert H. Lehman to Ralph Barton Perry, November 1, 1952, Senate Legislative Files, "44. Internal Security Act," HHL). Another report described the Douglas contribution this way: "Senator Paul Douglas (D, Ill.) spent a weekend studying the problem and decided that the emergency-detention system established by the British during the last war might

emergency detention legislation as a response to the Mundt bill. According to his account, as the second session of the Eighty-first Congress was drawing to a close, Majority Leader Scott Lucas inadvertently allowed a motion to consider the Mundt bill, with its registration provisions, to be introduced on the Senate floor. In response, Douglas and his "progressive group immediately asked Joe Rauh and Frank McCulloch [of the Senate Office of Legislative Counsel] to draft an alternative . . . [because the liberal senators] did not want to take a purely negative position when some real danger to the nation was involved."[45] Douglas suggested three reasons why the senators offered their emergency detention proposal:

> [First,] . . . we thought we might derail the Mundt-Nixon-Mc-Carran steamroller with an affirmative substitute. Second, we hoped to change the focus of public attention from Communist speech and association (which were not the greatest dangers) to the genuine problems of sabotage and espionage. Third, and equally high in our thinking, was the fact that J. Edgar Hoover had just made clear that the Federal Bureau of Investigation was ready to seize some 12,000 dangerous persons in case of war with Russia. We thought there should be procedures for their release where there was no danger of sabotage or espionage.[46]

The first motivation is certainly consistent with reports of the meeting between the liberal senators and the president on September 6.[47]

---

be the answer. . . . Douglas convinced a handful of his liberal colleagues that they would make a far better showing against the McCarran-Mundt proposals by offering the British system as an alternative than by merely advocating tightening our present espionage and immigration laws as recommended by the President" (*New Republic*, September 25, 1950, p. 7).

45.   Douglas explained as follows: "Truman wanted to keep this bill [Mundt-Nixon] off the Senate floor in 1950 in order to kill it by inaction. Scott Lucas made the parliamentary mistake, however, of failing, as the session was drawing to a close, to schedule another bill for action after we had passed a relatively unimportant one. So there was an apparently unnoticed parliamentary vacuum on the floor. Late that night Mundt arose with a smile and introduced the Nixon bill. Since Lucas had left the floor to me while he took some much-needed rest, I at once called for a quorum, but it was too late. The motion was in order, and the Senate had to deal with the issue" (*In the Fullness of Time: The Memoirs of Paul H. Douglas* [New York: Harcourt Brace Jovanovich, 1971], p. 306). Douglas's account, here and elsewhere, is rather simplistic. Lucas might not have been able to withstand pressure from McCarran indefinitely, and conservative senators had the option of attaching their internal security proposals to other bills as riders.

46.   Ibid., p. 306.

47.   Douglas was apparently more optimistic than some of his liberal colleagues:

But more, as the Baldinger memos indicate, the senators felt that the executive had dropped the ball. They had waited for leadership and for realistic legislation to emerge from the White House so that a Democratic Congress could attempt to table the more drastic bills. Not only had proposals failed to materialize in a timely fashion, but when they did come, they contained little that was new, either in content or legislative strategy. In this leadership vacuum, the liberal senators faced an adversary southern wing in their own party, and found themselves up against the formidable talents and powers of the chairman of the Judiciary Committee, Pat McCarran.[48] It is, therefore, probable that Douglas's account can be taken at face value in this particular: the liberals proposed the Emergency Detention Act as a desperate move to capture initiative and leadership in the politics of internal security and to assert their own approach.

On the second point, there can be little doubt that the liberal senators sought to divert the thrust of internal security measures then pending in Congress away from efforts to control thought, speech, and free association. Their intent—and this is the central logic of the EDA—was to redirect internal security back to its origins in a wartime setting by concentrating on the hazards of espionage and sabotage. The liberals refused to take the metaphor of the cold war as seriously as did their more conservative colleagues. To be sure, they paid it lip service, but they were, for the most part, unwilling to abandon their own approach to internal security. Perhaps they believed that their detention proposals would never be activated. A few Communists in government, a handful of convicted spies, and even armed conflict with Communist powers in Korea did not justify such measures.

Douglas's final point—that the liberals proposed the Kilgore bill to regulate detention of "dangerous persons" by the FBI and to set up

---

"Some sponsors of the 'Red detention' substitute voiced doubt that the new measure or anything the Administration can devise at this point can avert passage of the Mundt-Ferguson registration plan and many other sweeping provisions of the McCarran bill" (*Washington Post*, September 7, 1950, p. 13).

48. In contrast with several of the liberals, who were first-term senators, Pat McCarran was a grand master of legislative politics. According to one account, "McCarran . . . had a swift and sure instinct for the traditional levers of congressional power. He exercised baronial authority over the Senate Judiciary Committee, and through his control of all judicial appointments he was able to exact tribute from the administration and his fellow senators alike. He could extort from Attorney General James P. McGranery, in return for the latter's confirmation, the promise that the Justice Department would press perjury charges against Owen Lattimore. And he could browbeat a deputy attorney general into promising that—'Cross my heart'—he would carry out a demand made by the chairman" (Griffith, *Politics of Fear*, p. 118).

"procedures for their release"—is somewhat misleading. J. Edgar Hoover did make a statement before the Senate Appropriations Committee on September 7 to the effect that "the FBI has tagged [the] 12,000 most dangerous Communists, and is ready to seize them in case of war with Russia." And Hoover was quoted as requesting 835 new agents and 1,218 additional clerical workers to establish surveillance close enough "to put these people to bed at night and get them up in the morning."[49] But Hoover's testimony followed the introduction of the Kilgore bill by one day and so could not have served as a direct motivation for it.

The FBI director's statement was interpreted by some as support for the nascent emergency detention legislation.[50] Hubert Humphrey relentlessly used the testimony of the FBI director to bolster the detention initiative and to attack the McCarran bill four days later on the floor of the Senate.[51] This is not to suggest, however, that liberals were unconcerned with the rights of individuals who might be incarcerated under their proposals. Their legislation was, indeed, selective. It steered away from indiscriminate mass internment of national or racial classes of persons, focusing on suspected spies and saboteurs. In short, the liberals intended to avoid a repetition of the concentration camps established for the nisei during World War II.[52]

Whether there was direct coordination between the FBI director and the liberal senators over the issue of emergency detention would seem to be one of those questions that cannot definitely be decided and probably is not very important. That there was extensive mutual and reinforcing support is beyond question. The timing of Hoover's state-

49.   *Washington Post*, September 8, 1950, p. 19.

50.   "A question arose as to whether they [American citizens] could be interned summarily without new Congressional authorization. In some quarters this was seen as a strong argument for adoption of the bill offered by Senator Harley M. Kilgore" (*New York Times*, September 8, 1950, p. 1).

51.   In this regard, Humphrey stated: "J. Edgar Hoover has testified that 12,000 [Communists] whom he considers to be dangerous he would have to pick up. We provide the means [in the EDA] by which he can pick them up, and do a thorough job of picking them up. The McCarran bill does not provide that means" (*Congressional Record*, September 11, 1950, p. 14493).

52.   One of the sponsors of the Kilgore bill explained it this way: "We felt that since the security agencies of the federal government would undoubtedly move to detain Communists in the event of war in any case, as they did in the case of enemy aliens and sympathizers in World War II, there was some advantage in making legislative provision for this contingency and surrounding it with the best safeguards we could" (Herbert H. Lehman to Ralph Barton Perry, November 1, 1952, Senate Legislative Files, "44. Internal Security Act," HHL).

ment lent credibility to the emergency detention bill, providing the liberals with powerful arguments in support of their cause célèbre. Indeed, the FBI director had gone on record in opposition to banning the Communist party or registering its membership.[53] He had instead recommended securing congressional authorization for his own clandestine emergency detention programs on August 5, 1946, and had reiterated his request to the attorney general on subsequent occasions.[54]

One can only speculate on the motivations of the FBI director. Did he attack efforts to register and outlaw communism because he did not want specific legislation defining the role and powers of his agency? Perhaps he preferred undefined grants of authority that would allow greater latitude in his lifelong crusade against the red menace. Did he then request congressional authorization for his detention programs because he feared that they would be discovered and embarrass the FBI in the absence of specific legislation?

For their part, the liberal senators celebrated the director and his agency, invoking his power and prestige to bolster their approach to internal security. They sang his praise on the floor of the Senate and in the pages of the mass media. In describing the Kilgore detention proposal Senator Lehman said, "It would dovetail with the plans and designs of the FBI for the protection of our internal security. This is the kind of a law the FBI would welcome. . . . a real security bill—a real anti-Communist bill."[55]

53.   J. Edgar Hoover apparently was not alone in his opposition to major provisions of the McCarran bill: "The Department of Justice, the Department of Defense, the Department of State, the Central Intelligence Agency and the F.B.I. were unanimous that the [McCarran] bill would actually hamper their efforts to protect us against the real dangers of communist espionage and sabotage" (Representative Franklin D. Roosevelt, Jr., October 18, 1950, from a document entitled "Six Minute Speech on Senator Lehman by FDR, Jr.," p. 2, Special Files, "759. FDR, Jr.," HHL).

54.   Church, bk. 3, p. 46.

55.   Lehman continued, "It [the Kilgore bill] would not require the FBI to show its hand, to disclose its sources, and to neutralize its effectiveness before the day comes when the FBI may need to show its hand and act to protect the very life of our Nation. . . . In times of internal danger, we would round up those whom the FBI knows to be Communists and threats to the national security, and put them under detention and surveillance. The individuals concerned would not be asked to register. The FBI would register them. But they would have full opportunity to prove that they are not what the FBI says they are" (*Congressional Record* reprint entitled "Statement by Senator Lehman on S. 4130, The Internal Security and Internment Bill," September 11, 1950, Senate Subject Files, "Internal Security Bill S. 4130," HHL).

There was another motivation behind the decision to propose emergency detention legislation. As late as September 4, two days before the Kilgore bill was introduced, many questions remained concerning its sponsorship, content, and strategy.[56] No doubt, the liberals were anxious to go on record as opposing communism in preparation for the election only four weeks away.[57] They were fully cognizant of the antidemocratic aspects of the detention proposal. An aide to Senator Lehman, Julius Edelstein, specifically advised the senator, "The operational weaknesses of this amendment are many and its constitutional weaknesses are, in my judgment, profound."[58]

Although Edelstein suggested a number of improvements to the measure, his ambivalence was clear: "I would very much like to recommend your going along but I am forced reluctantly to the conclusion that this is a pretty bad bill, even though superior in most respects to Mundt-Ferguson." On balance, however, he did urge that Lehman sponsor the Kilgore bill because "the political logic of the situation requires that you go along." That political logic was, of course, that the bill might possibly preempt the McCarran and Mundt proposals and, in the process, make a show of liberal anti-Communist politics.

56. Senator Lehman's administrative aide, Julius C. C. Edelstein, advised: "It is difficult for me to make a final recommendation because the form of this amendment [the emergency detention proposals] is still undecided. It is even undecided whether the amendment will be introduced. I understand that Senator Kilgore proposes to call Senators Douglas, Graham, Kefauver, and yourself, into an informal caucus Tuesday morning [September 5] to decide what to do" (J.C.C.E. to Senator Lehman, September 4, 1950, Senate Subject Files, "97. Internal Security. Constitutionality of Bills," HHL).

57. Senator Douglas explained his vote in favor of the final Senate version of the McCarran bill—which contained the Mundt-Ferguson registration provisions as well as the EDA: "The administration forces decided to give in and accept the revised bill. They would thus escape being branded as pro-Communists and opponents of internal security. To oppose the bill would mean being labeled pro-Communist. It was with heavy hearts that Humphrey and I conferred together just before the roll call and decided that as a practical matter we would vote for the bill" (Douglas, *In the Fullness of Time*, pp. 306–307). Their colleague, Senator Lehman, did not join them.

58. The aide continued, "It [the EDA] seeks to set aside . . . the right of *habeas corpus* proceedings. While this amendment does not state that the right of habeas corpus is suspended, it very clearly seeks to shut the door against any such writ. I would doubt very much if the Courts could sustain it on this point. On the other hand if the writ of habeas corpus were granted, the amendment would be of questionable effectiveness" (Julius C. C. Edelstein, "Memorandum on Amendment to S. 4061," n. d., p. 2, Senate Subject Files, "97. Internal Security. Constitutionality of Bills," HHL).

"I think the legislation will certainly impress the public with the fact that you are determined to act against communists," Edelstein observed. "I cannot conceive of the libertarians being anything but very unhappy over this amendment, although I believe that they will withhold their fire, recognizing it for what it is."[59]

The sponsors of the Kilgore bill moved boldly, and they hoped to involve the liberal organizations in their plans. Two years later, when the Bureau of Prisons established six internment camps to comply with the EDA,[60] Senators Hubert Humphrey and Herbert Lehman recalled the ACLU participation. Humphrey argued that he had always opposed concentration camps and that the Kilgore bill was "by no means a 'concentration camp' bill, but a bill perfectly within the traditions of our country and our civil liberties and received the approval of the leaders of the American Civil Liberties Union."[61] Senator Lehman remembered that a "number of major changes were made to conform with the suggestions of the ACLU experts."[62]

The fact of the matter is that the ACLU attempted to hedge its bets. On one side, the liberal lawyers did review the emergency detention proposals and suggest revisions.[63] And on the other, they came out

59. Ibid, pp. 5, 3.

60. NCLCH Bulletin, May 1952. Liberal concern about the camps increased after January 1952, when Senator James O. Eastland "introduced a bill calling for the immediate declaration of a state of emergency so that the McCarran Act detention camp provisions [would] go into effect at once" (A. Reitman to M. Baldinger, January 30, 1952). Journalist I. F. Stone commented on the construction of the camps: "This is an election year. Truman began his Smith Sedition Act roundups in the last election year, 1948. Will he stage new roundups under the Emergency Detention Act this year as another way of striking fear into anyone who may oppose expansion of the war?" (cited documents are in vol. 42, 1952, "1. Concentration Camps," ACLU).

61. Hubert Humphrey to Henry Olson, September 30, 1952, p. 1, 23.L.9.4F, Box 545, "Attacks on Humphrey—Communist 1952–1954," HHH.

62. Herbert H. Lehman to Ralph Barton Perry, November 1, 1952, Senate Legislative Files, "44. Internal Security Act," HHL.

63. On September 8, Baldinger attached the following note to a two-page technical memorandum that largely added procedural safeguards to the Kilgore bill: "Attached are suggested changes to be incorporated in a 'clean' version of S. 4130 on Monday [September 11, 1950]. We don't know whether or not all of them will be accepted by the sponsoring Senators, but at least they are being presented" (note and attachment, MAB to Herbert [Levy], September 8, 1950, vol. 22, 1950, "7. ACLU Memos and Policy Statements," ACLU). Levy received a response from Frank McCulloch of the Senate Office of Legislative Counsel: "Thank you very much for your letter of September 8th with its detailed comments and suggestions on S. 4130. You may be interested in the technical

decidedly against the Kilgore bill on the eve of the final vote in the Senate.[64] Although the ACLU board split on its vote not to support the Kilgore bill, it was technically "unequivocal" in its opposition.[65] The press release and telegram in which the ACLU stated its position were, however, somewhat less than unequivocal. They used the words "at this time" and "under the present circumstances" and stated that "more consideration is warranted." The ACLU policy statements did not attack the EDA on constitutional grounds or as a matter of principle, but specifically left the door open for further study of the detention concept.

In addition, when the liberal organizations released their statement supporting the administration bill (S. 4061), they apparently felt the need to present their anti-Communist credentials. They opposed the McCarran, Mundt, and Wood legislation, but were "conscious of the need for adequate internal security" and "united in their opposition to all totalitarian political movements," as well as "committed to the preservation of the democratic way of life at home and abroad."[66] The statement reads something like a loyalty oath. The ACLU position on communism was, apparently, not entirely alien to that which the liberal senators had advocated in the preamble to the Kilgore bill. In another important respect, the ACLU leaders distinctly resembled the liberal senators—they sought to establish cordial relations with the FBI.

Two months before the EDA was passed, ACLU executive director Patrick Malin wrote J. Edgar Hoover to commend him for the "fine bal-

---

changes which we did make in the Kilgore bill in the course of the final debate. I am attaching a copy of those perfecting amendments" (Frank W. McCulloch to Herbert M. Levy, September 18, 1950, vol. 22, 1950, "5. Correspondence with Congressional Leaders," ACLU).

64.   In a telegram to Senator Lucas, the leaders of the ACLU stated: "We are also opposed at this time to the Kilgore bill under the present circumstances, since neither the people nor the Congress nor interested persons or organizations have had the opportunity to examine and discuss the provisions of a bill which might result in imprisonment of hundreds of thousands of persons. More consideration is warranted" (Ernest Angell and Patrick Murphy Malin to Majority Leader Scott Lucas, September 11, 1950, vol. 22, 1950, "5. Correspondence with Congressional Leaders," ACLU).

65.   "The [ACLU] Board voted to oppose unequivocally the Kilgore Bill at this time and under present circumstances. Mr. Pitzele and Mr. Fry are recorded as voting in the negative" (ACLU Board notes, section entitled "ACLU Position on Kilgore Bill for Detention of Security Risks in Event of National Emergency," September 11, 1950, vol. 22, 1950, "7. ACLU Memos and Policy Statements," ACLU).

66.   NCLCH release, August 28, 1950, Senate Subject Files, "93. Internal Security. Administration Bill (Pro)," HHL.

ance" he had demonstrated in his statement of July 26, 1950, on "the serious and intricate problem of national security in relation to civil liberties." Malin quoted, with approval, Hoover's admonition that "hysteria, witch-hunts and vigilantes weaken internal security." But he did not stop there. He also cited some of the more controversial language in the Hoover statement: "We in the Union are conscious of the fact that Communists 'utilize cleverly camouflaged movements, such as some peace groups and civil rights organizations, to achieve their sinister purposes.' " Malin apparently sought to put some distance between the ACLU and the suspect groups and perhaps to ingratiate himself with the director. "Our own activities, as you know," he stated, "are an open book: we defend civil liberties *for* everybody, but work *with* nobody who is anti-democratic in belief or practice."[67]

Hoover had released his statement of July 26 in relation to a presidential directive issued two days earlier. The Truman directive is particularly important because it stated explicitly, and for the first time, that the FBI should "take charge of investigative work in matters relating to espionage, sabotage, subversive activities and related matters."[68] It thus constituted an executive authorization for domestic security investigations by the FBI of subversives, without first defining that term.[69]

It is significant, then, that the ACLU leaders chose this occasion to write in support of the FBI director's public statements pursuant to the president's directive. As the constitutional watchdogs of American government, they could not have failed to grasp the implications of the presidential grant of new authority.[70] A likely interpretation is that the

67. Patrick Murphy Malin to J. Edgar Hoover, July 31, 1950, vol. 15, 1950, "B. FBI," ACLU.

68. The president requested that "all Enforcement Officers, both National and State . . . [and] all patriotic organizations and individuals likewise report all such information relating to espionage, sabotage and subversive activities to the Federal Bureau of Investigation" (White House statement signed by Harry Truman entitled "Information Relating to Domestic Espionage, Sabotage, Subversive Activities and Related Matters," July 24, 1950, vol. 15, 1950, "B. FBI," ACLU).

69. Earlier directives by Franklin Roosevelt had not used this language, and "President Truman's statement clearly placed him on record as endorsing FBI investigations of 'subversive activities.' Neither the President's statement nor the secret NSC charter nor the confidential Delimitations Agreement defined 'subversive activities' or 'subversion' " (Church, bk. 3, p. 463).

70. Among the president's advisers, the new directive was greeted without enthusiasm: "President Truman's domestic policy aides were surprised by the release of the statement. One noted, 'This is the most inscrutable Presidential statement I've seen in a long time.' Another asked, 'How in the H——[sic] did this get

ACLU leaders supported the concept of investing greater domestic security investigative powers in the FBI and wished to make their support known to its director.

For his part, J. Edgar Hoover moved swiftly to consolidate his new authority.[71] In his statement, which Malin had referenced and endorsed in his letter, Hoover seized the opportunity to advance his conception of Communist intrigue:

> The forces which are most anxious to weaken our internal security are not always easy to identify. Communists have been trained in deceit and secretly work toward the day when they hope to replace our American way of life with a Communist dictatorship. They utilize cleverly camouflaged movements, such as some peace groups and civil rights organizations, to achieve their sinister purposes. While they as individuals are difficult to identify, the Communist Party line is clear. Its first concern is the advancement of Soviet Russia and the godless Communist cause. It is important to learn to know the enemies of the American way of life.[72]

Malin concluded his communication by requesting a meeting with the director, "perhaps in company with our chairman, Ernest Angell, who is also chairman of the Second Regional Loyalty Board."[73]

Malin was not the only ACLU official who sought to curry favor with the FBI director. Morris L. Ernst, counsel for the ACLU, published an

---

out?' A third replied, 'Don't Know—I thought you were handling.' Even before the statement was issued, one of these aides had warned the President's counsel that the Justice Department was attempting 'an end run' " (Church, bk. 3, p. 463).

71. In addition to the Hoover release of July 26, the FBI issued posters that referred to the presidential directive and asked the public to assist the FBI by reporting subversive activities.

72. FBI press release, "Statement of J. Edgar Hoover, Director, Federal Bureau of Investigation," July 26, 1950, vol. 15, 1950, "B. FBI," ACLU. The reference to peace and civil rights organizations is noteworthy because it presaged by ten years a full-scale FBI domestic intelligence operation aimed at infiltration, investigation, and disruption of such groups.

73. Hoover responded, "I wish to acknowledge your kind letter of July 31, 1950, pertaining to the position of the FBI in the current situation. It was very encouraging to have your observations on our position which, of course, merely was a restating of a policy that we have long adhered to. I would be most happy to meet both Mr. Angell and you sometime when you are in Washington, D.C." (J. Edgar Hoover to Patrick Murphy Malin, August 3, 1950, vol. 15, 1950, "B. FBI," ACLU).

article in the *Reader's Digest* entitled "Why I No Longer Fear the FBI." It is as vehement in its defense of J. Edgar Hoover and the FBI as it is in its attack on communism. Ernst wrote that "a real 'smear' campaign has been carried on against Hoover's work. Those who feared the bureau—as I once did—will be glad to know the facts. The FBI is unique in the history of national police. It has a magnificent record of respect for individual freedom. It invites documented complaints against its agents. It has zealously tried to prevent itself from violating the democratic process."[74]

Ernst's personal relationship with Hoover spanned a period of twenty-five years, during which they exchanged over three hundred letters. The two appear to have shared a "fear and hatred of communism." The letters and related documentation indicate that Ernst regularly passed sensitive information from the ACLU—including letters from clients—to the FBI, and that he mistakenly trusted Hoover not to copy his many enclosures before returning them.[75] Ernst was also the author of a plan in 1948 that would have forced Communist and other organizations to disclose their financial records and membership lists publicly.[76]

If the ACLU hedged its bets on the Kilgore bill and the Truman directive, the same and more might be said of the liberal senators with regard to the McCarran omnibus legislation. On September 12, 1950, Majority Leader Lucas proposed to substitute Title II of the Kilgore bill (the EDA) for the registration provisions of the McCarran bill. This amendment was defeated roundly by a vote of 29 to 45. Then Lucas—who was not a sponsor of the EDA and who faced a tough reelection battle—unexpectedly proposed to add the emergency detention bill to the McCarran legislation as Title II. This second Lucas amendment was narrowly defeated by a vote of 35 to 37. By this point there was considerable confusion and shouting on the floor of the Senate.

After some clarification, Kilgore offered his bill as a substiute for the entire McCarran bill, as the liberals had originally agreed, and was overwhelmingly defeated, 23 to 50. In this environment, it seemed that if anything untoward could happen, it would, and it did. First, the conservatives, Mundt, Ferguson, and McCarran, co-opted the detention

---

74. Morris L. Ernst, "Why I No Longer Fear the FBI," *Readers Digest*, December 1950, p. 139.

75. Harrison E. Salisbury, "The Strange Correspondence of Morris Ernst and John Edgar Hoover, 1939–1964," *Nation*, December 1, 1984, pp. 576, 579.

76. Robert Bendiner, "Civil Liberties and the Communists: Checking Subversion without Harm to Democratic Rights," *Commentary* 5 (1948): 430.

initiative and, after making several alterations,[77] attached their version to the McCarran bill as Title II by voice vote.[78] And second, when the McCarran omnibus measure finally did come to a vote, liberal senators Humphrey, Douglas, Kilgore, and Benton—who had argued vigorously against it—voted with the majority, 70 to 7, in favor of passage. In the closing minutes of the debate, Herbert Lehman, the only senator facing an election who voted no, predicted, "Some of my colleagues whom I highly respect will vote for the McCarran bill. . . . The time will come when they will regret that."[79]

And it did. That evening, Humphrey and Douglas commiserated with each other into the next morning.[80] And within two weeks, ten liberal senators signed a statement calling for the repeal or drastic modification of the McCarran Act.[81] Humphrey sent form letters to his constituents that stated: "There is no doubt in my mind that a majority of the American people, once aware of the dangerous implications of the McCarran bill, will call for its repeal or severe modification."[82] It would be difficult to sort out the motivations that led several

77. These changes added several important safeguards to the liberals' original proposal (William Randolph Tanner, "The Passage of the Internal Security Act of 1950" [Ph.D. diss., University of Kansas, 1971], pp. 452–53). In another account, the changes were described this way: "A Red 'concentration camp' measure, tossed out by Administration adherents as a substitute for the McCarran subversive catch-all, was toned down and made part of the omnibus bill" (*Washington Post*, September 13, 1950, p. 1). As Senator Lucas put it, "We'll have signs on our concentration camps. They'll read, 'It's not comfortable, but its constitutional' " (*Newsweek Magazine*, September 25, 1950, p. 34).

78. The Kilgore bill put the conservatives in an awkward position: "If they defeated the amendment, the Administration could tell the country that it was rebuffed in a real attempt to cope with the Communist menace. If they let it be carried, the President could use the unconstitutional elements in the amendment as an argument for vetoing the entire bill" (ibid.).

79. *New Republic*, September 25, 1950, p. 8.

80. "The liberal Sen. Humphrey had trouble sleeping the night after he cast his reluctant vote for the drastic Communist control bill—which he had earlier lambasted on civil-rights grounds. Well after midnight he phoned his Fair Deal colleague Sen. Paul Douglas, who made the same unexpected switch. Douglas was awake too—for the same reason. The pair commiserated on the cruel realities of politics well into the small hours" (*Newsweek Magazine*, "The Periscope," September 25, 1950, p. 17).

81. The liberals' statement said, "We now hope that when Congress reconvenes in the calmer post-election atmosphere, it may repeal or drastically modify this unwise law and enact a postitive, effective security program" (*New York Times*, October 2, 1950, p. 7).

82. Hubert H. Humphrey to Mr. William G. Kubicek, October 21, 1950, 23.L.4.7B, "Form Letters–1950 2nd Session–81st Congress," HHH).

key sponsors of the EDA to vote in favor of the McCarran proposals, but it is significant that they did not recant their support for the concept of emergency detention.[83]

The senators who sponsored the EDA and who saw the FBI as the legitimate repository of internal security powers were not without allies among liberal intellectuals. Two years later, Richard Rovere wrote in defense of FBI critic Alan Barth, "He feels, as I do, that the provision of the McCarran Act which calls for the internment of all Communists known to the F.B.I. immediately upon outbreak of war is sound and necessary." Minimizing the EDA's "violation of principle," Rovere observed that the FBI had been the most effective means of combating communism. "In every case but one," he wrote, "Communist spies have been apprehended by the F.B.I. F.B.I. agents provided most of the evidence by which the Communist leaders were convicted under the Smith Act."[84]

This attitude permeated the editorial pages of the mainstream liberal press. On the day before the Senate vote, the New York Times attacked the McCarran proposals and praised the Kilgore bill (the EDA) as having "the great merit of striking directly at the heart of the matter." In the best liberal tradition, the Times conceived of the problem as a clash between conflicting requirements of providing for the national security while ensuring democratic freedoms. The Kilgore bill provided a solution to this dilemma because "it would give the F.B.I. a legislative basis for speedy and effective police action against the most likely enemies of our country when and if the emergency comes."[85] It was, therefore, clearly superior to all other proposals.

In the days following the final vote on internal security legislation in the Senate, the Washington Post and the New York Times called for a presidential veto, assuming virtually identical positions against the McCarran Act but in support of its emergency detention provisions.[86]

83. About a week after the EDA was added to the McCarran bill, Senator Estes Kefauver introduced another cloned version of the Kilgore bill. He described the new bill, S. 4163, this way: "It goes further to declare an automatic internal security emergency when our armed Forces are fighting for the United Nations, as they now are [in Korea]" (Estes Kefauver to Ernest Angell, September 21, 1950, vol. 22, 1950, "5. Correspondence with Congressional Leaders," ACLU). It is possible that the Senator overstated his case. For the applicable provisions, see Senate Bills, 81st Cong., 2d sess., S. 4163, pp. 7–8.

84. Richard H. Rovere, "Communists in a Free Society," Partisan Review 19, no. 3 (1952): 344.

85. Editorial, New York Times, September 12, 1950, p. 26.

86. The liberal press was by no means unanimous in its support for the emergency

The editors of the *Post* reasoned, "Admittedly there are grave constitutional questions involved . . . [but] the Kilgore-Douglas proposals represent a conscientious, careful attempt to reconcile security and freedom."[87] The *Times* confirmed this positive reaction to the EDA: "On the credit side, it [the McCarran bill] now includes as a last-minute addition the Kilgore detention-center bill, which goes to the heart of the Communist problem."[88]

But more, the *Times* stressed the efficacy of the FBI as the agency best suited to deal with the issue of internal communism and subversion. In so doing, the editors developed the liberal theory to its logical, and, for that matter, administrative, limits. Citing J. Edgar Hoover's reference to "12,000 dangerous Communists," the *Times* concluded, "The Kilgore bill would give a legislative basis, replete with constitutional guarantees, for the police action that undoubtedly should be taken [by the FBI] against this 'hard core' [of Communists] in an emergency."[89]

When the liberal senators wrote the Kilgore emergency detention bill, they lifted, verbatim, anti-Communist language that served as a statement of legislative intent for the Mundt-Ferguson and McCarran bills. This language had been conspicuously absent from the administration proposal, S. 4061. By adopting such language, as well as the concept of communism that it advanced, the liberals shut the door to a more sophisticated view of domestic communism and the actual magnitude of the threat it posed after 1950 to American government and society. They adopted the bipolar thinking that came to dominate the field of internal security for a generation. The actions of the liberal senators in introducing the detention legislation and their consistent

---

detention concept. The *Chicago Daily News* ran a strong attack against Douglas, Kilgore, and the EDA on its editorial page, September 25, 1950.

87.   In an odd twist, the *Post* argued against additional safeguards that had been added to the detention proposals: "Quite needlessly, in our opinion, it [the Senate] also adopted an amendment by Senator Ferguson stating that nothing in the detention provisions should abridge any right guaranteed by the Fifth and Sixth Amendments or suspend habeas corpus unless in conformity with the Constitution. This seems sheer surplusage" (editorial, *Washington Post*, September 15, 1950, p. 18).

88.   Following a standard liberal approach, the *Times*'s editors also wrote, "The real danger to our country lies far more in actual or potential espionage or sabotage at the hands of Russian sympathizers who may or may not be members of the Communist party than in the public expressions of Communist belief, however offensive, mendacious and contemptible such expressions may be" (editorial, *New York Times*, September 14, 1950, p. 30).

89.   Ibid.

support for the FBI, the backing of the liberal press, and the attitude of liberal organizations all buttressed the view that internal security powers should be centralized in the FBI as administrative functions.

Support from these quarters resonated with the grant of executive authority that President Truman had conferred on the FBI in his directive of July 24. In writing the EDA, the liberals sought to vest in the FBI legislative authorization and controls for the most extreme actions that they felt the federal police might have to take in an emergency. As events unfolded in the late summer and autumn of 1950, an anti-Communist consensus, characterized by a myopic vision of monolithic communism, enveloped the capitol. The liberal theory of internal security was brought to fruition; it would reach the status of unquestioned dogma and official policy.

The *Philadelphia Inquirer* summed up the liberal view in a statement that would go largely unchallenged for more than two decades: "Handling Communists and pro-Communists and their threat to national security is an FBI responsibility. Whatever that agency wants in new legislation and new authority should be granted immediately. But it is folly to pass laws [specifically, the Wood bill to register communists (H.R. 9490)] that are ineffective, unworkable and unconstitutional."[90]

The Liberal Theory

If the legislative politics of the EDA made manifest the principal elements of the liberal approach to internal security, the administrative logic of the law pushed liberal theory one step farther—but did so more by implication than by explicit legislative intent. Whereas the act clearly designated communism as the enemy, sabotage and espionage as the evils to be avoided, and detention as the remedy, it did not suggest a specific mechanism for gathering information to indicate who should be detained.[91] Because the legislators sought to prevent conspiracy before the fact, it became necessary to find some "reasonable ground," other than the crime itself, to indicate that an individual was

90. Editorial, *Philadelphia Inquirer*, August 31, 1950, p. 10.

91. To establish "reasonable ground" for detention, however, the Kilgore bill did authorize the attorney general to consider evidence such as training in sabotage or espionage by a foreign government, membership in the Communist party after January 1, 1949, and "other evidence of conduct of the same degree of gravity." The important distinction here is between the decision to investigate and the decision to intern. The act spoke to the latter but not to the former. See *Senate Bills*, 81st Cong., 2d sess., S. 4130, pp. 40–41.

a person who "may engage in, or may conspire with others to engage in acts of espionage or of sabotage."

The liberal senators believed that the FBI already had identified potentially dangerous persons.[92] Their intent was to authorize and set standards for FBI domestic security operations. Senator Humphrey said as much: "Our internal security today requires competent and effective counterintelligence . . . to prevent espionage, sabotage, and subversive activities. Our bill is designed to serve this end."[93] The administrative logic underlying the EDA demanded a set of criteria or guidelines to determine whom to investigate. The act implied that Communists would be good candidates for internment, but it left the actual selection to the discretion of the attorney general and did not address the central issue of investigation.[94]

Implementation of the EDA necessitated—by implication and as a functional requisite—that domestic security intelligence investigations be carried out to determine who the potential saboteurs and spies might be and to gather a continuous flow of information regarding their whereabouts and activities. The act did not require an emergency situation before intelligence investigations could be initiated, but rather assumed—without so stating—that such investigations would become a routine process of administration in preparation for the day when the president might declare an internal security emergency and invoke the power of internment.

Such preparations thus forced a distinction between criminal investigations and investigations for the purpose of gathering intelligence. The former would be limited in duration, conducted upon probable cause, lead to a charge to be levied against an individual in a court of law, and be subject to due process and other constitutional guarantees. The latter would be of indefinite duration, undertaken at the discretion of an administrator, unrelated to the court system or other adversarial proceeding, and immune to the usual constitutional safeguards.[95] For-

92.   As Hubert Humphrey stated, "The FBI knows who these people are. J. Edgar Hoover came before the Appropriations Committee and said he needed $6,000,000 more to hire agents so as to keep track of 12,000 really dangerous Communists. And he said, 'I can pick them up like that'—snapping his fingers. We provide in our substitute [the Kilgore bill] the way to pick them up" (*Congressional Record*, September 11, 1950, p. 14463).

93.   Ibid.

94.   *Senate Bills*, 81st Cong., 2d sess., S. 4130, pp. 26, 40.

95.   In general, domestic intelligence investigations do not and historically have not resulted in criminal prosecutions. One reason is that relaxed investigatory standards would, in most cases, make the evidence inadmissible in a court of law. In

mally, then, the EDA opened the door to ongoing investigation of a substantial and ill-defined group of individuals at the discretion of the administrator in charge, and it did not provide for judicial or administrative relief.[96]

Through the mechanism of the Emergency Detention Act, liberal theory generated a rationale, legal authority, and legitimacy for domestic security intelligence investigations as well as for the concept of summary internment. There was, however, very little in the EDA that had not previously been instituted by the executive branch under emergency conditions related to World War II. The new twist was that Congress, not the president, took the initiative and that internal security plans were exposed to the glare of publicity and open debate. At that time, and afterward, Congress was unaware of the nature and extent of FBI domestic security operations in general or of the fully developed emergency detention program in particular.[97]

Nevertheless, each of the principal elements of liberal theory, as exemplified in the EDA, can be traced to its origins in the Roosevelt administration under the auspices of such noted liberals as Frank Murphy, Robert Jackson, and Francis Biddle. The liberal impulse in the late 1930s was to centralize internal security operations in the FBI on civil libertarian grounds.[98] Liberals felt they could control the agency and hoped to avoid vigilante activity, such as the excesses of the American Protective League (APL) during World War I.[99] Attorney General Mur-

---

addition, intelligence officials are usually reluctant to present information gained in an intelligence investigation as evidence in a criminal proceeding because their sources and methods would have to be revealed to the accused.

96.   The question of relief is noted here because some investigative techniques can be so intrusive as to constitute harassment. These include breaking and entering, use of informers, wiretapping, and numerous personal interviews with employers, associates, friends, or the person under investigation. This should not be confused with judicial and administrative safeguards in the act applicable to persons actually detained.

97.   "The development of plans during this period [1946 to 1950] for emergency detention of dangerous persons and for intelligence about such persons took place entirely within the executive branch. . . . These plans were not only withheld from the public and the Congress but were framed in terms which disregarded the legislation [the EDA] enacted by Congress" (Church, bk. 3, p. 436).

98.   "The basic policy of President Roosevelt and his four attorneys general was to centralize civilian authority for domestic intelligence in the FBI. Consolidation of domestic intelligence was viewed as a means of protecting civil liberties" (Church, bk. 2, p. 33).

99.   For an excellent treatment of the APL, see Joan M. Jensen, *The Price of Vigilance* (Chicago: Rand McNally, 1968).

phy stated, "Twenty years ago, inhuman and cruel things were done in the name of justice; sometimes vigilantes and others took over the work. We do not want such things done today, for the work has now been localized in the FBI."[100]

By "localized" Murphy meant that wide investigative authority had been conferred on the FBI through delegation of inherent executive powers. This authority was primarily for the purpose of gathering intelligence for use by the executive in a crisis situation and was unrelated to any act of Congress.[101] President Roosevelt laid the foundations of the nation's internal security apparatus and established authority for the FBI's domestic intelligence programs in a series of verbal and written communications beginning in 1936. In August of that year, the FBI director personally advised the chief executive of the existence of a highly advanced Communist plot to take over the West Coast Longshoremen's Union, the Newspaper Guild, and the United Mine Workers. As Hoover recounted in a secret memorandum, "I told him that my information was that the Communists had planned to get control of these three groups and by doing so they would be able at any time to paralyze the country in that they stop all shipping in and out through the [Harry] Bridges organization; stop the operation of industry through the Mining Union of [John L.] Lewis; and stop publication of any newspapers of the country through the Newspaper Guild."[102]

According to Hoover's account, President Roosevelt authorized at that time an expansive domestic intelligence system to investigate "subversive activities in the United States, particularly Fascism and Communism." The president reportedly also requested "a broad picture of the general movement and its activities as may affect the eco-

100. Quoted in Church, bk. 2, p. 33. See also *New York Times*, October 1, 1939, p. 38; "Murphy Pledges Liberties in War," *New York Times*, October 14, 1939.

101. "A central feature of the FBI domestic intelligence program authorized by President Roosevelt was its broad investigative scope. The breadth of intelligence-gathering most clearly demonstrates why the program could not have been based on any reasonable interpretation of the power to investigate violations of the law" (Church, bk. 3, p. 412).

102. Church, bk. 3, p. 394. The Church citation is to "Hoover memorandum, 8/24/ 36." Hoover based his appeal to Roosevelt on what the Church Committee called the "theory of subversive infiltration." This rationale was closely allied with the ideas of preventive and pure intelligence. The former is collected for the purpose of preventing subversive acts such as sabotage, and the latter, to provide the executive with information with which to make informed decisions. See Church, bk. 3, pp. 412–13, for a more detailed discussion.

nomic and political life of the country as a whole."[103] These meetings, as well as the administrative planning and programs they spawned, were kept secret from the Congress and the public at the request of the director of the FBI. In a memorandum for the president, Hoover opposed seeking congressional authorization for "expansion of the present structure of intelligence work" in order to maintain secrecy and "to avoid criticism or objections which might be raised to such an expansion by either ill-informed persons or individuals having some ulterior motive."[104]

A second element of liberal theory, that of prevention, was set side by side with the concept of centralization of authority in a confidential Roosevelt directive to department heads dated June 26, 1939. In this communication the president ordered the various departments not to conduct any investigation "into matters involving actually or potentially any espionage, counterespionage, or sabotage." These would be "controlled and handled" by the FBI and the military intelligence services.[105] Apart from the issue of centralization, the key word here is "potentially." It is a reference to preventive intelligence, an animating concept behind the EDA and liberal theory. Although President Roosevelt did not here or elsewhere specifically request investigations or actions in writing against potential saboteurs or spies, there is no doubt that the FBI director interpreted the presidential order as such an authorization, and it is certain that Roosevelt intended that he should.[106]

A third pillar of liberal theory, that intelligence activity should be

103. Ibid., p. 394. The Church citation is to "Hoover memorandum, 8/25/36."
104. Church, bk. 3, p. 392. The Church citation is to "Letter from Attorney General Homer Cummings to President Roosevelt and [Hoover] enclosure, 10/20/38." Hoover further observed, "It would seem undesirable to seek any special legislation which would draw attention to the fact that it was proposed to develop a special counterespionage drive of any great magnitude" (Hoover memorandum, enclosed with letter from Cummings to the president, 10/20/38, reprinted in part in Church, bk. 3, p. 398).
105. Church, bk. 2, pp. 26–27. The Church citation is to "Confidential Memorandum for the President to Department Heads, 6/26/36."
106. After a detailed examination of extensive evidence, the Church Committee reports concluded: "President Roosevelt never formally authorized the FBI or military intelligence to conduct domestic intelligence investigations of 'subversive activities,' except for his oral instruction in 1936 and 1938. His written directives were limited to investigations of espionage, sabotage, and violations of the neutrality regulations. Nevertheless, the President clearly knew of and approved informally the broad investigations of 'subversive activities' carried out by the FBI" (Church, bk. 3, p. 405).

related to emergency conditions, is also grounded in Roosevelt's actions of this period. On September 6, 1939, following the outbreak of hostilities in Europe, J. Edgar Hoover suggested that President Roosevelt issue a statement "to all police officials in the United States" requesting that they deliver to the FBI "any information obtained pertaining to espionage, counterespionage, sabotage, and neutrality regulations." That same day a statement was drafted by the attorney general, signed by the president, and disseminated widely to the media.[107] Two days later, the president declared a national emergency and issued an executive order increasing the investigative staff of the FBI "in connection with the national emergency."[108]

Pursuant to these events, the FBI first began to search its files and to conduct "confidential investigations" for the purpose of identifying individuals "on whom there is information available to indicate that their presence at liberty in this country in time of war or national emergency would be dangerous to the public peace and the safety of the United States Government."[109] This program generated the Custodial Detention List, which—though unrelated to the internment of Japanese-Americans in 1942—would become a subject of much bureaucratic wrangling in connection with the EDA after 1950.

In one final respect, the liberal approach to internal security in the late 1930s anticipated the content of the EDA in 1950. It is the view that the primary threat to internal security is international communism. Roosevelt did tolerate the participation of some Communists in the New Deal and sometimes refused to take communism in government as a serious issue. It may have been Hoover's intention to disabuse him of this posture in 1936, when the FBI director reported that Communists were preparing to take over unions that would be of strategic importance to the defense of the nation in an emergency. It was

107. Church, bk. 3, p. 404. At a news conference held on the same day, Attorney General Murphy reaffirmed the liberal faith in the FBI on libertarian grounds: "There will be no repetition of the confusion and laxity and indifference of twenty years ago. We have opened many new FBI offices throughout the land. Our men are well prepared and well trained. At the same time, if you want this work done in a reasonable and responsible way it must not turn into a witch hunt. We must do no wrong to any man. Your government asks you to cooperate with it. You can turn in any information to the nearest local representative of the Federal Bureau of Investigation" (New York Times, September 7, 1939, p. 8, quoted in Church, bk. 3, p. 405).

108. Church, bk. 3, p. 405.

109. Letter from J. Edgar Hoover to special agents in charge re Internal Security, December 6, 1939, reprinted in Church, vol. 6, pp. 409–11.

more on the basis of the communist threat than the danger of a Nazi fifth column that Roosevelt authorized the first major expansion of FBI domestic intelligence programs in 1936.[110]

A parsimonious explanation of the liberal view of communism during this period is precluded by the complexity of world war and shifting alliances. Nonetheless, as Diana Trilling observed in 1950, even before the war, "the ranks of American liberalism were broken into two profoundly antagonistic groups—those whose only enemy was fascism; and those who had two enemies, both fascism and Communism."[111] Subsequent to the Nazi-Soviet pact, when the United States and the Soviet Union became allies, and even after the war, Roosevelt lost no opportunity to praise the Soviets in his public statements.[112] If the liberal attitude toward communism and Communist states fluctuated, it is clear that the liberal approach to internal security did not. From the outset, the basic domestic intelligence structure installed in the FBI was designed primarily to mitigate the threat of Communist subversion, temporary preparations to meet a supposed Nazi fifth column notwithstanding. This nearly exclusive focus on Communist subversion and infiltration would become an obsession at the FBI, extending several decades into the future.

By 1950, the liberal theory of internal security had generated an administrative as well as a legislative politics related to emergency detention. Although the liberals and the Congress generally did not know it, the FBI had maintained a central index of persons to be detained in an emergency since 1941. After 1943, the existence of this list was also unknown to the executive branch. In that year, Attorney General Francis Biddle ordered that the wartime Custodial Detention List be terminated. His order stated, "There is no statutory authorization or other present justification for keeping a 'custodial detention' list of citizens" and challenged the reliability of the evidence used to compile the list.[113]

In addition, he attacked the central underlying premise of the program itself: "The notion that it is possible to make a valid determina-

110. "The nature of the President's interest is also reflected in the information FBI Director Hoover provided at their crucial meeting in August 1936. Except for a reference to Hoover's previous report on Father Coughlin and General Butler, it dealt exclusively with Communist activities" (Church, bk. 3, p. 393).

111. Trilling, "Memorandum on the Hiss Case," p. 491.

112. Freeland, *The Truman Doctrine*, pp. 40–41.

113. Memorandum from Frances Biddle to Hugh B. Cox and J. Edgar Hoover, July 16, 1943, reprinted in Church, vol. 6, pp. 412–13.

tion as to how dangerous a person is . . . without reference to time, environment, and other relevant circumstances, is impractical, unwise, and dangerous."[114] Within a month the FBI director apparently decided to disregard Biddle's order; instead, Hoover integrated the Custodial Detention List into a new list, called the Security Index, and took extraordinary and successful precautions to ensure that its existence would not be detected by anyone outside of the FBI.[115]

Perhaps the FBI director had misgivings about his decision to circumvent Biddle's order, but in any case, in a 1946 communication, Hoover informed Attorney General Tom C. Clark that the FBI had "found it necessary to intensify its investigation of Communist Party activities and Soviet espionage cases." In an apparent reference to the Security Index, he explained that the FBI was "taking steps to list all members of the Communist Party and any others who would be dangerous in the event of a break in diplomatic relations with the Soviet Union." In such a crisis, the FBI director suggested, it might become necessary "to immediately detain a large number of American citizens." He recommended a study be undertaken "to determine what legislation is available or should be sought to authorize effective action . . . in the event of a serious emergency."[116] On at least three subsequent occasions, Hoover requested in writing that the Justice Department seek "statutory backing for detention" and was overruled.[117]

Instead, FBI and Justice Department officials put together in 1949 an "Emergency Detention Plan," also known as the "Attorney General's Portfolio." It was instituted "pursuant to an agreement executed

114. Ibid.

115. "Henceforth, the cards previously known as Custodial Detention Cards will be known and referred to as Security Index Cards, and the list composed of such cards will be known as the Security Index. . . . The Bureau will continue to investigate dangerous and potentially dangerous individuals. . . . It will also continue to prepare and maintain Security Index Cards. The fact that the Security Index and Security Cards are prepared and maintained should be considered as strictly confidential, and should at no time be mentioned or alluded to in investigative reports" (letter from J. Edgar Hoover to special agents in charge, August 14, 1943, reprinted in Church, vol. 6, pp. 414–15). For a detailed treatment of Hoover's decision and the various FBI dangerousness classifications and lists, see Church, bk. 3, pp. 417–22; Theoharis, *Spying on Americans*, pp. 40–64.

116. Personal and Confidential Memorandum from Hoover to the Attorney General, 3/8/46, quoted in Church, bk. 3, p. 430.

117. Hoover made requests for legislative approval of FBI detention programs in August 1946, October 1947, and March 1948. See Church, bk. 3, pp. 436, 438, 439.

on February 11 by Secretary of Defense James Forrestal and Attorney General Clark." During this period, the FBI informed the Justice Department of the existence of the Security Index but not of the more extensive "Communist Index" or of special targeting programs to investigate "top functionaries" and "key figures," among others.[118] Again, Hoover exercised extraordinary administrative caution to ensure that a variety of FBI programs would remain unknown to the Congress, the public, and Justice Department officials. He thus instructed his top agents that "no mention must be made in any investigative report relating to the classifications of top functionaries and key figures, nor to the Detcom or Consab Programs, nor to the Security Index or the Communist Index. These investigative procedures and administrative aids are confidential and should not be known to any outside agency."[119]

It was against this background that the legislative politics of emergency detention collided with the administration of internal security in 1950. The problem was that the public policy of emergency detention mandated different and more restrictive standards than the secret programs and policies of the FBI and the Department of Justice. The following specific differences, among others, were cited in an in-depth FBI analysis: The Attorney General's Portfolio provided for suspension of the writ of habeas corpus, and the EDA did not. The portfolio contained a master arrest warrant, whereas the EDA called for "individual warrants obtained only upon probable cause supported by oath or affirmation." Only the portfolio envisioned searches and confiscation of property. The EDA required preliminary hearings within forty-eight hours as opposed to forty-five days under the portfolio plan. And finally, unlike the portfolio, the EDA provided for rules of evidence as well as judicial review in a court of law.[120]

Despite these discrepancies, Attorney General J. Howard McGrath verbally directed J. Edgar Hoover to disregard the provisions of the

---

118. The Justice Department was unaware of some of the FBI's most important intelligence and detention programs: "The FBI kept secret from the [Justice] Department its most sweeping list of potentially dangerous persons, first called the 'Communist Index' and later renamed the 'Reserve Index,' as well as its targeting programs for intensive investigation of 'key figures' and 'top functionaries' and its own detention priorities labeled 'Detcom' and 'Consab' " (Church, bk. 3, p. 436).

119. SAC Letter no. 97, Series 1949, 10/19/49, quoted in Church, bk. 3, p. 441.

120. D. M. Ladd to Director, FBI, November 13, 1952, pp. 4–5, reprinted in Church, vol. 6, pp. 416–26.

EDA and to "proceed with the [portfolio] program as previously outlined."[121] In addition, just two weeks after the EDA was passed, the
Justice Department formally advised Hoover that, under emergency
conditions, "all persons now or hereafter included by the Bureau on
the Security Index should be considered subjects for immediate apprehension, thus resolving any possible doubtful cases in favor of the Government in the interests of the national security."[122]

But the matter did not end here. The department was reluctant to go
on record as authorizing the FBI to ignore an act of Congress. The FBI
did not want to continue to use standards for its detention programs
that were clearly at odds with congressionally mandated public policy.
The result was a complex series of bureaucratic maneuvers in which
J. Edgar Hoover finally prevailed. After nearly two years, Attorney
General James McGranery authorized the FBI director to ignore the
standards set forth in the EDA and gave full approval to the "Bureau's
concepts of the Detention Program and the Security Index standards."[123]

One stated purpose of the EDA was to provide legislative standards
for FBI emergency detention programs. In this respect, the act exerted
pressure on the FBI in the direction of increased accountability. For a
few months in 1950, internal security policy was exposed to congressional intervention and to public debate, suggesting the possibility of
an agency of internal security based on the model of a bureau of domestic intelligence. But because Congress did not insist on oversight of
the agency, the FBI—after some internal struggle—ignored the EDA and
constructed its own separate security plans in this area. The bureau
had, accordingly, achieved sufficient insularity of operations to apply
detention standards that were at variance with those mandated by law.
The Attorney General's Portfolio and the Security Index suggested the
emergence of an agency that resembled more the model of a secret police.

121.   Church, bk. 3, p. 442.

122.   Memorandum from Peyton Ford, Deputy Attorney General, to the FBI Director,
       12/7/50, quoted in Church, bk. 3, p. 442.

123.   The memo stated: "I wish to assure you that it is the Department's intention in
       the event of emergency to proceed under the program as outlined in the Depart-
       ment's Portfolio, invoking the standards now used. This approval, of course, in-
       dicates agreement with your Bureau's concepts of the Detention Program and
       the Security Index standards as outlined in your memorandum of June 28,
       1951" (Attorney General to the Director, FBI, re "Public Safety of the United
       States," November 25, 1952, reprinted in Church, vol. 6, p. 427).

Unintended Consequences

The basic approach to internal security, forged by liberals from Franklin Roosevelt to Hubert Humphrey, spawned a variety of unforeseen and, to the liberal mind, often unacceptable consequences. These originated both from internal inconsistencies in the theory itself and as logical outcomes of its constituent elements. They were manifested in open legislative acts of Congress, such as the EDA and the Communist Control Act (CCA) of 1954, as well as in secret administrative policies of the FBI and the Department of Justice. This is not to suggest that liberal theory failed in some respect to serve the ends of its promoters. It did not. In the short run, liberals got what they wanted.

In the late 1930s Franklin Roosevelt desired an executive-centered national security apparatus that would protect the security interests of the United States and, at the same time, provide an intelligence data base to assist in making presidential decisions.[124] He got both. In the early 1950s, the liberal senators who sponsored the EDA hoped to remove the issue of communism from politics and install it in the FBI as an electorally neutral administrative solution to the problem of ensuring domestic security.[125] The practicality of this course seemed evident by the middle 1950s. The FBI had contributed significantly to the demise of American communism, the force of McCarthyism was spent, and the battle cry of communism in government had faded to a mild susurration.

If liberal theory provided adequate means to meet the political needs of its supporters, it also contained internal contradictions that created political liabilities. The hypothesis of one-communism, for example, when pushed to its logical extension, is inconsistent with the requirements of free association and freedom of thought. That is, a theory that

124. For examples of political intelligence provided by the FBI to President Roosevelt, see Church, vol. 6, pp. 452–56, Exhibits 34, 35–1.

125. Senator Humphrey argued that he fought for the Communist Control Act of 1954 to this end: "When the White House opposed my amendment [to outlaw the Communist party] and tried to water it down in the conference committee, I successfully led a move in the Senate to send the bill back to conference again in order to strengthen its language. . . . I insisted on my amendment for the very reason that I *do* think it is time we took this very serious issue out of the political arena, and make it a matter of law enforcement rather than denunciation for the sake of votes" (Humphrey to J. R. Rohn, September 11, 1954, 23.L.10.3B, Box 104, "Leg.: Communism—HH Amendment to Butler Bill—Outlawing C.P.," HHH).

defines communism as a monolithic movement bent on the destruction of Western society cannot discriminate between dangerous activity—such as sabotage and espionage—and relatively harmless intellectual pursuits such as reading Marx or Lenin and studying political ideology in connection with the Communist party.

If a person joins the Communist party, the theory holds, he or she is a member of an international conspiracy directed by a hostile foreign power and an enemy of the American state. The thoughts and associations of such a person cannot be tolerated. This view led Senator Hubert Humphrey to propose the Communist Control Act of 1954, which made membership in the party a federal crime. The liberal logic that supported this action is preserved in a number of communications through which Humphrey hoped to mollify an outraged section of the liberal community.

Many Humphrey supporters attacked the senator for proposing and rushing through the anti-Communist legislation, particularly at a time when American communism no longer appeared to pose a significant threat. One close associate, Arthur M. Schlesinger, Jr., was particularly forceful on this point. He wrote Humphrey that the Communist Control Act amounted to "a confession of weakness, which can only persuade the rest of the world that we have indeed gone mad."[126]

In response to a torrent of criticism, Humphrey set forth his reasons for banning communism. He compared his legislation with the effort to "meet aggressive fascism with force, and even outlaw the German-

126. Following the passage of the Communist Control Act of 1954, Schlesinger published an attack on the legislation and on Humphrey in the *New York Post*. He wrote to Humphrey at length, partly to apologize for his *Post* column but also to underscore his opposition: "It is absurd to say that the Communist Party presents a greater threat today than it did in 1946, when you and I in our various ways were trying to awaken the liberal community to the Communist danger. It is absurd to say that the Communist Party presents a greater threat today than it did in 1936. Yet the republic survived without resort to drastic measures in the thirties and forties; and I do not think that the exercise of combatting Communist candidates, Communist arguments, Communist agents and Communist spies has weakened America. We licked a strong Communist movement to a frazzle by democratic means. For us now to say before the world that we no longer can cope with Communism by these means, that we dare not have the party operate or permit it access to the ballot or the mails—at a time when U. S. Communism has faded to a whisper—all this seems to me a confession of weakness, which can only persuade the rest of the world that we have indeed gone mad" (Arthur Schlesinger, Jr., to Hubert H. Humphrey, September 14, 1954, p. 2, 23.L.10.3B, Box 104, "Leg.: Communism—HH Amendment to Butler Bill—Outlawing c.p.," HHH).

American Bund in this country."[127] He charged that party members had "stolen" the atomic and hydrogen bomb secrets "and passed them directly to the Soviet Union."[128] He denied that the Communist party was a political party and characterized it as "a conspiracy against the government of the United States, directed and controlled by a hostile foreign power with the object of destroying our government by any means whatever."[129] Humphrey reasoned that if communism was indeed an "international conspiracy," and not a bona fide political party, then membership should be a criminal offense "because members of such a conspiracy are, in fact, conspirators to overthrow the government of the United States by force and violence."[130]

It is precisely here that the one-communism hypothesis, when elevated to the status of political ideology and official public policy, collided with the liberal tenet of preserving democratic rights such as freedom of association and thought. If a person joined the Communist party for private reasons but without subversive intentions the 1954 law made him a criminal. Here, association and thought, whatever their character, were condemned because they were inconsistent with liberal principles of internal security as codified in the law. But by 1954, many liberals veiwed anticommunism as a politico-religious conviction.[131]

127. Humphrey to K. L. Shisler, September 16, 1954, 23.L.10.3B, Box 104, "Leg.: Communism—HH Amendment to Butler Bill—Outlawing c.p.," hhh.

128. Humphrey to Professor Leo Marx, October 9, 1954, 23.L.10.3B, Box 104, "Leg.: Communism. HH bill outlawing cp Continued," hhh.

129. Humphrey to Richard F. Cornwell, September 13, 1954, 23.L.10.3B, Box 104, "Leg.: Communism—HH Amendment to Butler Bill—Outlawing c.p.," hhh.

130. Humphrey to Marvin Rosenberg, August 27, 1954, 23.L.10.3B, Box 104, "Leg.: Communism. HH bill outlawing cp Continued," hhh. This letter also contains an interesting view of contemporary liberalism in relation to the liberal tradition: "The American liberal movement has refused to face up to this question [of outlawing communism]. It has rested its case primarily on thinking done in the 17th, 18th, and 19th centuries by men like John Stuart Mill. I think it is time for the American liberal movement to do some 20th century thinking in order to face 20th century problems. I believe in my own heart and soul—and I still believe this—that in the long run I am doing the liberal movement and my country a service by my firm convictions that the Communist Party has no place for recognition in a democratic society" (p. 4).

131. A Humphrey campaign position paper on the Communist Control Act explained to staff and supporters: "Effective, courageous anti-Communism is thoroughly consistent with intelligent sincere liberalism. . . . In acting constructively, concisely and directly against specific members of the Communist Party, Senator Humphrey, as a leading spokesman of American liberal democracy, has

The liberal approach to domestic security contained a second internal contradiction, which centered on the administrative logic of the EDA. Security measures aimed at preventing conspiracy, when applied to ideological groupings through legislative enactment, blurred the distinction between thought and action and conflicted with the requirement of preserving democratic rights. The tension arises because the concept of preventing possible conspiracy removes remedial government action from the realm of actual law enforcement. Domestic intelligence investigations conducted pursuant to the EDA, for example, were not intended to foil acts of sabotage as a primary goal. Their mission was to discover, for the purpose of preemptive incarceration, persons who might commit such an act—or might conspire to commit such an act—at some future date and in the event of an emergency.

The investigation, the act, and the administrative logic were thus several steps removed from the crime itself. First, they projected a hypothetical emergency condition, which, in fact, never materialized. Second, they focused not on the crime itself but rather on the possibility that such a crime might be committed. And third, they entered the murky realm of potential conspiracy to commit a crime, specifying ideological orientation, that is, membership in the Communist party, as a reasonable ground and appropriate evidence.

The distinction between thought and action breaks down. It is not possible to make an investigative finding that a person is likely to conspire to commit a crime at some future date under extraordinary conditions without examining the person's mental processes. Since this is still very difficult to accomplish in a democratic society, the next best course of action is to discover the person's ideological persuasion and make a judgment on that basis. The latter is exactly the course envisioned in the EDA and pursued by the FBI. It is a direct and unintended consequence of liberal theory that cannot be reconciled with the principle that government may not inquire into the thought and speech of individuals.

In addition to these endogenous factors, other aspects of liberal theory, either singularly or in combination, generated unintended consequences that conditioned the character of internal security up until the early 1970s. By 1950, the liberal conception of communism had become indistinguishable from that of conservatives like Senators Mundt

---

performed a great service to his country, to his political principles and to the Democratic Party" (attachment to form letter, Hubert H. Humphrey to Dear Friend, entitled "The Humphrey Anti-Communist Amendment," September 6, 1954, p. 1 of attachment, 23.H.9.10F, Box 551, "HH Campaign Anti-Communist Bill," HHH).

and McCarran. Indeed, it was legislatively identical because liberals had adopted verbatim the anti-Communist language of the Mundt and McCarran proposals.[132] The most visible consequence was an anti-Communist consensus that blanketed the political landscape.

While it is clear that liberal intellectuals of this period varied significantly in their construction of anticommunism, few were prepared to extend to Communists the full protections of the Constitution and the Bill of Rights. Extreme anti-Communists like Irving Kristol, the powerful managing editor of *Commentary*, attacked more moderate liberals, including Henry Steele Commager, Zechariah Chafee, and William O. Douglas, who feared that indiscriminate anticommunism would eventually weaken civil liberties and, by extension, liberalism itself.[133] But liberal luminaries such as Robert Bendiner, Sidney Hook, Leslie Fiedler, Arthur Schlesinger, Daniel Bell, Richard Rovere, and others lent support and offered justification for anti-Communist measures instituted throughout government.[134]

The liberal contribution was in part obscured at the time because of the theatricality of Senator McCarthy's charges and the overwhelming media attention that he commanded after February 1950. Participation by liberals in the anit-Communist consensus tended to subdue responsible criticism of reckless accusations leveled against native Communists and persons only tangentially related to them. By adopting the anti-Communist party line, liberals surrendered their moral authority to uphold the rights of the accused. After 1950, their attempts to oppose McCarthy and his rantings often seem anemic at best.

But perhaps of more lasting significance, the anti-Communist consensus also inhibited responsible criticism of the FBI. Liberals were historically and ideologically the natural watchdogs of the central police. By venerating the FBI and delegating large and undefined internal security powers to that agency, liberal theory and practice positioned the FBI in an extraconstitutional terrain, beyond the reach of the law and the traditional system of checks and balances.

132.   Compare S. 4130 (the EDA), pp. 19–24, with S. 2311 (the Mundt bill), pp. 1–6, in *Senate Bills*, 81st Cong., 2d sess., and 81st Cong., 1st sess., respectively.

133.   Irving Kristol, " 'Civil Liberties,' 1952—A Study in Confusion," *Commentary* 13, no. 3 (1952): 228–36. This article is strongly rebutted by Alan F. Westin who maintained—against the tide of liberal thinking—that it was necessary to protect the civil liberties of Communists to preserve the rights of all citizens. See "Our Freedom—and the Rights of Communists: A Reply to Irving Kristol," ibid. 14, no. 1 (1952): 33–40.

134.   Richard H. Pells, *The Liberal Mind in a Conservative Age: American Intellectuals in the 1940s and 1950s* (New York: Harper & Row, 1985), pp. 265–70.

In particular, by conferring the internal security powers on a single intelligence agency, especially in the context of an anti-Communist consensus across the spectrum of political elites, liberal theory delegated the dominant policy role to the FBI in the internal security arena. The function of policy formation was shifted to administrative levels, well below the executive and congressional offices. This is, in part, exactly what liberals wanted. It was a way to turn a damaging political issue into a routine process of administration.

This is not to say that liberals acted only out of self-interest and without conviction. In part, their motivation stemmed from sincere alarm at the injustices that resulted from "trial by administrative ruling and Congressional investigation" in "star-chamber proceedings."[135] But by mixing political expediency with a certain naiveté they got more than they bargained for. The policy machinery of domestic security receded to an administrative limbo beyond the reach of the liberals and the Congress. The failure of the FBI to comply with Attorney General Biddle's orders in 1943 and with the provisions of the EDA after 1950 are just two examples of what hindsight shows might reasonably have been expected. They represent, in fact, merely the tip of an iceberg.

The liberal principle of preventive security, when combined with the doctrine of inherent executive emergency powers, led to unaccountable FBI programs and policies. Because liberal theory helped to generate a crosscutting consensus against communism and did not rely on congressional authority in the area of internal security, the Senate liberals—and Congress generally—were excluded from the domestic security policymaking process. Internal security matters took on a special status, colored by public hysteria and pervasive administrative and bureaucratic secrecy.

By the middle 1950s, and for the following two decades, Congress found itself both unable and unwilling to exercise its oversight and approval powers over the FBI. Indeed, the FBI had not been established pursuant to any legislative charter, and many of its domestic intelligence powers and programs were not exercised under the authority of specific congressional enactments. Neither were they subject, in general, to review by the courts. Regulation and oversight of FBI programs devolved, accordingly, to the executive branch and did not surface except at the bureaucratic level under the expansive and largely unaccountable authority of the director of the FBI.

As the bureau assumed greater discretionary powers in relation to

---

135.   Humphrey to Richard F. Cornwell, September 13, 1954, 23.L.10.3B, Box 104, "Leg.: Communism—HH Amendment to Butler Bill–Outlawing C.P.," HHH.

the rest of the American state, it left behind its resemblance to the model of a bureau of domestic intelligence. As the decade of the 1950s advanced, so too did the increasing autonomy with which the FBI selected its policy orientation as well as the degree of insularity its operations enjoyed from the rest of government and the society in general. But it was not until the middle 1960s that the bureau passed through and beyond the model of a political police. This change could be identified clearly, after 1964, in the covert attempt by the FBI to disrupt the activities of indigenous American groups, in particular, the Ku Klux Klan, that had no connection either to the Communist party or to the agency of a foreign power.

CHAPTER THREE

A Politics of Equivocation: The Liberals, the Klan, and Dr. King

THE PREVIOUS chapter investigated the way in which the liberal theory of internal security developed from the politics of anticommunism in 1950 and explored some of the consequences of that approach. Here, the politics of civil rights offers a similar opportunity to establish the underlying factors that motivated the liberal political community and the FBI to undertake a federal assault against the Ku Klux Klan in the early 1960s. Both inquiries help to explain how liberal theory and practice enabled the FBI to circumvent the legal system in conducting many of its domestic security activities. Specifically, liberal tolerance of FBI autonomy in creating its own internal security policies and liberal acceptance of the official secrecy and insularity of FBI operations contributed to the growth and maintenance of a domestic intelligence state within the national state that would ultimately prove to be incompatible with basic liberal values.

In this chapter, examination of the White Hate Groups Cointelpro, an intelligence program to disrupt the Klan, is intended to demonstrate the autonomy and insularity that the FBI had achieved in domestic security affairs by 1964. The chapter also assesses the extent to which liberal leaders of the 1960s directly or indirectly sanctioned the FBI's covert programs to destroy the Klan and the Communist party. This analysis explores the modifications to liberal theory that were required before the federal police force could be sent to infiltrate and neutralize the Klan under the rubric of internal security. Finally, an exposition of the role of the FBI in civil rights in relation to liberal expectations provides empirical validation of the liberal contribution to internal security in the 1960s and its relation to that of the previous decade.

In September 1964, the FBI launched a secret domestic Cointelpro, or counterintelligence program, designed to infiltrate and disrupt the Ku Klux Klan and a number of indigenous fascist and Nazi organizations. The program was instituted without the knowledge of the Congress or the attorney general and "required only the recommendation of the Assistant Director in charge of [the Domestic] Intelligence Division and the approval of the FBI Director." It was conceived by a federal bureau operating without oversight, and it exemplified the "virtual independence of the FBI in matters relating to domestic security."[1]

The program, known in FBI parlance as the White Hate Groups Cointelpro, was an administrative child of the FBI. Its provenance suggests that by 1964, the application of the liberal theory of internal security to domestic politics had replaced the usual constitutional checks and other legal requirements of liberal government. Because the White Hate Cointelpro was designed to circumvent the justice system and to apply state-initiated coercion against American citizens who were not Communists, it is an indication that the FBI had come to resemble an agency based on the model of an internal security state.

But the FBI did not create the White Hate Cointelpro without precedent, and the program was related to the political context of the civil rights movement of the middle 1960s. It was, in fact, an amplification of and variation on existing secret counterintelligence programs—aimed against the Communist party and its Trotskyite rival, the Socialist Workers party—that had been implemented by the FBI in 1956 and 1961, respectively. Like these earlier Cointelpros, the FBI effort to destroy the Klan emerged from the center of a larger politics of liberalism. The former involved a politics of anticommunism; the latter, a politics of civil rights in which the Klan sought to block implementation of the Civil and Voting Rights Acts of 1964.

There was, as former attorney general Nicholas Katzenbach pointed out, "a basic identity of constitutional and political interest" between the Kennedys on one hand and Martin Luther King and the civil rights movement on the other. Support for King and civil rights was, he explained, "an essential ingredient in the Kennedy administration" and "the necessary predicate to all subsequent events,"[2] especially FBI efforts to discredit King and to disrupt and destroy the Klan.[3] Without question, organized terrorism perpetrated by Klansmen against Negroes and civil rights workers threatened to undermine the drive for

1. Richard D. Cotter, "Notes toward a Definition of National Security," *Washington Monthly*, December 1975, pp. 15, 9, 6. Cotter is a former chief of the Research Section of the FBI's Domestic Intelligence Division and a twenty-six-year veteran of the bureau.

2. "Statement of Nicholas deB. Katzenbach, Former Attorney General of the United States," Church, bk. 6, p. 208.

3. A major confrontation evolved between Martin Luther King and J. Edgar Hoover over the role of the FBI in the enforcement of civil rights for Negroes in the South. This issue will be addressed in detail below.

integration and voting rights in the South. But equally important, FBI interference with King's activities and organization strained the political alliance between the civil rights movement and the Kennedy and Johnson administrations.

In their approaches to internal security, both the FBI and the liberal political community exhibited peculiar inconsistencies. The liberals' position was incongruous because they put their political muscle on the line to force civil rights for Negroes and at the same time rolled over the constitutional rights of Klansmen. The FBI was inconsistent because it conducted high-profile criminal investigations of specific Klan murders and at the same time disrupted various Klan organizations through covert intelligence operations. Moreover, the bureau claimed it lacked jurisdiction to intervene in violent acts against Negro voters in the South. At the same time, it found the authority to press intensive intelligence investigations of King and the SCLC and to drive home its secret campaign against the Klan.

To eradicate the Klan, the FBI mounted two major offensives in 1964. The first involved large-scale, highly publicized investigations of a series of Klan murders. It was ordered by the president, complete with nationally televised statements by the chief executive that cases would be solved by the FBI in the near future. As a result, FBI presence and jurisdiction expanded in the South, particularly after President Johnson signed the Civil Rights Act in July. The second was the White Hate Cointelpro.

The underlying purpose of both efforts was to reestablish law and order in the South, using federal powers to repair a breach of the internal security by neutralizing the various branches of the Klan. The breach consisted of the organization of malcontents into terrorist groups that would resist, by force and violence, the implementation of federal civil rights policies in the South. In this respect, the Klan offered a challenge to the sovereignty and political will of the liberal state. The Klan hoped to subvert recent laws of Congress that it did not accept through alliance with white citizens' groups and local law enforcement officials who were in sympathy with that cause. Klan actions constituted an attempt to break the state's monopoly on the legitimate use of violence to achieve its ends.

It is often difficult to sort out covert counterintelligence actions from publicly acknowledged FBI criminal investigations aimed at the Klan. The two efforts were distinct at the administrative level in Washington. The former was run by the FBI's General Investigative Division, and the latter fell to the Domestic Intelligence Division. But they were integrated at the level of the field office. In most cases, the same special agents conducted intensive, publicly acknowledged criminal investigations and secret Cointelpro operations against the same Klan organizations. Intelligence and investigative reports were shared in the field office and at headquarters.

The line between observation, or information gathering, and counterintelligence was often indistinct. The mere presence of a highly placed informant within a group, or an agent conducting interviews, could cause internal dissension and mistrust. But the distinction can be made theoretically if not always operationally. Criminal investigation focuses on gathering information that leads eventually to a proceeding in a court of law. Counterintelligence activity gathers intelligence and acts upon it with the intent of influencing or damaging an individual or group in the absence of due process.

Nice distinctions notwithstanding, liberal politicians and civil rights leaders demanded that the FBI eradicate Klan violence in the early 1960s. But the theory of internal security, under which liberals had endorsed infiltration and disruption of the Communist party, required modification before it could be applied to home-grown, even anti-Communist, groups like the Klan. Indeed, the White Hate Cointelpro marks the first instance in which the FBI moved against a group that did not have ties to a foreign government and that was entirely the product of endogenous factors in American history. In this respect the White Hate Cointelpro was a watershed, a precursor of programs and events that would characterize domestic security intelligence activities for the balance of the decade.

Dimensions of the White Hate Cointelpro

The covert program to disable the Klan was advanced most forcefully by William C. Sullivan, the FBI assistant director in charge of the Domestic Intelligence Division (DID). He argued that "the investigation and penetration" of Klan organizations should be transferred to the DID "on the premise that the KKK and supporting groups are essentially subversive in that they hold principles and recommend courses of action that are inimical to the Constitution." He pointed out that actions of these organizations did not "constitute the same menace as the Communist Party inasmuch as they are not controlled by a foreign power." Transfer of the intelligence responsibility for the Klan to the DID would not effect "investigation of individual cases, i.e. bombings, murders, police brutality, etc., [which] should [continue to] be handled by the General Investigative Division." What Sullivan had in mind was the creation of a new "disruptive counter-intelligence program against the Klan and other hate groups" that would treat them as subversive organizations.[4]

Another reason for assigning the task of infiltrating the Klan to the Domestic Intelligence Division was offered by the FBI Inspection Division. The inspector pointed out that increased activity by the Communist party in the area of civil rights indicated a "definite need for an intelligence type penetration of these racial and hate groups so as to keep abreast of and ahead of their plans and activities."[5] This logic is incomplete because there is no clear connection between alleged Communist party actions in the civil rights field and the need for a counter-intelligence program to disrupt the Klan.

It might have been argued that the Communist party used the Klan to stir up trouble in the South, but that argument was not made, and no one suggested that Communists had infiltrated the Klan. Sullivan contended that "the Communist Party is increasing its activities in the field of racial matters and civil rights, directing more and more of its fire against the KKK and similar organizations to confuse the issue."[6] But, again, there is no logical connection between the Communist party's antipathy for the Klan and the need for an FBI program to penetrate and destroy Klan organizations. In this case, the FBI and the Communists would presumably have been on the same side.

These FBI executives apparently felt a need to link the Communist party with the Klan, even if only by juxtaposition in the text of the memorandum through which they hoped to gain approval for the initiation of a new counterintelligence program. By 1964, the issue of communism in government, and domestic communism generally, had

4.   J. H. Gale to Mr. Tolson, "Investigation of Ku Klux Klan and Other Hate Groups," July 30, 1964, pp. 1–2. This document is a decision memorandum in which Gale presents the positions of various FBI administrators regarding transfer of investigative responsibility for the Klans from the General Investigative Division to the Domestic Intelligence Division. Gale and Sullivan were close friends. The memorandum was written to Tolson because, by the middle 1960s, Tolson functioned as a clearinghouse for any important decisions on their way to Hoover.

5.   The inspector, working from Sullivan's data, attempted to link the proposed program to increased Communist party activity in the civil rights movement: "Today it seems clear from information developed by Domestic Intelligence Division that the Communist Party now has evidenced a definite interest in the racial problem, is becoming deeply enmeshed therein, and appears to be exploiting it to an ever-increasing extent" (ibid., p. 3).

6.   Ibid., p. 1.

receded from center stage in American politics. It was largely external-
ized through a cold war focus on the arms race with the Soviet Union
and a nascent military operation to contain Communist forces in
Southeast Asia. But in the mind of J. Edgar Hoover, and to a lesser
extent in those of his chief subordinates, the threat of internal communism was unmitigated and grave.

There is an element of contradiction in the FBI's two most common
claims regarding the Communist party. The first was that the party
was always seeking new ways to undermine American society and to
overthrow the government of the United States by force and violence.
The reported entrance of Communists into the civil rights fray was
merely a new tactic by an ancient and deadly enemy. The second was
that the FBI had successfully infiltrated and disabled the party, breaking up its nefarious activities and largely neutralizing it as a force in
American politics.

This contradiction was, of course, resolved through the person of
the FBI director, who was equally adept at portraying the towering
menace of Communist subversion and the eternal vigilance of the FBI
in protecting the nation's internal security.[7] It is possible that the director's subordinates reasoned they would gain his approval for their am-
bitious new program if they could convincingly link Klansman and
Communist.[8] This was Sullivan's intention in introducing the party
into the discussion and labeling the Klan "essentially subversive," even
though he conceded the absence of a controlling foreign power.

There are at least two ways to determine that a particular group and
its members are sufficiently subversive to merit disruption by the government. One is to develop a theory that will single out and stigmatize
the target. This was the case with the Communist party. A second
method is to damn the group by its association with or similarity to

7.   At least one political journalist noted this propensity: "There seems to be little
     doubt that Hoover regularly exaggerates both the exploits of the Bureau, and
     the dangers posed by those it opposes" (Joseph Kraft, "J. Edgar Hoover: The
     Complete Bureaucrat," *Commentary*, February 1965, p. 60).

8.   Sullivan, in particular, understood Hoover's focus on the Communist party and
     hoped to overcome his resistance to implementing a counterintelligence pro-
     gram against the Klan. "Although Sullivan repeatedly followed a Hoover
     dogma alleging communist infiltration of the civil rights movement—insisting,
     for example, that the 1963 March on Washington had included some two
     hundred Communist party members trying to exploit the occasion for their own
     purposes—he also took the position that the Ku Klux Klan was hurting the na-
     tion and urged that the FBI use its substantial resources against that organiza-
     tion, something Hoover had always seemed reluctant to do" (Unger, *FBI*, p.
     300).

persons or organizations already known to be subversive. It seems likely that the FBI executives were groping toward an analogy between the Klan and the Communist party that they were unable to work out in its entirety before establishing the White Hate Cointelpro.

In either case, the group must be sufficiently evil to justify infiltration and disruption by federal police in lieu of due process in a court of law. As constructed by liberals in the early 1950s the theory of internal security could not reach the Klan because it required that a group or individual be part of a criminal conspiracy, directed by a hostile foreign power, intent on the overthrow of the government of the United States by force and violence. The Klan was both anti-Communist and patriotic in its orientation. Accordingly, the FBI chose an alternate course, attempting to establish subversion by drawing a close analogy between the new target group and the old Communist party.

J. Edgar Hoover discovered numerous parallels between the two groups. He noted, for example, that the Klan organization "makes wide use of cover names or front organizations as a façade behind which it carries on it activities." Like the Communist party, the Klan was far more popular in 1964 than its relatively small membership would suggest: "The Klan's resurgence has brought its current hard-core membership to over 14,000, plus tens of thousands more inactive members, supporters and sympathizers." The Klan also represented "a thoroughly repugnant ideology and force inimical to the welfare of our country." As with the party, government efforts would "not be sufficient by themselves to bring the Klan under control. . . . [The public] must join with governmental bodies in a constructive, systematic, coordinated and total effort against the Klan."[9]

In August of 1964, Hoover authorized Sullivan "to give consideration to the application of counterintelligence and disruptive tactics to hate groups."[10] His recommendation was to apply to the Klan the same techniques that had proven successful in combating the Communist party over the past eight years.[11] This approach reflected Sulli-

9.   J. Edgar Hoover, "The Resurgent Klan," *American Bar Association Journal* 52 (July 1966): 618–20. In this article, the Communist party is not mentioned; the Klan stands alone as the bête noire of internal security.

10.   F. J. Baumgardner to W. C. Sullivan, "Counterintelligence Program/Internal Security/Disruption of Hate Groups," August 27, 1964, p. 1.

11.   "It is our recommendation that we immediately initiate a hard-hitting, closely supervised, coordinated counterintelligence program to expose, disrupt and otherwise neutralize the Ku Klux Klan (KKK) and specified other hate groups. This new counterintelligence effort will take advantage of our experience with a

van's view that disruption was an intrinsic part of the intelligence process. As he put it, "We might as well not engage in intelligence unless we also engage in counterintelligence. One is the right arm, the other the left. They work together." Sullivan explained his contribution in developing the White Hate Cointelpro: "In 1956 . . . the decision was made to incorporate all counterintelligence operations into one program directed against the Communist Party. I merely redirected the use of those techniques toward investigating the Klan."[12]

On September 2, 1964, the White Hate Cointelpro was launched in an administrative letter from the FBI director to seventeen field offices located primarily in the South; it stated that "the purpose of this program is to expose, disrupt and otherwise neutralize the activities of the various Klans and hate organizations, their leadership and adherents." It listed twenty-six Klan and "hate" groups and set up quarterly reporting requirements from the field offices. Hoover's authorization indicated the proper role of the new program in relation to ongoing investigations of various Klan groups: "Counterintelligence action directed at these groups is intended to complement and stimulate our accelerated intelligence investigations." And, finally, the memorandum underscored the importance of secrecy: "You are cautioned that the nature of this new endeavor is such that under no circumstances should the existence of the program be made known outside the Bureau and appropriate within-office security should be afforded this sensitive operation."[13]

The White Hate Cointelpro depended on the creativity, expertise, and enthusiasm of FBI special agents and informants in the field. Most proposals for disruptive counterintelligence actions emerged from routine investigative work. They were forwarded to FBI headquarters by the special agent in charge (SAC) of the field office and were either approved or denied on a case-by-case basis by the director. Each field office designated one special agent to take charge of and coordinate Klan counterintelligence.[14] This agent normally worked in the field,

---

variety of sophisticated techniques successfully applied against the Communist Party, USA, and related organizations since 1956" (ibid.).

12.   William C. Sullivan with Bill Brown, *The Bureau: My Thirty Years in Hoover's FBI* (New York: W. W. Norton, 1979), p. 128.

13.   Director, FBI (157-9-Main), to SAC, Atlanta, "Counterintelligence Program/Internal Security/Disruption of Hate Groups," September 2, 1964, pp. 1, 4. Letters from the director to a particular SAC often contained instructions for additional field offices. In this case the instructions were applicable to seventeen field offices.

14.   "At the present time, over 100 separate counterintelligence operations [Klan

supervised Klan informants, and had access to the investigative reports of other special agents who conducted ongoing criminal investigations of the Klan. All agents were expected and encouraged to submit creative counterintelligence suggestions, based on their expert knowledge of the specific Klan groups and cases to which they had been assigned.[15]

This system generated diverse disruptive actions against the Klan. In what is perhaps an isolated case, "the FBI assisted an informant in the Ku Klux Klan in his efforts to set up a new state-wide Klan organization independent of the regular Klan."[16] The new Klan issued charters and gained a membership of about two hundred persons. On one occasion, there was an armed face-off between members of the old Klan and the new FBI-sponsored Klan. The director of the Bureau of Investigation of the state in which the new Klan was formed "testified that he witnessed the FBI informant address a Klan rally attended by several thousand persons and heard the informant state: 'We are going to have peace and order in America if we have to kill every Negro.' "[17]

In a more mundane instance, the FBI sent anonymous postcards to six thousand members of the Klan in several southern states. The cards featured derogatory cartoons with captions such as "Klansman, trying to hide your identity behind your sheet? You received this—someone knows who you are."[18] Although the FBI maintained strict secrecy regarding the existence of the White Hate Cointelpro, it anonymously informed the various Klan groups that they had been penetrated by FBI informants as a means of creating suspicion and distrust among mem-

---

and Communist party combined] are in various stages of enactment. The various counterintelligence plans and techniques are handled and supervised by the Agent assigned to the program in each participating office by the use of a single control file" (F. J. Baumgardner to W. C. Sullivan, "Communist Party, USA/ Counterintelligence Program/Internal Security—C" and "Counterintelligence Program/Internal Security/Disruption of Hate Groups," January 6, 1965, p. 3).

15.   The FBI director was explicit in this regard: "All investigative personnel responsible for Klan-type and hate group investigations should be alerted and encouraged to submit counterintelligence recommendations relating to their individual investigations. The responsibility for counterintelligence action should not be delegated exclusively to the Agent assigned to the Program, who should be acting in the capacity of coordinator" (Director, FBI [157-9-Main], to SAC, Atlanta [157-826], "Counterintelligence Program/Internal Security/Disruption of Hate Groups," October 4, 1965, p. 1). These instructions were sent to seventeen field offices.

16.   Church, bk. 3, pp. 251–52.

17.   Ibid., p. 252.

18.   F. J. Baumgardner to W. C. Sullivan, "Proposed Postal Cards for Mailing to Known Klan Members/Counterintelligence—Klan," April 20, 1966.

bers of the groups.[19] The number of FBI informants in the Klan reached a peak in 1965 of approximately six hundred.[20]

A single, well-placed informant can create enormous security problems for an organization, particularly if the group, like the Klan, is a secret society. Gary Thomas Rowe was an FBI informant in the Klan from 1959 through March 1965. He reported all aspects of Klan life to his FBI contacts. His "mission was 'total reporting,' including membership lists, financial matters, and political positions, as well as Klan violence." He was present at the Klan murder of Viola Liuzzo, although he stated that he did not participate and was unable to prevent it.[21]

Rowe rose within the Klan organization, gaining a position in the "Klan Bureau of Investigation," which was responsible for security matters and for investigating new members. To get information on Klan violence, "the FBI instructed Rowe to join a smaller group of Klan members, a so-called 'Action Group,' which conducted violent acts against blacks and civil rights workers." In this capacity Rowe participated in Klan violence, giving the FBI notice of many actions in advance. The Klan even asked him to be an action group squad leader. Here the FBI drew the line, telling Rowe he would have to refuse the promotion if he wanted to remain an FBI informant.[22]

Domestic counterintelligence activities often focused on Klan leaders, particularly Robert M. Shelton, Imperial Wizard of the United Klans of America, Inc. (UKA), and James R. Venable, an Atlanta attor-

19.   F. J. Baumgardner to W. C. Sullivan, "Counterintelligence Program/Internal Security/Disruption of Hate Groups/ (Cartoons and Caricatures)," January 19, 1965.

20.   Bureau estimates on informants are unreliable, but they do indicate the scope of the operation: "*Senator Schweiker*: Back in 1965, during the height of the effort to destroy the Klan, as you put it a few moments ago, I believe the FBI has released figures that we had something like 2,000 informers of some kind or another infiltrating the Klan out of roughly 10,000 estimated membership. . . . *Mr. Adams*: Well, this number, 2,000 did include all racial matters, informants at that particular time, and I think the figures we tried to reconstruct as to the actual number of Klan informants in relation to Klan members was around 6 percent [or about 600]" (Church, vol. 6, p. 144). James B. Adams was assistant to the director of the FBI and deputy associate director (investigation) in 1975 when he gave this testimony.

21.   As an informant, Rowe reported to the FBI that he was present at a Klan bombing in 1963 and that he shot an unidentified black man who was part of a crowd that was attacking his car ("Summary of Results of the Department of Justice Task Force Investigation on Gary Thomas Rowe, Jr.," U.S. Department of Justice, 1980, pp. 9, 11).

22.   Church, bk. 3, pp. 239–44; ibid., vol. 6, pp. 116–17, 130.

ney and Imperial Wizard of the National Knights of the Ku Klux Klan. Bureau headquarters in Washington requested the field "to develop compromise-type data" on these men, among others, "indicative of the immorality, dishonesty and devious tactics of leaders of the Klan." The information was gathered specifically for use "as a disruptive counter-intelligence technique."[23] In Shelton's case, for example, the FBI requested copies of his IRS tax returns to determine if he had secret sources of income or a "depository used by him for the Klan organization." If damaging financial information came to light, it would be useful in "exposing Shelton within the Klan organization, publicly or by furnishing information to the Internal Revenue Service."[24]

The FBI also obtained a letter written by Shelton that contained his signature stamp and the initials of his stenographer. The proposal was to make exact replicas of the letterhead and signature stamp in order to enable the bureau "to direct letters, on a highly selective basis, and over Shelton's signature, which will be designed to cause dissension within the leadership of the United Klans of America, Inc."[25]

In an effort coordinated among twenty-two field offices, the FBI director requested comment from the field on a proposal to disrupt the organizational structure of the United Klans of America. The purpose was "to force the United Klans of America, Inc. (UKA), to consider holding a National Klonvocation [convention]." The basic strategy centered on increasing factionalism among the constituent state Klan organizations by developing "a 'smear campaign' . . . against Shelton which will begin with rumors and slowly grow in substantial strength until our objective is accomplished." Hoover specified the relevant methods: "This proposal can be moved through informants, established news sources, anonymous communications, the Bureau-controlled fictitious anti-Klan organization, the National Committee for Domestic Tranquility, chain letters, cartoons, compromise of Klansmen and other means too numerous to mention."[26]

The FBI created a paper organization, the National Committee for

23. Director, FBI (157-9-Main), to SAC, Atlanta (157-826), "Counterintelligence Program/Internal Security/Disruption of Hate Groups," April 29, 1965, p. 1.

24. F. J. Baumgardner to W. C. Sullivan, "Counterintelligence Program/Internal Security/Disruption of Hate Groups/ (Robert M. Shelton)/(United Klans of America, Inc.)," November 18, 1964, p. 1.

25. F. J. Baumgardner to W. C. Sullivan, "Counterintelligence Program/Internal Security/Disruption of Hate Groups/ (Robert Shelton)," October 5, 1966, p. 1. It is not known whether this action was approved.

26. Director, FBI (157-9-4), to SAC, Birmingham (157-833), "Counterintelligence Program/Internal Security/Disruption of Hate Groups/(United Klans of America National Klonvocation)," September 27, 1966, pp. 1–2.

Domestic Tranquility (NCDT), to "provide a vehicle for attacking Klan policies and disputes from a low key, common sense and patriotic position." The bulletin of the organization was prepared by the FBI "under the signature of Harmon Blennerhasset, an obscure figure in American history who gave financial support to Aaron Burr." Its dateline was "Dayton," a name shared by nineteen municipalities across the United States. The object was to "heighten Klan disputes, discredit leaders and hotheads in the various hate groups, and possibly enhance the development of certain subjects as informants." The NCDT newsletters carried the slogan, "Quit the Klan; and back our boys in Vietnam."[27]

Secrecy surrounding this campaign was strict, even by FBI standards. Hoover admonished the twenty field offices involved in this operation to "regard this development as a highly confidential counterintelligence technique. Information concerning the NCDT should not be set forth in the details of any communication prepared for dissemination." Further, it could not be divulged to other intelligence agencies, even when specifically requested. According to the FBI director, the NCDT was set up as a "growth-type organization."[28] The group established a mailing address in Dayton, Ohio, acquired an actual membership, and, in at least one instance, offered an enthusiastic individual "a leadership position as representative of our organization [the NCDT] in the 5th Congressional District, Louisiana."[29] Despite FBI secrecy, the United Klans of America, Inc., guessed that the FBI was behind the NCDT, as well as other disruptive activities, and published an article in its newsletter, *The Fiery Cross*, to warn members.[30]

There is no discussion of or reference to legislative or executive authority in any of the documents that led to the creation of the FBI pro-

27. F. J. Baumgardner to Mr. W. C. Sullivan, "Counterintelligence Program/Internal Security/Disruption of Hate Groups/(The National Committee for Domestic Tranquility)," March 10, 1966, pp. 1–3.

28. Director, FBI (157-9-12), to SAC, Dallas (157-689), "Counterintelligence Program/Internal Security/Disruption of Hate Groups/(The National Committee for Domestic Tranquility)," May 12, 1966, pp. 1–2.

29. F. J. Baumgardner to W. C. Sullivan, "Counterintelligence Program/Internal Security/Disruption of Hate Groups/(The National Committee for Domestic Tranquility)," September 21, 1966; C. D. Brennan to W. C. Sullivan, "Counterintelligence Program/Internal Security/Disruption of Hate Groups/(The National Committee for Domestic Tranquility)," January 24, 1967.

30. SAC, Birmingham (157-9-4), to Director, FBI (157-835) (P), "Counterintelligence Program—Klan/Racial Matters (Klan)," August 6, 1966. The Klan article, which is retyped in this memorandum, concludes with the following question: "Could there be agents from the Anti-Defamation League who have infiltrated the F.B.I.? What is the Anti-Defamation League of B'nai B'rith?"

gram to disrupt the Klans. No regulation was published and no outside opinion sought. The program was not implemented pursuant to any legislative act of Congress, and no records have come to light that would indicate involvement of the White House. There is some question whether the FBI informed the president and the attorney general of the existence of the White Hate Cointelpro after the fact, and without naming it, but there is no doubt as to the effectiveness of the program in disrupting and disintegrating the Klan.

By the FBI's public accounting, Klan membership had reached ten thousand in 1965 and was growing, largely as a reaction to passage of the Civil Rights Act of 1964. By 1969, the total number of Klansmen had fallen to about sixty-eight hundred.[31] In late 1964, Hoover stated publicly, "We have been able to penetrate the Klan. There are 480 Klansmen in Mississippi. . . . I had our agents in Mississippi interview every member of the Klan."[32] One internal FBI report indicated that after only four months, "tangible results are beginning to be realized and the field has demonstrated an enthusiasm for counterintelligence techniques [directed at the Klan]."[33]

By 1969, high-ranking FBI officials could point to "excellent results achieved through counterintelligence in smashing the Klan effectiveness in North Carolina." Part of the strategy had been "the use of selected racial informants, friendly press media and other logical counterintelligence techniques . . . to split the North Carolina Klan from the national Klan [UKA]." The effort was apparently effective, as symbolized in one instance by Klan ritual: "One hundred and fifty UKA membership cards were attached to a cross and burned, signifying a split in the Klan."[34]

One year after the White Hate Cointelpro was established, a senior

31.   These figures constitute only a very rough indication because they were released in a public relations context (see the *FBI Annual Report*, 1965, p. 29, and 1969, p. 24). That number could vary when it suited bureau purposes; for example, the Klan membership figure was given in the 1968 *FBI Annual Report* as twelve thousand (p. 23). Both high and low figures could be cast in a favorable light: a large or increasing Klan membership indicated a growing menace and a need to supplement bureau funding, whereas a small or decreasing Klan membership indicated that the FBI was doing a good job.

32.   *Newsweek*, December 7, 1964, p. 24.

33.   F. J. Baumgardner to W. C. Sullivan, "Communist Party, USA/Counterintelligence Program/Internal Security—C" and "Counterintelligence Program/Internal Security/Disruption of Hate Groups," January 6, 1965, p. 1.

34.   G. C. Moore to W. C. Sullivan, "Counter-intelligence Program/Disruption of Klan and White/Hate Groups, United Klans of America, Inc. (UKA)/Racial Intelligence," September 16, 1969, p. 1.

FBI official set forth the results the program had obtained in a memorandum to Clyde Tolson, the number-two man in the bureau. Although the memo is too highly censored to give an accurate picture of Klan counterintelligence, it contains a handwritten note initialed by J. Edgar Hoover that states: "Send letter to Watson giving our accomplishments."[35] Pursuant to the director's order, two letters containing the same information were prepared and sent, one to a special assistant to the president, Marvin Watson, and the other to Attorney General Nicholas deB. Katzenbach.

Although he did not mention the word "Cointelpro," the FBI director disclosed that "nearly two thousand of our informants and sources are being operated to obtain up-to-date intelligence data concerning racial matters." He added that 774 of these had been developed over the past twelve months—one year to the day since the White Hate Cointelpro had been established. He stressed the importance of the informant program: "Particularly significant has been the high-level penetration we have achieved of Klan organizations. At the present time, there are 14 Klan groups in existence. We have penetrated every one of them through informants and currently are operating informants in top level positions of leadership in [deleted][36] of them." Finally, Hoover stated, "We are also seizing every opportunity to disrupt the activities of the Klan organizations." The memorandum, addressed to the attorney general, was captioned "Penetration and Disruption/Of Klan Organizations/Racial Matters."[37]

Liberal Theory Revised—1964

Attorney General Katzenbach wrote in response, "May I take this opportunity to congratulate you on the development of your informant system in the Klan organizations and on the results you have obtained through it." He expressed regret that the effectiveness of FBI anti-Klan operations would be compromised "if too extensive publicity were given to them" and stated his hope that one day it might "be possible to place these achievements on the public record, so that the Bureau can receive its due credit." His response is captioned "Your memoran-

35.   A. H. Belmont to Tolson, "Recent Shootings in Alabama,/Louisiana and Mississippi/Civil Rights," August 31, 1965, p. 3.

36.   Five typewritten letters are deleted here, so the missing word is either "three," "seven," or "eight."

37.   Director, FBI, to The Attorney General, "Penetration and Disruption/Of Klan Organizations/Racial Matters," September 2, 1965, pp. 1–2.

dum of September 2, regarding penetration and disruption of Klan Organizations."[38]

Ten years later, in testimony before the Church Committee in Congress, Katzenbach acknowledged approving the FBI program to infiltrate the Klan.[39] But he denied ever having heard the word "Cointelpro" or giving his sanction to any improper activities against the Klan.[40] His position in this matter—as well as his conception of propriety—is of interest because the FBI understood his written approval to be an authorization for the White Hate Cointelpro.[41] But more, Katzenbach's views on the government's efforts to penetrate and disrupt the Klan are critical in determining the precise status that the liberal theory of internal security had come to assume.

Like most liberals in 1964, Katzenbach believed that Klan violence in the South had to be brought to an end if civil rights policies were to be implemented. The federal government was the appropriate vehicle because, he believed, the "situation in 1964 in Mississippi was a desperate one. There was no law enforcement agency in Mississippi that was worth a damn, and none would protect the rights of clients."[42] He acknowledged the role of the FBI in this task: "The Bureau did, to my certain knowledge, investigate, penetrate and disrupt activities of the Ku Klux Klan. It did so vigorously, actively, overtly and with outstanding success." This was necessary, he claimed, to bring "to an end the

38. Nicholas deB. Katzenbach to J. Edgar Hoover, September 3, 1965.

39. Katzenbach stated: "[FBI investigative and informant] techniques were designed to deter violence—to prevent murder, bombings and beatings. In my judgment, they were successful. I was aware of them and I authorized them. In the same circumstances I would do so again today" (Church, vol. 6, p. 207).

40. The testimony is as follows: "*Mr. Smothers*: Do you recall a memorandum [cited above] originating from you back to Mr. Hoover indicating your satisfaction with the Bureau's efforts against the Klan as reflected by that memorandum [cited above]? *Mr. Katzenbach*: Yes, sir, I do, and they [the efforts of the FBI] were magnificent. *Mr. Smothers*: Did you approve the Bureau's cointelpro effort against the Klan? *Mr. Katzenbach*: I never heard the word cointelpro as such. I certainly approved everything described to me in that memorandum" (ibid., pp. 230–31).

41. "The Bureau interpreted this letter as approval and praise of its White Hate Cointelpro. Mr. Katzenbach has said that he has no memory of this document [cited above], nor of the response [cited above]. He testified that during his term in the Department [of Justice] he had never heard the terms 'Cointel' or 'Cointelpro,' and that while he was familiar with the Klan investigation, he was not aware of any improper activities such as letters to wives" (Church, bk. 3, p. 67).

42. Church, vol. 6, p. 231.

Klan's criminal conspiracy of violence that scourged the South, especially Mississippi, in the middle 1960's."[43]

The phrase "criminal conspiracy" is important because it connects the logic of the attack on the Klan with the old liberal theory of internal security. Hubert Humphrey had used the same words in the reasoning with which he justified outlawing the Communist party to the liberal community.[44] The difference was that with the party, the connection between membership and criminal conspiracy was a great deal less direct than it was with the Klan. Liberals assumed that the Communist party was part of an international conspiracy that might one day rise up against the government, using force and violence to attain its ends. As regards the Klan, no assumption of criminality was necessary. There was abundant prima facie evidence that members of so-called Klan action groups had entered into and carried out conspiracies to intimidate, bomb, and murder Negroes and civil rights workers. With the Klan, it was unnecessary to derive criminal conspiracy because it could easily be proved.

To the liberal mind, Klansmen and Communists alike forfeited a measure of their own civil rights because they were prepared to violate the civil rights of others. This attitude is perhaps best captured by the phrase "intolerance against the intolerant," which has been advanced "as essential for maintaining and particularly for establishing a democracy as 'tolerance for the tolerant.' "[45] Without doubt the main object of the Klan after 1964 was to block implementation of the Civil Rights Act, passed in July of that year. It was appropriate, then, if seemingly incongruous, that Klan murders of Negroes and civil rights workers in the South often could be prosecuted under federal statutes only as conspiracies to deny civil rights.

In retrospect, Katzenbach justified, even applauded, FBI efforts to disrupt the Klan on the assumption that the actions Klansmen advocated and carried out against Negroes put them in a special cate-

---

43.   Ibid., p. 213.

44.   As Humphrey put it: "If we are correct in our assumption that the Communist movement is such an international conspiracy—and I believe the facts are overwhelmingly in favor of this conclusion—then I am convinced that membership in that conspiracy should be punishable as a criminal offense, because members of such a conspiracy are, in fact, conspirators to overthrow the government of the United States by force and violence" (Hubert H. Humphrey to Marvin Rosenberg, August 27, 1954, 23.L.10.3B, Box 104, "Leg.: Communism. HH bill outlawing CP Continued," HHH).

45.   Kurt Lewin, *Resolving Social Conflicts: Selected Papers on Group Dynamics* (New York: Harper and Brothers, 1948), p. 37.

gory outside the usual protections of the Constitution. "The Bureau," he argued, "was investigating [the Klan] and attempting to prevent violence. To equate such efforts with surveillance or harassment of persons exercising constitutionally guaranteed rights is in my view unmitigated nonsense." To the attorney general and the liberal administration he served, the Klan was a fit object for internal security measures and was properly subjected to the same techniques that had been used against the Communist party in the previous decade.[46] He underscored the disruptive effect FBI penetration inflicted on the Klan and its necessity:

> I have no doubt that the Bureau's investigation of the criminal activities of the Klan was tough, intensive, harassing and thorough. I expected no less, the President asked for no less, and the Nation deserved no less. . . . Klansmen in Mississippi—the Klan leadership—were not ordinary citizens [seeking to exercise their constitutional rights]. They were lawbreakers of the most vicious sort—terrorists who intimidated, bombed, burned and killed, often under the watchful and protective eyes of their brethren in the local law enforcement agencies.[47]

In this view, the Klan and the Communist party merited like treatment because they were essentially the same. The party tried to subvert American government and values, and the Klan attempted to undermine the constitutionally guaranteed rights of Negro citizens and white civil rights activists. Yet the term *subversive* did not seem to fit the anti-Communist and professed Klan patriots quite so well as *extremist*, which was applied to the Klan by the FBI and added to the 1964 Democratic party platform at the request of President Johnson.[48] The extremist plank lumped the Klan together with other radical groups: "We condemn extremism, whether from the right or left, including the extreme tactics of such organizations as the Communist Party, the Ku Klux Klan and the John Birch Society." A nearly identical position had earlier been rejected by the Republican party, led by conservative presidential candidate Barry Goldwater.[49]

46.   As Katzenbach testified, "In an effort to detect, prevent, and prosecute acts of violence, President Johnson, Attorney General Kennedy, Mr. Allen Dulles, myself and others urged the Bureau to develop an effective informant program, similar to that which they had developed with respect to the Communist Party" (Church, vol. 6, p. 207).

47.   Ibid., p. 215.

48.   *New York Times*, August 5, 1964, p. 1.

49.   Ibid., August 25, 1964, p. 1.

To accommodate these perspectives, and a full attack on the Klan, the liberal theory of internal security required subtle but significant modifications to make it more versatile without transforming its basic structure. The revised theory diverged from precedent because it eliminated the requirement that the group in question be dominated by a hostile foreign power. In its place, liberals substituted criminal conspiracy on the part of the Klan for assumption of conspiracy by virtue of membership in the Communist party. In several celebrated cases, the FBI investigated and arrested Klan members under criminal statutes. But even here, indictment and prosecution were difficult because local juries and law enforcement officials were often sympathetic to the goals and activities of the Klan organizations.

Whereas Communists were thought to be subversive, the Klan was known to be extremist, which was itself considered to be a variety of subversion. Such groups sought to undermine the Constitution and laws of the United States by using force and violence to deny civil rights to American citizens. It is likely that the liberal political community supported a hard-hitting FBI campaign to infiltrate the secret Klan orders because there was no other effective way to reach and prevent Klan violence. Sophisticated intelligence sources and methods became necessary because it would be futile to wait until after a crime occurred to look for its perpetrators.

And, finally, the term *Klan terrorism* entered the liberal internal security lexicon as a stand-in for Communist sabotage and espionage. With these modifications, the liberal theory was refitted so that Klan violence could be addressed as a breach of internal security. The formidable powers of the national domestic security police could now be leveled against the designated threat. The requirement that the group in question be dominated by a hostile foreign power dropped out because it was no longer needed to substantiate the charge of conspiracy. In this way, the liberal theory was modified to meet the new contingency of internal subversion through organized, indigenous terrorism.

In important respects, however, the liberal approach to internal security in 1964 remained strikingly similar to that of the previous decade. The primary responsibility for internal security continued to reside with a single intelligence agency, the FBI, now swollen by a host of new responsibilities and a decade of generous appropriations.[50] In

50.   In fiscal year 1964, for example, the House Appropriations "committee's cutting drive hit all the big agencies except the Federal Bureau of Investigation, which asked for and received $146,900,000. Its allotment would permit the employment of 350 more clerks and 200 more field agents" (ibid., June 16, 1963, p. 23). In the previous fiscal year, when the FBI asked for $127,216,000, Appro-

fact, the bureau stood alone among federal agencies in the flexibility, autonomy, and secrecy of its budget and expenditures.[51] As in 1950, liberals still subscribed to preventive and disruptive intelligence measures, designed to discover and foil conspiracies and other threats to internal security before the fact. The liberal commitment to freedom of speech and association also remained largely intact, but not—as already indicated—for those who would withhold such freedoms from others.

If the FBI efforts to attack the Klan are disaggregated, one group of activities might be called the attorney general's program, and the rest, the director's. The former was conducted pursuant to acknowledged public policy and was ordered by the president. Its mission was to penetrate the Klan for the purpose of prosecuting and preventing Klan violence. The latter was a covert FBI campaign—the White Hate Cointelpro—designed to fragment and destroy the Klan organizations and to disable Klan leadership. The difference was more than a matter of degree. And it was a difference that held with regard to the Communist party as well as the Klan.

Both cases resulted from two trends in liberal theory and practice of internal security that tended to weaken and undermine liberalism over time. The first was a persistent inclination on the part of Congress and the executive alike to delegate internal security policymaking to the FBI. It was a result of a strong liberal conviction—a hangover from the McCarthy years—that internal security policy should not be forged in the heat of acrimonious public debate. It should be transferred to professional administrators, who could be depended upon to act in the

---

priations Committee chairman John Rooney commented, " 'The confidence which the Committee has in the Federal Bureau of Investigation under the highly capable and efficient leadership of Director J. Edgar Hoover is best illustrated by the fact that this is the tenth consecutive year that not one penny of the funds he has requested of the Committee has been denied' " (Navasky, *Kennedy Justice*, p. 38). In fiscal year 1965, Rooney's committee allocated a budget of $150,445,000 to the Bureau and accepted "five FBI special agents on loan . . . to help with the committee's work" (*Newsweek*, December 7, 1964, p. 23).

51. Only a small percentage of the FBI budget was divided into line items. The bulk of the "funds appropriated to the Bureau come in one lump sum, to be expended not necessarily as the Director said they would during his congressional appearances, but as he wishes." As Hoover testified, "I can frankly say we have seldom been denied funds by the House Subcommittee on Appropriations. . . . The Bureau of the Budget and the Congress . . . have always been most considerate of our needs." By 1971, the FBI budget had grown to $334 million, almost as large as that of the Department of State (Walter Pincus, "The Bureau's Budget: A Source of Power," in Pat Watters and Stephen Gillers, eds., *Investigating the FBI* [New York: Doubleday, 1973], pp. 64–65).

public interest rather than from political motivations. The second was an apparently limitless liberal tolerance of pervasive official secrecy in internal as well as national security affairs. This tendency made it easy for FBI bureaucrats to insulate their security operations not only from the Congress but also from higher executive authority, the press, and the general public.

Taken together, tolerance of pervasive official secrecy and delegation of unspecified security powers led to greater and greater divergence between liberal leaders, on one hand, and FBI bureaucrats and the programs they administered on the other. The attorney general certainly authorized penetration and disruption of the Klan, insofar as he understood the meaning of those terms. He held the position that "you cannot do a criminal investigation of any organization properly without having some disruptive influence." He went further: "Where you have reason to know that the [Klan] organization and its members are engaged in acts of violence, then by George, you want to disrupt those acts of violence."[52]

The attorney general's program envisioned FBI activities to disrupt Klan violence that were within the law and would bring Klansmen to the bar of justice, and he assumed adherence to due process. Although he probably guessed that the FBI sometimes stepped across the line, it was all in a good cause and could be ignored because secrecy meant that he was not officially aware of it. The director's program was quite another matter. Almost no one outside the bureau has gone on record as approving the methods and techniques that were used in the White Hate Cointelpro.[53] Former Attorney General Ramsey Clark testified: "I think that any disruptive activities such as those that you reveal, regarding the Cointel Program and the Ku Klux Klan, should be absolutely prohibited and subjected to criminal prosecution."[54]

52.   Church, vol. 6, p. 231.

53.   Among prominent academics, James Q. Wilson is apparently alone in endorsing Cointelpro techniques: "One's immediate instinct is to condemn such acts as contemptible, as indeed they are. But that does not cover the matter. Granted that they are dirty tricks, are they always inappropriate applied to any organization under any circumstances? Against the Soviet secret police? Against an illegal conspiracy bent on terrorist bombings, such as the Weather Underground? Against even the Klan . . . But if there are circumstances in which one might reasonably contemplate authorizing such acts, there obviously should be some effort to define, in the most limiting manner, what those circumstances might be" (James Q. Wilson, *The Investigators: Managing FBI and Narcotics Agents* [New York: Basic Books, 1978], pp. 84–85).

54.   Clark added, "I believe the police investigation, the criminal investigation and

But the FBI director did not see it that way. He and his subordinates took their cues from the administration in power—in this case, to extinguish Klan violence—and from their own peculiar ideas about what measures were necessary to protect the internal security of the United States. As time passed, secret Cointelpros proliferated, and disruptive intelligence techniques were applied to dozens of indigenous American protest groups—without the knowledge of liberals or the benefit of their theoretical elucidations. The FBI attack on the Klan was a break with the past and a gateway to the future. It is therefore necessary to discover its origins in the politics of civil rights.

The FBI and Civil Rights in the South

If the FBI worked against the Klan after 1964 with devastating efficiency, it had entered the civil rights arena with hesitancy and, to a great extent, on its own terms. The bureau was unwilling to yield control of its agents to a young and headstrong attorney general, who was intent on enforcing federal civil rights policies in the South.[55] This attitude resulted in part from precedent. The FBI director had exercised ironclad authority over his agents for nearly forty years. It was part strategy. He had built the bureau on a principle and a public posture of impartiality, which might be compromised by the partisan politics of the president's younger brother. It was partly the result of insubordination by the FBI director.[56] And, finally, the director was reluctant

---

accumulation of data files or dossiers should be prohibited, except in actual ongoing criminal investigations initiated where there was probable cause to believe the crimes have been committed, or is about to be committed" (Church, vol. 6, p. 221).

55.   "Mr. Hoover's price for reluctantly going along in civil rights was that he have control of his own troops, that the FBI oversee its own men, use its own systems, follow its own rules, provide parallel rather than integrated services. . . . The long-range results of [Attorney General] Kennedy's enlisting the FBI in civil rights were (a) to enlarge the Justice Department's law enforcement capability, but (b) at the same time to give the FBI effective veto power over each and every civil rights activity in which it was a participant" (Navasky, *Kennedy Justice*, p. 113).

56.   As Katzenbach described the situation, "There was, especially in the area of civil rights, a good deal of tension between the Director on one hand and the Attorney General and his principal assistants on the other. I was very conscious of the fact that there was often a lack of candor in relationships between the Bureau and the Department; that Mr. Hoover was opposed to many of the views of Mr. Kennedy, Mr. Clark and myself, and that he expressed his views privately, and occasionally publicly; that the Bureau leaked stories to the press which were embarrassing to me and to my predecessor. I did occasionally pursue those leaks

to sour relations with southern law enforcement officials, upon whom he depended for assistance in solving cases unrelated to civil rights.[57]

For most of the Kennedy administration, there was considerable distance between the role the FBI actually played in civil rights and the expectations of liberals and Negro leaders—who demanded that the FBI intercede on the side of justice. Roy Wilkins, the executive director of the NAACP, explained why Negroes could not accept the traditional alliance between the FBI and law enforcement authorities in the South, or the studied detachment with which agents approached civil rights confrontations:

> Negroes have been prosecuted and persecuted under local ordinances and traditions, by local police force[s], the local judges, the local law-enforcement machinery, and the FBI simply stood by taking notes of this and that . . . sometimes taking pictures, and sought out to see wherein technically a federal law has been violated. All the while Negroes are suffering physical bloody persecution. Negroes just don't see how a federal police agency can stand by and look at this happening and fold its hands and say, "Well, we can't step in here."[58]

Despite such criticism—and the bureau's subsequent covert action program to destroy the Klan—the FBI never altered its public stance regarding its role in civil rights. This position involved several elements, some of which were unpopular in liberal and civil rights circles. First and foremost, the FBI maintained that it was not a federal police agency.[59] "Our principal function," Hoover often stated, "is the gathering of information—strictly investigative in character." Second, agents were directed not to intervene when they witnessed civil rights violations involving violence to persons. Hoover explained the FBI policy: "We do not have the authority to give personal protection to any-

---

but the Bureau invariably denied that it was the source" (Church, vol. 6, p. 200).

57.   The FBI had no field office in Mississippi until after 1964 and so depended on close ties with state and local law enforcement officials.

58.   Quoted in *U.S. News & World Report*, December 7, 1964, pp. 45–46.

59.   Hoover stated his position: "I am inclined toward being a States' righter in matters involving law enforcement. That is, I fully respect the sovereignty of State and local authorities. I consider the local police officer to be our first line of defense against crime, and I am opposed to a national police force" ("Interview with J. Edgar Hoover," *U.S. News & World Report*, December 21, 1964, p. 38).

one. . . . We make the investigations, gather the facts, [and] submit the evidence to the Justice Department attorneys."[60]

The FBI agent's responsibility in such a situation was to take careful notes.[61] "If the agent should become personally involved in the action," one report stated, "he would be deserting his assigned task and would be unable to fulfill his primary responsibility of making objective observations."[62] And finally, the bureau was unable to assist in efforts to integrate the South because, as the FBI director explained, "The Civil Rights Act of 1964 has no criminal provisions: hence, there is no authority under which an arrest can be made." What could the FBI do? "We would conduct a preliminary investigation to determine the facts of the complaint," Hoover continued, "and furnish the results of this to the Department of Justice."[63] If the FBI intervened in local civil rights matters, Hoover argued, it would run the risk of becoming a national police force—a threat to American freedoms.[64] The director's position dismayed civil rights activists, many of whom believed

60.   Ibid., p. 36. On another occasion, Hoover stated to a group of women reporters: "The bureau is not a police agency . . . we don't guard anybody. We are fact finders. . . . We simply can't wet nurse everybody who goes down to try to reform or re-educate the Negro population of the South" (*Newsweek*, November 30, 1964, p. 29).

61.   "The Justice Department assumed the FBI's unavailability and called in special deputized federal marshals while FBI agents looked through windows and took notes. . . . In addition to obtaining (or relaying) information and not moving to protect the [freedom] riders . . . the FBI also did not apparently even consider— nor was it suggested that they should—making on-the-spot arrests of visible outlaws. As a result, the FBI early established its reluctance to antagonize local law enforcers, and the Administration early learned to assume that it was without what might have been its most valuable race-relations asset: a manpower pool permitting flexible response in crisis situations" (Navasky, *Kennedy Justice*, pp. 139–40).

62.   U.S. Commission on Civil Rights, *Law Enforcement: A Report on Equal Protection in the South* (Washington: GPO, 1965), p. 166, quoted in Navasky, *Kennedy Justice*, pp. 139–40.

63.   "Interview with J. Edgar Hoover," *U.S. News & World Report*, December 21, 1964, p. 37.

64.   Attorney General Robert Kennedy reportedly agreed. "Kennedy, furthermore, bought Hoover's favorate bromide—that too much FBI involvement in anything the FBI didn't want to become involved in would inevitably lead to a national police force—yet ironically, by permitting Hoover dictatorial control over the FBI's ranks, rules and systems while enlarging its numbers, budget and paper jurisdiction, Kennedy was perpetuating and enlarging whatever danger there was that the FBI might function as a national police force" (Navasky, *Kennedy Justice*, p. 142).

that if the FBI was unwilling to oppose racist law-enforcement officials in the South, it must be in league with them.[65]

The FBI director was not a little disingenuous in his public pronouncements. For many years, the bureau had conducted secret activities that were largely unrelated to investigation of federal crimes and had nothing to do with Justice Department prosecutions. These ranged from counterintelligence actions against the Communist party and the Socialist Workers party to electronic surveillance of Martin Luther King, including his organization and his associates.[66] Hoover was able to manipulate the issue of the role of the FBI in civil rights to suit his purposes. If he was unwilling to involve his agents in enforcing voting rights or integration policies, perhaps because he did not want to strain relations with local police, he would conclude that the FBI lacked jurisdiction in such matters and defer to municipal or state authorities.[67]

At the same time, however, he cited the growing number of FBI civil rights investigations to back up his requests for additional agents and used civil rights as a way to expand his agency and extend its influence into the South. As demands for an end to racial violence mounted in late 1963 and 1964, the FBI discovered the jurisdiction to involve itself deeply and solved several major civil rights crimes of the period. The

65. Roy Wilkins, executive director of the NAACP, stated: "They [Negroes] feel that the FBI's traditional method of operation—that is, co-operation with local police agencies—cannot produce results in the South, and that unless the FBI departs from this formula, the FBI will be working in co-operation with some of the very forces that have oppressed Negroes" (U. S. News & World Report, December 7, 1964, p. 45). Wilkins's comment echoed the findings of the Truman Committee on Civil Rights in 1947: "The tendency of FBI agents to work in close cooperation with local police officers has sometimes been detrimental to the handling of civil rights investigations. At times, these local officers are themselves under suspicion. Even where this is not so, the victims or witnesses in civil rights cases are apt to be weak and frightened people who are not encouraged to tell their stories freely to Federal agents where the latter are working closely with local police officers" (quoted in James A. Wechsler, "The FBI's Failure in the South," Progressive, December 1963, p. 21).

66. In his public statements on the mission of the FBI, Hoover apparently did not take into account the Cointelpro operations, which were, from their beginning in 1956, "a complete aberration of the FBI's investigative function and a breach of a cardinal article of faith: that the Bureau was strictly a fact-finding agency" (Cotter, "Notes toward a Definition of National Security," p. 14).

67. At a news conference on July 10, 1964, Hoover stated: "We most certainly do not and will not give protection to civil rights workers. The FBI is not a police organization. It is purely an investigative organization. The protection of individual citizens, either natives of this state or coming into the state, is a matter for local authorities" (Nation, July 27, 1964, p. 21).

key, of course, was political pressure emanating from liberal quarters, especially the president, the attorney general, and their friends in the civil rights movement. In the aftermath of a Klan bomb attack on a Birmingham church, in which four Negro children were killed in September 1963, ADA spokesman Joseph L. Rauh, Jr., advanced a position that would come to dominate liberal thinking on the subject of racial terrorism: "The failure or reluctance of the F.B.I. to infiltrate [the] rightwing subversive element in the United States becomes more apparent with each additional tragedy in the South. The total infiltration of the Communist party by the F.B.I. demonstrates the capacity of the bureau to forestall criminal activity. The failure to infiltrate the [White] Citizens Council[s], the Ku Klux Klan and other racist organizations is inexcusable in this current crisis."[68]

The Birmingham murders followed a series of racial disorders that had occurred four months earlier, during which federal troops had been stationed in outlying areas. In the Birmingham case, the Kennedy administration opted not to send troops. The FBI instead launched an intensive investigation involving twenty-five special agents, which was conducted under provisions of the Civil Rights Act of 1960.[69] The murders and subsequent violence were treated by the press and the Kennedys as major national events. Negro leaders, including Martin Luther King, repeatedly demanded federal intervention. Assistant Attorney General Burke Marshall was dispatched to the scene of the crime. And the president issued a statement in which he deplored the bombings, commended nonviolent Negro leaders, and stated that "bomb specialists of the Federal Bureau of Investigation are there [in Birmingham] to lend every assistance in the detection of those responsible for yesterday's crime."[70]

In an odd twist of events, the FBI investigation of the Birmingham murders was cut short when the Alabama Highway Patrol decided— in a highly unusual procedure—not to inform the bureau before mak-

68. From a telegram to President Kennedy, quoted in *New York Times*, September 17, 1963, p. 25.

69. In this case, the FBI investigation was authorized under a section of the law which "bans interstate transport of explosives meant to damage any building 'for the purpose of interfering with its use for educational, religious, charitable, residential, business or civic purposes. . . . If death results [the convicted persons] shall be subject to imprisonment for any term of years or for life, but the court may impose the death penalty if the jury so recommends' " (*New York Times*, September 16, 1963, p. 1).

70. Ibid., September 17, 1963, p. 1.

ing arrests.[71] Both suspects in the case had "Ku Klux Klan records, [and] had been under surveillance for about a week by a large force of investigators from the F.B.I." and local police.[72] Despite the frenzy of activity on the part of the Kennedy administration and highly publicized involvement by the FBI, the case continued to invite comparisons between the bureau's infiltration of the Communist party and its lack of similar interest in the Klan.

Liberal writers and editors attacked the FBI specifically on this point, focusing on the Birmingham events. They questioned not whether the FBI possessed legal authority to initiate intelligence investigations but, rather, why the bureau had failed to infiltrate the Klan and prevent violence. Liberals considered the evil so great that they glossed over legal formalities in search of any remedy.[73] As one editor suggested, "If only a fraction of the FBI manpower dedicated to the care and feeding of the Communist treasury [dues paid by FBI informants] had been allocated to undercover work in the rightist network, perhaps at least a few of the more deadly Southern explosions might have been forestalled."[74]

Liberals from the president on down endorsed this reasoning because they were presented with an intractable problem. Officials responsible for running the criminal justice system at state and local levels in the South were often sympathetic to the goals of the Klan.[75] In

71. One year later, the FBI commented on the surprise arrests: "This investigation [of the Birmingham bomb murders] was prejudiced by premature arrests made by the Alabama Highway Patrol, and, consequently, it has not yet been possible to obtain evidence or confessions that would insure successful prosecution although the FBI has identified a small group of Klansmen believed to be responsible" (*U.S. News & World Report*, December 7, 1964, p. 46).

72. *New York Times*, October 1, 1963, p. 1.

73. In a related area, the American Civil Liberties Union did insist upon the letter of the law. Ten days after the Birmingham bomb murders, the ACLU argued before the Supreme Court that freedom of speech had been denied to the leaders of the National States Rights Party, a radical segregationist organization, because local authorities had obtained and enforced an injunction prohibiting the group from distributing its literature (ibid., September 26, 1963, p. 29).

74. Wechsler, "The FBI's Failure in the South," p. 22. At that time, Wechsler was editor of the editorial page of the *New York Post*.

75. The FBI understood the problem as well. As James B. Adams, assistant to the director of the FBI, testified: "[Our strategy was to] create enough disruption that these [Klan] members will realize that if they go out and murder three civil rights workers, even though the sheriff and other law enforcement officers are in on it, if that were the case and with some of them it was the case, that they would be caught" (Church, vol. 6, p. 148).

many cases of Klan brutality and even murder, there was no federal law to make the punishment fit the crime. And when Klansmen were charged under state murder statutes, it was often difficult to obtain convictions, even when there was abundant evidence of guilt. In the nationally publicized murder of Lemuel Penn near Colbert, Georgia, for example, four Klan members were acquitted in the face of overwhelming evidence compiled by the FBI, including signed confessions. "While the jury was out," one account stated, "there was no excitement or tension. Everybody had known the verdict from the beginning—acquittal, 12 to 0."[76]

Just as frequently, local police turned a blind eye on the violent exploits of the Klan and sometimes colluded actively with Klansmen, as happened in at least one Birmingham incident. The Klan attacked a busload of freedom riders at the suggestion of a detective and a high-ranking officer in the Birmingham Police Department. The Klansmen "were promised 15 minutes with absolutely no intervention from any police officer whatsoever." According to one Klansman, an FBI informant who participated in the beatings, "You would look over from the bus station and see city hall and you would see as many as 100 police officers walking. They couldn't help but see us." After the beatings had been in progress for about fifteen minutes, a police officer reportedly ran up to the Klansmen and stated, "Godammit, godammit, get out of there. Get 'em out of here. Your 15 minutes are up and we're sending the crew."[77]

Because Klan violence often met with approval from local law-enforcement personnel, it created a crisis for the liberal Kennedy and Johnson administrations. It threatened to undermine the drive for civil rights and perhaps to alienate a large Democratic constituency consisting of Negroes and sympathetic whites in the North. This is perhaps what former attorney general Nicholas Katzenbach had in mind when he referred to the "identity of constitutional and political interest" between King and the Kennedy and Johnson administrations.

Because they could not depend on local or state police to stem racial terrorism, liberals embraced the FBI as a viable alternative to calling out troops and instituting martial law in the South. After the fall of 1963, the nation was shocked by a succession of brutal Klan murders.

76. William Bradford Huie, "Murder: The Klan on Trial," *Saturday Evening Post*, June 19, 1965, p. 88.

77. Testimony of Gary Thomas Rowe, Jr., who also stated that the freedom riders were "beaten very badly" and that the Klansmen carried visible weapons: "We had baseball bats, we had clubs, we had chains, we had pistols sticking out of our belts. It was just unbelievable. Not one officer in the Birmingham Police Department asked us what was going on" (Church, vol. 6, p. 118).

One FBI official later recalled that "the newspapers, the President, and Congress . . . [were] concerned about the murder of the civil rights workers, the Lemuel Penn case, the Viola Liuzzo case, the bombings of the church in Birmingham. We were faced with one tremendous problem."[78] As the pace of Klan violence escalated, so too did the visible presence of the FBI in combatting the hooded menace.[79]

When three civil rights workers—Michael Schwerner, Andrew Goodman, and James Chaney—disappeared near Philadelphia, Mississippi, on June 21, 1964, the FBI mounted what would become the most extensive manhunt in the history of that state.[80] But the investigation, which was initiated during the climax of the congressional debate over the Civil Rights Act, failed to produce quick results. The bodies of the missing men were not discovered until August 4, even though President Johnson ordered four hundred navy men to assist in the search.[81] Sensational events surrounding the crime immediately captured national media attention, which was sustained for six months, until after the case was solved.[82] On December 4, FBI agents arrested twenty-one persons in connection with the murders, including a number of Klan members, the Neshoba County sheriff, and his deputy.[83]

In the interim, the case and its fallout contributed materially to three developments that help to explain the relationship between the FBI and the liberal community during this period. First, the FBI director personally opened an expansive new field office in Jackson, Mississippi, in July—at the specific request of President Johnson who was deeply interested in the case.[84] Second, Hoover engaged in an open and bitter

78.   Testimony of James B. Adams, assistant to the director of the FBI, in Church, vol. 6, p. 144.

79.   Even the *Nation* reluctantly admitted, "Of recent months, the FBI has been doing a good job, by all accounts, in checking on violations of the civil rights of Negroes. But it did not act until it was ordered into action, first by President Kennedy and later by President Johnson. Its previous record on civil rights was miserable" (November 30, 1964, p. 394).

80.   *Newsweek*, December 14, 1964, p. 21.

81.   *New York Times*, August 5, 1964, p. 1.

82.   The case created one sensational headline after another because of its timing in relation to other Klan murders and the Civil Rights Act, as well as the mysterious way in which the facts unfolded.

83.   *Time*, December 11, 1964, p. 29.

84.   According to an account authorized by the FBI, in the early stages of the investigation, President Johnson discussed the case with J. Edgar Hoover as often as four times a day. He received the parents of two of the missing workers at the White House several weeks before the bodies were discovered. In a discussion

feud with Nobel laureate Martin Luther King, Jr., over the FBI's apparent failure to put an end to racist violence against Negroes in the South. And third, the bureau conceived and implemented the White Hate Cointelpro.

The new FBI office in Jackson, initially staffed with 153 agents, provided a powerful base from which the FBI could monitor Klan activities and undertake civil rights investigations throughout the state.[85] The Jackson office increased the number of agents permanently assigned to Mississippi by a factor of 10.[86] But more, the process by which it was established demonstrates both the priority that liberals assigned to halting Klan terrorism and the logic that enabled them to approach this task as an internal security matter.

In the early summer of 1964, Attorney General Robert Kennedy and his key assistants, Nicholas Katzenbach and Burke Marshall, became increasingly alarmed about the violent activities of the Klan in Mississippi. In the first week of June, Kennedy sent a special team of experienced Justice Department criminal lawyers to Jackson and southwestern Mississippi to make an informal investigation and get the facts. Based on their report, Marshall, who had headed the team, drafted a memorandum that was sent to President Johnson over Kennedy's signature.[87]

The memorandum cited "an increase in acts of terrorism" in Mississippi and stated that "law enforcement officials, at least outside Jackson, are widely believed to be linked to extremist anti-Negro activity, or at the very least to tolerate it." Based on the uniqueness of the situation, the attorney general recommended that the FBI consider devel-

---

with Secretary of Defense Robert McNamara, Johnson approved the use of helicopters from the Meridian Naval Air Station to assist in the search. He ordered Hoover to fly to Jackson to open the new FBI office and provided him with a presidential jet for that purpose. Finally, the president approved infiltration of the Klan, telling Hoover, "Edgar, I want you to put people after the Klan and study it from one county to the next. I want the FBI to have the best intelligence system possible to check on the activities of these people" (Don Whitehead, *Attack on Terror: The FBI against the Ku Klux Klan in Mississippi* [New York: Funk & Wagnalls, 1970], pp. 69, 88, 91, 93).

85.   During this period, the Klan was active in other parts of Mississippi as well: "From June through September, 1964, a series of bombings occurred in McComb, Mississippi. After intensive FBI investigation, nine members of the Ku Klux Klan were arrested and charged with bombing homes and churches at McComb" (Director, FBI, to Attorney General, "Ku Klux Klan/FBI Accomplishments," December 19, 1967, reprinted in Church, vol. 6, p. 519).

86.   *New York Times*, July 11, 1964, p. 1.

87.   Church, bk. 3, pp. 470–71.

oping new methods to identify persons involved in acts of racial terrorism and their friends in law-enforcement circles:

> In the past the procedures used by the Bureau for gaining infor-
> mation on known, local Klan groups have been successful in
> many places, and the information gathering techniques used by
> the Bureau on Communist or Communist related organizations
> have of course been spectacularly efficient. . . . The techniques
> followed in the use of specially trained, special assignment
> agents in the infiltration of Communist groups should be of
> value. If you approve, it might be desirable to take up with the
> Bureau the possibility of developing a similar effort to meet this
> new problem.[88]

The timing of this communication was prescient. It preceded the dis-
appearance of the civil rights workers in Philadelphia, Mississippi, by
about a week. Kennedy had predicted the violence, it had come to pass,
and the president was ready to act on his recommendations. As a first
step, Johnson ordered an intensive FBI investigation. "Working closely
with Mr. Kennedy," Katzenbach recalled, "and using all the powers of
his office, he [the president] asked [former CIA director] Allen Dulles
to confer immediately with Mississippi officials as his personal emis-
sary."[89] On his return, Dulles recommended increasing the FBI presence in Jackson, and, shortly thereafter, J. Edgar Hoover was dispatched to Mississippi to dedicate the new office.

More important than the timing of these events was the way liberals
framed the problem and, ultimately, its solution. In his memorandum
to the president, Kennedy suggested that the techniques that had been
applied to the Communist party might be useful in controlling the
Klan. But though the problem of dealing with a terrorist organization
that enjoyed "the sanction of local law enforcement agencies" was
new, the tried and true solution lay in the domain of internal security.
He referred to the "use of specially trained, special assignment agents
in the infiltration of Communist groups" and recommended that such
techniques be applied to the Klan.

The attorney general must be assumed to have comprehended fully
the techniques he advocated because he was in receipt of detailed information from Hoover, which set forth the particulars of the "FBI's

88. Large portions of this memorandum are reproduced in Navasky, *Kennedy Justice*, pp. 118–19, and in Church, vol. 6, p. 214. Kennedy's recommendations to
the president parallel closely those Sullivan made to Hoover regarding establishing the White Hate Cointelpro.

89. Church, vol. 6, pp. 214–15.

counterattack against the cpusa."[90] The administration's logic combined political expediency with the liberal doctrine that government should greet the intolerant with intolerance. Politically, the president and his party were looking to a national election in only five months. They could not fail to address the issue of racist terror against Negroes in the South and, at the same time, maintain credibility in the drive for equal citizenship, symbolized by the Civil Rights Act of 1964. There were, however, few attractive alternatives. Mobilize the National Guard? But for how long and to what end? Send in the Marines? Definitely an unpopular move. But the FBI, with its impeccable reputation, offered the possibility of an effective response combined with popular appeal.

In the spring of 1964, President Johnson had done his part to burnish the image of the aging superbureaucrat and national hero J. Edgar Hoover. Hoover had served under eleven attorneys general as director of the FBI since May 10, 1924, almost forty years to the day.[91] On this occasion, the president signed an executive order exempting the FBI director from the requirement that he retire in seven months on his seventieth birthday. At a ceremony held in the Rose Garden, Johnson praised Hoover, stating that his name was a "household word" and describing him as "a hero to millions of citizens and an anathema to evil men." He characterized the director as a "quiet, humble and magnificent public servant."[92] At the time, Hoover was thought to be closer to Johnson than to any of the previous six presidents he had served.[93]

90. J. Edgar Hoover to Honorable Robert F. Kennedy, January 10, 1961, with attachment entitled "Communist Party, USA," reprinted in Church, vol. 6, pp. 821–26.

91. The fortieth anniversary of Hoover's appointment as director of the FBI was treated by the media as an important event. In a retrospective piece, for instance, the *New York Times* noted: "The Director is unassailable. The reputation of his organization as one of the most efficient police forces in the world is rarely challenged even by those who feel uneasy over the pervasive power of the F.B.I" (May 10, 1964, p. 58).

92. Ibid., May 9, 1964, p. 12. Anthony Lewis had earlier characterized Hoover as "a phenomenon without any known equivalent in Washington—an official who rarely if ever receives anything but praise from politicians of either party" (ibid., May 4, 1964).

93. On an autographed picture of the president, which was displayed in the director's office, Johnson had written the words: "To J. Edgar Hoover—Than whom there is no greater—From his friend of 30 years" (ibid., May 10, 1964, p. 58). The affinity of the two men was no secret: "Mr. Hoover's relations with President Johnson are reported to be closer than with any of the previous six Presidents under whom he has served. The two have known each other for many

For his part, the president knew how to use the prestige of the FBI director to advantage, as he demonstrated at a press conference later that summer. In a prepared statement on the murder of the three civil rights workers in Mississippi, the president placed the bureau's reputation on the line. "I have just talked with Mr. J. Edgar Hoover," he said. "He assures me that the investigation in Mississippi is going exceedingly well; that substantive results can be expected in a very short period of time."[94] Despite the president's optimism, the case remained unsolved for an additional four months, and relations between the Negro leadership and the FBI continued to deteriorate.[95]

Hoover versus King

Martin Luther King was perhaps the foremost critic of the FBI during this period. He was certainly the most prestigious and effective in gaining the attention of the director, who was known to be very sensitive to any criticism of the bureau. "We have had remarkable success in our civil-rights cases," Hoover asserted, "but to hear Martin Luther King you wouldn't think so."[96] King, for example, was paraphrased as saying that "since the FBI can reassemble a dynamited airplane and convict the dynamiters, why can't it similarly punish murderers and dynamiters in Mississippi?"[97]

The public dispute between King and the FBI director was initiated when Hoover made his annual appearance before a House subcommittee on appropriations. "The infiltration, exploitation, and control of the Negro population," he told the committee, "has long been a [Communist] party goal and is one of its principal goals today." In his testimony, which was widely quoted in the news media, Hoover argued that "Communist [party] influence" existed in the civil rights movement. "It can be the means," he warned, "through which large masses are caused to lose perspective on the issues involved and, without realizing it, succumb to the party's propaganda lures."[98]

---

years, often lunch together" (*U.S. News & World Report*, May 18, 1964, p. 20).

94. *New York Times*, August 9, 1964, p. 1.

95. On November 30, 1964, the *New York Times* ran a front-page article entitled "Role of F.B.I. Distrusted by Negro in Rights Cases."

96. Quoted in *Newsweek*, December 7, 1964, p. 24.

97. William Bradford Huie, "The FBI as Missionary," *New Republic*, November 21, 1964, p. 10.

98. *U.S. News & World Report*, May 4, 1964, p. 33. Hoover's comments conflicted with the views of Attorney General Kennedy, which had been drafted earlier in

King immediately took the offensive. "It is very unfortunate," he replied, "that Mr. J. Edgar Hoover, in his claims of alleged communist infiltration in the civil rights movement, has allowed himself to aid and abet the salacious claims of southern racists and the extreme right-wing elements." He castigated the FBI in what must have appeared to the director to be a personal insult:

> It is difficult to accept the word of the FBI on communist infil-
> tration in the civil rights movement, when they have been so
> completely ineffectual in resolving the continued mayhem and
> brutality inflicted upon the Negro in the deep south. It would be
> encouraging to us if Mr. Hoover and the FBI would be as dili-
> gent in apprehending those responsible for bombing churches
> and killing little children as they are in seeking out alleged com-
> munist infiltration in the civil rights movement.[99]

Indeed, Hoover's assessment of the extent of Communist influence in the civil rights movement was a matter of contention within the FBI. In the month preceding the March on Washington in August of 1963, the FBI's most experienced domestic intelligence officers had reported to the director that there had been "an obvious failure" on the part of the Communists "to appreciably infiltrate, influence, or control large numbers of American Negroes" and that Communist influence on the civil rights movement was "infinitesimal."[100] Hoover refused to accept this assessment and forced his subordinates to capitulate[101] and to un-

---

consultation with the FBI: "Based on all available information from the F.B.I. and other sources, we have no evidence that any of the top leaders of the major civil rights groups are Communists, or Communist-controlled. It is natural and inevitable that Communists have made efforts to infiltrate the civil rights groups and to exploit the current racial situation. In view of the real injustices that exist and the resentments against them, these efforts have been remarkably unsuc- cessful" (Robert F. Kennedy to Senator A. S. Monroney, July 23, 1963, quoted in *New York Times*, April 22, 1964, p. 30).

99. Excerpted from an FBI transcription of King's statement to the press, reprinted in Church, bk. 3, p. 155.

100. F. J. Baumgardner to W. C. Sullivan, August 22, 23, 1963, quoted in Church, bk. 3, p. 480.

101. The head of the FBI's Domestic Intelligence Division wrote, "We regret deeply that the memorandum [minimizing Communist influence in the civil rights movement] did not measure up to what the Director has a right to expect from our analysis." In another internal communication, he recanted, "It is obvious that we did not put the proper interpretation upon the facts which we gave to the Director. . . . [We must] do everything humanly possible to develop all facts nationwide relative to Communist penetration and influence over Negro leaders

dertake massive intelligence investigations to uncover Communist influence on civil rights leaders, including King, and within their protest organizations.[102]

The following month, Hoover and King again traded charges. The director reiterated his statements concerning Communist influence in the civil rights movement to a UPI reporter, and King rebutted them on a nationally televised news program, "Face the Nation."[103] But the director's greatest ire and subsequent indiscretion were provoked by a report that King had said that FBI agents in Albany, Georgia, were failing to act on the complaints of Negroes because the agents were white southerners.[104] In a news conference with women reporters that was "as remarkable for its three-hour length as for its mere occurrence," Hoover threw caution to the winds and "loosed a broadside of uncharacteristic public charges" against a variety of targets.[105]

He attacked the findings of the Warren Commission, which had criticized the FBI for its failure to inform the Secret Service that Lee Harvey Oswald was in Dallas.[106] The Warren Report, he said, was "unfair" and "the most classic example of Monday-morning quarterbacking I have ever read." The FBI's civil rights investigations had been bogged down in Mississippi, he asserted, because the area was "filled with

---

and their organizations" (W. C. Sullivan to A. Belmont of August 30, 1963 and September 25, 1963, quoted in Church, bk. 3, pp. 480–81).

102. "This exchange [between Sullivan and Hoover] set in motion a disastrous series of events. The Domestic Intelligence Division recommended asking the Attorney General to approve a wiretap on Dr. Martin Luther King, intensifying field investigations to uncover 'communist influence on the Negro' using 'all possible investigative techniques,' and expanding Cointelpro operations using 'aggressive tactics' to 'neutralize or disrupt the Party's activities in the Negro field' " (Church, bk. 3, p. 481).

103. Ibid., pp. 155–56.

104. Although the FBI director objected specifically to remarks he attributed to King concerning agents in Albany, Georgia, there does not appear to be a contemporary source that substantiates Hoover's complaint. Instead, it appears likely that the FBI director recalled a statement that King had made two years earlier: "One of the great problems we face with the FBI in the South is that the agents are white Southerners who have been influenced by the mores of the community. To maintain their status, they have to be friendly with the local police and people who are promoting segregation. Every time I saw FBI men in Albany [Georgia], they were with the local police force" (*Atlanta Constitution*, November 19, 1962, p. 18, quoted in Church, bk. 3, p. 90).

105. *New York Times*, November 19, 1964, p. 1.

106. Ibid., September 28, 1964, p. 1. At that time, as was his custom regarding any criticism of the bureau, the FBI director took pains to rebut the findings of the Warren Commission. See *Newsweek*, October 5, 1964, p. 63.

water moccasins, rattlesnakes and red-necked sheriffs, and they are all in the same category as far as I am concerned."[107] But he reserved his most severe comments for Martin Luther King, whom he characterized as "the most notorious liar in the country" and, he added, "that is for the record."[108]

King, who was writing his Nobel Peace Prize acceptance speech at Bimini in the Bahamas, denied having made the comment about Hoover's agents and responded, "I cannot conceive of Mr. Hoover making a statement like this without being under extreme pressure. He has apparently faltered under the awesome burden, complexities and responsibilities of his office. Therefore, I cannot engage in a public debate with him. I have nothing but sympathy for this man who has served his country so well."[109]

Negro leaders rushed to King's defense, and liberal newspapers suggested it was time for the FBI director to retire. The day following Hoover's unwonted remarks, civil rights leaders Roy Wilkins, A. Philip Randolph, Whitney Young, Dorothy Haight, James Farmer, and Jack Greenberg met with the president at the White House and expressed their support for King. According to Wilkins, Johnson "simply listened and gave no comment and no opinion."[110] But one national news magazine gave a different report. In a cover story on the FBI director, *Newsweek* characterized Hoover as "an authentic folk hero" but noted that "suddenly J. Edgar Hoover has become a figure of controversy," who had alienated his friends. "One such disenchanted fan is Lyndon B. Johnson," the report said, "who had decided by last week that he must find a new chief of the FBI. . . . The search is on."[111]

The editors of the *New York Times* were even more direct. They questioned the wisdom of the president's earlier decision to waive mandatory retirement for the FBI director. "The adulation with which Mr. Hoover has been surrounded," the editorial said, "has made him resentful of criticism to an extent insupportable in any public official." Citing his verbal assaults on King, the justices of the Supreme Court, and the Warren Commission, the editorial advised that "under the circumstances, it would be wise to let the mandatory provisions of the

107.   *New York Times*, November 19, 1964, p. 28.

108.   *Newsweek*, November 30, 1964, p. 29.

109.   *New York Times*, November 20, 1964, p. 1.

110.   Ibid., p. 18. The meeting had been arranged before Hoover's news conference.

111.   *Newsweek*, December 7, 1964, p. 21. The White House press secretary George Reedy denied this report, but *Newsweek* countered in the next issue: "The information on which the Newsweek report was based came from a highly placed source within the White House" (*Newsweek*, December 14, 1964, pp. 22, 24).

Federal retirement law take effect on Mr. Hoover's 70th birthday."[112] The editors of the *Nation* were less charitable. In an editorial entitled "Hoover the Vulgarian," they wrote, " 'Liar' is an ugly word and notably so when used by a person of Mr. Hoover's prestige—false though it may be—and power, which is all too real."[113]

The public aspects of the controversy and feud between Hoover and King were laid to rest in a fortnight. Civil rights leaders followed King's largely conciliatory approach.[114] Roy Wilkins said on national television, for example, that the FBI director's "intemperate" language did not warrant his dismissal because he was "a good public servant," but "simply wrong" in his comments regarding King.[115] At a dinner in honor of his winning the Nobel Peace Prize, King telegraphed his intention to make peace: "I do not plan to engage in public debate with Mr. Hoover and I think the time has come for all this controversy to end, and for all of us to get on with the larger job of civil rights and law enforcement."[116]

According to public reports of the subsequent meeting, although Hoover did not apologize, he did "give King his pledge that he would take action against any FBI agent guilty of discrimination or injustice."[117] Although both men held fast to their positions during the seventy-minute session, King indicated that they had achieved "a much clearer understanding on both sides."[118] And, finally, on December 4,

112. Editorial, *New York Times*, November 20, 1964, p. 36.

113. *Nation*, November 30, 1964, p. 394. In addition, Methodist Bishop James K. Mathews called for Hoover's resignation (ibid., November 21, 1964, p. 8).

114. One writer explained King's position: "Dr. King and the Negro leaders who rallied to his defense were reluctant to be drawn into a test of strength between the civil rights organizations and Hoover's inchoate but powerful support" (William V. Shannon, "The J. Edgar Hoover Case," *Commonweal*, December 11, 1964, p. 375).

115. *New York Times*, November 23, 1964, p. 75.

116. UPI release, December 1, 1964, quoted in Church, bk. 3, p. 164. Internal FBI reports on this meeting and the observations of civil rights leader Andrew Young indicate that the meeting consisted largely of a "monologue that lasted for some fifty-five minutes. . . . [it was] essentially a briefing by Director Hoover on FBI operations relating to civil rights" (Church, bk. 3, p. 165).

117. *Newsweek*, December 14, 1964, p. 22.

118. *Time*, December 11, 1964, p. 30. In what must probably remain an enigmatic statement, FBI assistant director Cartha Deloach, who was present at the meeting, later recalled under oath: "It was more of a love feast; it was not a confrontation. It was a very amicable meeting, a pleasant meeting between two great symbols of leadership; Mr. Hoover . . . telling Dr. King that, in view of your stature and reputation and your leadership with the black community, you should do everything possible to be careful of your associates and be careful of

just three days later, the FBI arrested twenty-one suspects in connection with the Klan murder of the three civil rights workers near Philadelphia, Mississippi. To all appearances, Hoover and King had achieved a kind of choreographed peace, complete with media appearances and gestures of reconciliation.

As was so often the case in the 1960s, the liberal community and the public generally remained unaware of the FBI's extensive activities intended to discredit King and block his effectiveness as a civil rights leader. Although these efforts were intensified after 1964, they have been too well documented to merit recital here.[119] There are, however, two aspects of the bureau's campaign to discredit and neutralize Martin Luther King that are important to this study. The first concerns the precise status of the King investigation relative to liberal theory, and the second involves the contemporary reaction that it elicited from liberals.

In terms of liberal theory, the FBI efforts against Martin Luther King must be assigned a different status than the attack on the Klan, which took place at about the same time. Liberals and bureau administrators agreed that the Klan constituted a thoroughly pernicious and un-American influence. But for liberals, if not for the FBI director, King represented the forces of the just and the good. Even though both the civil rights movement and the Klan engaged in illegal activities, to the liberal mind they were differentiated on several levels. First, unlike the Klan, Martin Luther King and his followers were committed to a philosophy of nonviolence. Civil disobedience fractured the law, but it was a law of apartheid, with which liberals had never been comfortable.

---

your personal life, so that no questions will be raised concerning your character at any time. . . . I would like to repeat, it was a love feast more or less, rather than a bitter confrontation between these individuals" (Church, vol. 6, pp. 173–74).

119. In late 1963 and 1964, the bureau undertook sustained action to neutralize King as a civil rights leader: "The FBI's effort to discredit Dr. King and to undermine the SCLC involved plans touching on virtually every aspect of Dr. King's life. The FBI scrutinized Dr. King's tax returns, monitored his financial affairs, and even tried to establish that he had a secret foreign bank account. Religious leaders and institutions were contacted in an effort to undermine their support of him, and unfavorable material was 'leaked' to the press. Bureau officials contacted members of Congress, and special 'off the record' testimony was prepared for the Director's use before the House Appropriations Committee. Efforts were made to turn White House and Justice Department Officials against Dr. King by barraging them with unfavorable reports and, according to one witness, even offering to play for a White House official tape recordings that the Bureau considered embarrassing to King" (Church, bk. 3, p. 131). See "Dr. Martin Luther King, Jr., Case Study," in ibid., pp. 79–184; David J. Garrow, *The FBI and Martin Luther King, Jr.* (New York: Penguin Books, 1981).

Second, King embodied the very spirit of liberal tolerance, and he was also prepared to preach intolerance for the intolerant, as his comments on the FBI's inability to curtail Klan violence indicated. And, finally, there was, as Katzenbach insisted, an identity of political and constitutional interest between the liberal presidencies of the 1960s and the civil rights movement as a whole. In this regard, the FBI investigations of Martin Luther King, which were conducted in part to diminish his reputation and powers, were illiberal and posed a threat to the Johnson and Kennedy administrations as well.

Considering this view, the contemporary response of liberals to the FBI investigations of Martin Luther King and the SCLC may, at first glance, appear perplexing. It was, after all, the president's younger brother who first authorized wiretaps on King, his organization, and his associates. But when the FBI director attempted, in October 1963, to discredit the civil rights leader by circulating a damaging monograph entitled "Communism and the Negro Movement—A Current Analysis," Kennedy ordered that it be recalled.[120] When asked by the Congress in 1974 to produce evidence that past presidents or attorneys general "were aware of any FBI efforts to 'discredit' or 'neutralize' " King, the bureau replied that "a review of the King file in response to other items included in the request and a polling of all Headquarters personnel involved in that and previous reviews did not result in the location or recollection of any information in FBIHQ files to indicate any of the aforementioned individuals were specifically aware of any efforts, steps or plans or proposals to 'discredit' or 'neutralize' King."[121]

Responsible officials in the Kennedy and Johnson administrations did know, however, that since 1962 the bureau had conducted a Cominfil, or Communist Infiltration, investigation of the SCLC. There is also evidence that they knew of occasions on which the FBI had disseminated material that was unfavorable to King and that was not entirely or directly related to the question of Communist influence on the civil rights movement. But they tended to view these as isolated and unfortunate events, and they were, in any case, unaware of the formal pro-

---

120. Burke Marshall, who was Kennedy's assistant attorney general in charge of the Civil Rights Division, characterized the monograph: "[It was] a personal diatribe . . . a personal attack without evidentiary support on the character, the moral character and person of Dr. Martin Luther King, and it was only peripherally related to anything substantive, like whether or not there was communist infiltration or influence on the civil rights movement. . . . It was a personal attack on the man and went far afield from the charges [of possible Communist influence]" (Church, bk. 3, p. 133).

121. Ibid., p. 147.

grams and systematic efforts the FBI employed against Martin Luther King and his organization.

Once again, liberals demonstrated unqualified acceptance of pervasive official secrecy in national security matters. But, this time, the identified security menace was the preeminent leader of a great liberal cause. The attack on King gored the liberals' ox and presaged a trend that would continue beyond the 1960s until the end of FBI hegemony in internal security affairs. It consisted of a gradually widening gulf between FBI and liberal conceptions of what constituted a significant threat to the nation's internal security.

There was, to be sure, a certain degree of slippage in the liberal theory of internal security. According to the original theory, there was no place for communism in a democratic republic. The usual constitutional protections such as due process did not apply, and it was the duty of the government to create internal security programs in the FBI to meet the threat. As applied to the Klan, the theory required modification, but it proved to be sufficiently elastic to encompass the new threat. But that was an end to it. Liberal theory could not be extended to encompass the attack on Martin Luther King, nor did liberals ever contemplate any such application of their ideas or the institutions they had created.

As the nation plunged into a period of unprecedented social unrest and deep questioning of basic American values, the director became increasingly unassailable, and the FBI, increasingly necessary to the maintenance of law and order. Hoover and the FBI as an institution—its vast resources and ubiquitous agents—had become a kind of state unto itself. It was charged with upholding the law but was somehow above it. It operated as a strict hierarchical and paramilitary organization, but its director was subordinate to no one.[122] It drew authority from the laws and the Constitution but operated programs pursuant to no law, unknown to any lawmaker, and unenvisioned by the lawgivers.

122.   As Katzenbach explained, "The Director of the FBI is a subordinate of the Attorney General. In the 1960's J. Edgar Hoover was formally my subordinate; indeed, I had the formal power to fire him. Mr. Hoover was also a national hero, and had been for 30 years or more. I doubt that any Attorney General after Harlan Fiske Stone could or did fully exercise the control over the Bureau implied in that formal relationship. . . . In effect, he [Hoover] was uniquely successful in having it both ways; he was protected from public criticism by having a theoretical superior who took responsibility for his work, and was protected from his superior by his public reputation" (Church, vol. 6, p. 200).

CHAPTER FOUR

The End of the FBI-Liberal Entente

IN 1970, THE FBI was headed for a fall. It had also achieved perhaps the greatest independence of operations of any agency in the history of the American republic. It had been able to establish large-scale domestic counterintelligence programs in the absence of congressional or executive authorization and without judicial intervention. As staff to the House Appropriations Committee, its agents exercised investigative authority reaching throughout the entire executive branch.[1] By 1970, the FBI had received its budget as requested for decades running.[2] Unlike other agencies, in which an overall appropriation was divided among various programs or line items, the FBI's budget came in one lump sum, to be expended at the discretion of the director, and it was not subject to rigorous external review.[3]

Of all domestic agencies, the FBI alone was exempt from the rules and regulations of the Civil Service Commission, giving the director unparalleled authority over his agents. In 1970, the administrative forces of the FBI prepared to relocate to their new headquarters on Pennsylvania Avenue, the most expensive office building ever constructed by the government to that date.[4] And in 1970, President Nixon asked Congress for a supplemental appropriation to provide

1. Twenty-eight FBI agents worked as investigators for the House Appropriations Committee: "Three of the men, on leave of absence from the FBI are the only full-time investigators employed by the committee. They are in charge of directing all investigations for the committee into the financial affairs of government agencies and personnel. The other 25 agents do special case work for the committee" (*Congressional Quarterly Weekly*, April 23, 1971, p. 937).

2. Representative John Rooney, who chaired the subcommittee responsible for FBI appropriations, explained: "I have never cut his [Hoover's] budget and I never expect to. The only man who ever cut it was Karl Stefan. . . . When Stefan went home for election that year, they nearly beat him because he took away some of Hoover's money. When he came back he told me, 'John, don't ever cut the F.B.I. budget. The people don't want it cut.' "

3. Walter Pincus, "The Bureau's Budget: A Source of Power," in Pat Watters and Stephen Gillers, eds., *Investigating the FBI* (New York: Doubleday, 1973), pp. 64–65.

4. In late 1969, the cost of the new FBI building was estimated at $100 million. It would rise much higher (*New York Times*, November 5, 1969, p. 28).

one thousand additional FBI agents for the purpose of investigating arson and bombings on the nation's college campuses.[5]

Despite appearances, the FBI was more vulnerable than at any point since its establishment. In its zeal to protect the government from rising protest and civil unrest in the 1960s, the bureau risked direct confrontation with the liberal political community and with constitutional republicanism. This conflict arises formally because there is an outer limit at which efforts to maintain the state against public disorder lead to political degeneration of democratic and constitutional forms of government. Indeed, the nature of the internal security activity conducted at the margins of the liberal polity can alter or redefine the state in question. No state could, for example, be considered liberal if its security apparatus employed one in four persons and criticism of government policy was disabled through covert domestic intelligence operations.

The FBI was headed for a fall in part because, in the 1960s, it assumed internal security powers incompatible with the values of American liberals. Four factors delayed liberal condemnation of the FBI: habitual faith in the bureau linked to an earlier anti-Communist consensus; insularity and secrecy of agency operations; severity of social unrest; and public support for the bureau and adulation for its director. The liberal approach to internal security in the 1950s had been based largely on a belief that communism posed an immediate and violent threat to the American government and way of life. Liberals invested their trust in the FBI, not the Congress, as the instrument best suited to deal with insidious Communist conspiracy in the United States.

This habit of mind persisted largely because it was constantly reinforced by J. Edgar Hoover and his allies in the Congress and throughout the government, who testified and insisted on numerous occasions that Communists had infiltrated the civil rights and antiwar movements.[6] Nevertheless, as the anti-Communist consensus associated

---

5.   *Wall Street Journal*, September 23, 1970. Nixon's request was in addition to the approved fiscal year 1970 budget of $233 million, itself an increase of $13.2 million over the previous fiscal year. The FY 1970 budget already included funds to hire an additional 525 agents and 336 new clerks (*New York Times*, July 8, 1969, p. 24; *Congressional Quarterly Weekly*, December 26, 1969, p. 2703).

6.   For example, Hoover testified before the National Commission on the Causes and Prevention of Violence on September 18, 1968, "Communists are in the forefront of civil rights, antiwar and student demonstrations, many of which ul-

with the cold war relaxed in the early 1960s, liberals helped to shift the focus of domestic intelligence programs toward other enemies of the state, particularly the Klan in 1964. They discovered the political value of a domestic security police, even if it sometimes resisted their direction or acted sluggishly on their requests.

Second, liberal opinion against the FBI was mitigated and contained because liberals were never officially informed of the nature and extent of FBI activities against their causes. Blind faith and trust in the integrity of the agency tended to reinforce general ignorance of internal security operations. Because Congress and the executive were not privy to the specifics of FBI domestic security policies and programs, the bureau was able to avoid the usual scrutiny to which other agencies were subjected. The discipline and morale of the FBI were such that no agent came forward to make a sustained criticism of the bureau until 1970, and even then the existence of the domestic Cointelpros was not revealed.[7] The inviolate nature of the FBI files and a belief in the sanctity of the secret stamp encouraged liberals not to withdraw their support, even as evidence of improper domestic intelligence activities began to seep into the public record.

A third factor that inhibited liberal reaction against FBI domestic intelligence activity was the violent and volatile temper of the times. The civil rights demonstrations and ghetto riots of the early 1960s gave way to an era of widespread mass civil rights and antiwar protest that was sustained for the balance of the decade. Presidents and attorneys general of the middle 1960s faced mounting public demands for action against civil disturbance of all stripes. And by 1968, law-and-order candidate Richard Nixon easily defeated Hubert Humphrey, who was by then too closely associated with the unpopular war in Southeast Asia. Widespread opposition to public disorder was clearly registered in a CBS opinion poll: "Even with no clear danger of violence, 76 percent of those polled said they opposed the freedom of any group to organize protests against the Government."[8] In its efforts to protect the

---

timately become disorderly and erupt into violence" (*New York Times*, June 11, 1969, p. 32).

7. William W. Turner, *Hoover's FBI: The Men and the Myth* (Los Angeles: Sherbourne Press, 1970). In 1967, ex-FBI agent Norman T. Ollestad had published *Inside the FBI*, "a humorous and yet pathetic picture of this one-man agency" (*Saturday Review*, July 3, 1967, p. 6). Although his book skirted security issues, Ollestad was expelled from the Society of Former Special Agents because his writing was considered "detrimental to the good name or best interests of the society" (*New York Times*, August 1, 1967, p. 29).

8. *New York Times*, April 16, 1970, p. 37.

state from domestic turmoil, the FBI gained a measure of insularity and license it most certainly would not otherwise have enjoyed.

And, finally, liberal entente with the FBI was prolonged in the late 1960s because of the overwhelming popularity of the agency and its director. To the American people the FBI was the defender of freedom, the guardian of the American way, and J. Edgar Hoover was a living legend and authentic folk hero. Former Attorney General Katzenbach testified that, in his view, Congress was the only power capable of investigating the FBI and that such an investigation would not have been possible during the lifetime of its director.[9] A Gallup public opinion poll conducted in December 1965 confirms this assessment. When asked "How would you rate the following organization—Federal Bureau of Investigation?" 84 percent responded "highly favorable" and 12 percent reported "mildly favorable."[10] There appears also to have been a pervasive belief among more skeptical liberals that J. Edgar Hoover had files on everyone, and some were reluctant to oppose the bureau because they feared blackmail or exposure.[11]

In a decade, the alignment of political forces shifted dramatically. Not only liberals but opinion generally turned against the FBI and its domestic intelligence programs. Liberal senators proposed and put through Senate Resolution 21 on January 27, 1975. It established a select committee, headed by Senator Frank Church, to investigate "intelligence activities and the extent, if any, to which illegal, improper, or unethical activities were engaged in by any agency of the Federal Government."[12] It created a rupture in the security of FBI files unthinkable in the Hoover era. At various points, this book has devoted considerable attention to the question: How was J. Edgar Hoover able to retain the confidence of successive presidents and attorneys general? Part of the explanation is that Hoover built and maintained support for the FBI within the liberal community continuously after 1936, the

9.   "Mr. Hoover was a national hero, and had been for 30 years or more. . . . I do not think the practices this Committee has brought to light could have been exposed other than by Congressional investigation. It is also true, I suggest to the committee, that a Congressional investigation of the Federal Bureau of Investigation was not a political possibility during Mr. Hoover's tenure as Director, not simply because of his enormous and unique public prestige and power, but also because of the Bureau's reputation for total integrity" (Church, vol. 6, pp. 200–201).

10.   *Gallup Political Index*, Report no. 7, December 1965.

11.   *U.S. News & World Report*, "The Secret Files of J. Edgar Hoover," December 19, 1983, pp. 45–50.

12.   Church, bk. 2, p. 343.

year President Franklin Roosevelt first vested internal security powers in the bureau.

The extended process through which the FBI alienated its liberal constituency paralleled the rise of public disorder in the 1960s. As the bureau adopted more strenuous methods to counter security threats posed by increasing civil disturbance, antiwar protest, black militancy, and the organization of New Left groups, it also lost the ability to discriminate between dissent associated with liberal causes on one hand and subversive activity such as sabotage and espionage on the other. The failure to make this distinction transformed the FBI in the middle to late 1960s into an agency whose domestic security programs were incompatible with basic constitutional requirements. After 1964, FBI domestic security intelligence activity became increasingly hostile to the liberal community. It was only a matter of time before liberals and their sometime friends—like Senator Sam J. Ervin—with strict constitutionalist leanings would recognize the new internal security environment and take steps to contain it.

How, then—at what time and in what manner—did the FBI become vulnerable to political attack after three decades of increasing autonomy in policymaking and expanding insularity in its domestic intelligence operations? The answer is an empirical matter involving a number of mutually reinforcing explanations. First, the FBI could exercise hegemony over internal security policy only as long as it maintained its liberal constituency. As liberal support for the bureau eroded in the late 1960s, so too did the staying power of the agency. Second, continued FBI dominance depended on the ability to control the files, especially those that documented the actual ongoing activities of the bureau. When these files were exposed in the mass media, insularity was gravely impaired. Third, the man and the agency were the same. As J. Edgar Hoover weakened with age and succumbed to heart failure on May 2, 1972, so too did the political fortunes of his domestic security intelligence empire. Finally, Watergate revelations related to the Second Article of Impeachment, "Improper Use of Intelligence Agencies," so implicated the FBI as to make full congressional investigation and disclosure inevitable.

Each of these arguments helps to explain a portion of the rapid disintegration of FBI internal security powers in the 1970s. Throughout the middle and late 1960s, support for the FBI decreased as the liberal community acquired information that cumulatively suggested that the bureau was actively engaged in opposing and undermining various liberal causes. Just at the critical historical moment, in March of 1971, a clandestine group calling itself the Citizens Commission to Investigate the FBI stole more than one thousand documents from the resident FBI office in Media, Pennsylvania, and released them selectively to liberal politicians and newspapers, penetrating the insularity of the bureau. One year later, the FBI director, perhaps disheartened by successive demands for his resignation, passed away. And shortly thereafter, the Watergate committee—whose mandate was to probe a failed domestic intelligence operation at the Watergate offices of the Democratic National Committee—did indeed commence preliminary investigations of highly questionable intelligence activities related to the Nixon administration.

These explanations make sense when arranged, as above, in rough chronological order, but their significance and overlapping explanatory power are not so clear. It is therefore necessary to assess how much and what kinds of information liberals possessed about the activities of the FBI after 1964. The project here is to establish empirically the status of the liberal entente with the FBI through 1971, when the insularity of FBI secret domestic intelligence programs was ruptured by wide publication of information stolen from the FBI office in Media, Pennsylvania.

A comprehensive review of the periodical literature available on the FBI during the period in question suggests three distinct stages in the collapse of the FBI's liberal constituency. In the first, extending roughly from 1965 through May 1968, the FBI retained the support of the liberal community, although the relationship became increasingly strained and difficult. This stage commences at the outset of an uneasy truce between the liberals and the FBI, arranged by Martin Luther King, Jr., in the aftermath of the public feud between J. Edgar Hoover and the civil rights leader.[13] This conflict should not obscure the high level of support that the FBI enjoyed from liberals in early 1965. At that time, for example, President Johnson and Attorney General Katzenbach sponsored dramatic expansion of the FBI's Quantico training academy, which would centralize training programs for the nation's state and local police forces in the hands of the FBI director.[14]

A second stage began in the spring of 1968, when Democratic presidential candidate Senator Eugene J. McCarthy first called for Hoover's resignation, and ended in June 1969.[15] During this period, the FBI

13.   These events are discussed in detail near the end of chapter 3.

14.   Johnson and Katzenbach proposed to increase the FBI training capacity from 200 to 1,200 persons per year at an initial cost of $10 million (*New York Times*, May 27, 1965, p. 28).

15.   Ibid., April 22, 1968, p. 1.

director lost his vaunted immunity to public criticism, becoming an issue in the 1968 presidential campaign, in which the central themes included the war in Vietnam and law and order. But though the controversy centered on the competency of the agency and its director, liberals became increasingly concerned about a series of tough FBI statements aimed at a new threat to the internal security—extremism. They read largely unconfirmed reports that the FBI had apparently investigated and infiltrated groups as diverse as the Black Panther party, the Minutemen, and the National Association for the Advancement of Colored People.[16]

A final stage was initiated in June 1969, when FBI agents testified in open court that they had placed wiretaps on the telephones of Elijah Muhammad and Martin Luther King, Jr.[17] In this third stage, which ended with reports of a burglary of the FBI offices in Media, Pennsylvania, the liberal community focused on the threat to liberty posed by intelligence activities generally and on the authoritarian response to widespread dissent and public disorder advanced by the Nixon administration. But even here, the nature and extent of FBI domestic security operations was almost never questioned.

Stage I: Uneasy Alliance

From the outset of the FBI's difficulties, first with the civil rights movement and then within larger liberal circles, there was a tendency for liberal journalists to repeat the sins of the bureau, prolonging and cumulating whatever effect they exerted on the public. On the occasion of Hoover's seventieth birthday, for example, the *New York Times* ran what would become a perennial story, stating that the director planned to stay on despite his advanced years. It made reference to the dispute with King, already a month old, and reiterated, "Mr. Hoover called Dr. King 'the most notorious liar' in the country. The controversy died down at a peace meeting between Dr. King and Mr. Hoover in Washington."[18] But the controversy did not fade out completely because the press would not let it.

Six months later, in an Op-Ed piece entitled "Washington, The Junior G-Man Grows Senior," Tom Wicker, a persistent critic of the FBI, again raised the King issue and cited a variety of recent and not-too-

16.   *The Wall Street Journal*, October 15, 1968, p. 1.

17.   *Newsweek*, June 16, 1969, pp. 29–30; *New York Times*, June 21, 1969, p. 11.

18.   *New York Times*, January 1, 1965, p. 10.

recent indiscretions on the part of the FBI director.[19] "Over the years," he wrote, "the F.B.I. has become virtually an autonomous agency, only tenuously under the control of the Justice Department." But the account was balanced: "Mr. Hoover . . . has built a genuine record of effectiveness, and has provided very little evidence for those who fear the emergence of a secret police." He argued that the source of Hoover's power was not the files nor was it law enforcement. What made the FBI "sacred" was its director's genius for public relations, recent indiscretions to the contrary.[20]

If, the press launched an occasional salvo at the FBI in this period, the director controlled a far more powerful and pervasive media. Early in 1965, Hoover authorized Warner Brothers to produce "The FBI Story," a television series to be broadcast nationally by CBS in the fall. It would be based on the closed cases of the agency. Authorization was required because Public Law 670 prohibited use of the FBI name and seal without express permission from the agency. It also gave the FBI director, who could withdraw his consent at any time, complete control over the contents of the program. A spokesman for the bureau projected that the series would be a "means of educating the public as to the jurisdiction of the F.B.I."[21] He hoped it would increase public respect for and cooperation with the bureau, which were critical if the agency was to function effectively with only six thousand special agents in the field.[22] Although the *Times* suggested several negative implications and ran a front-page follow-up story on FBI security checks on actors in the series,[23] the director's vision of the agency prevailed, bombarding millions of living rooms across the nation every week via the impeccable credentials and demeanor of actor Efrem Zimbalist, Jr.[24]

19.   Wicker was one of two journalists who criticized the FBI continuously throughout the 1960s. The other was Alan Barth. Most of the rest of the lions of the Washington press corps maintained a noteworthy silence on this subject.

20.   *New York Times*. July 25, 1965, sec. 4, p. 10.

21.   The jurisdiction of the FBI was and had been an issue of hot contention over the preceding several years. Time and again Hoover claimed insufficient jurisdiction when he wanted to resist the orders of then attorney general Robert F. Kennedy to investigate civil and voting rights violations in the early 1960s. See Navasky, *Kennedy Justice*, pp. 131–34.

22.   *New York Times*, February 14, 1965, sec. 2, p. 13.

23.   Ibid., June 2, 1965, p. 1.

24.   As Zimbalist recalled, "Every script was approved by them [officials at the FBI]. . . . Writers would work with an FBI agent to produce a story that was close enough to something that had actually happened. When the agent was un-

During this period the mainstream liberal press and its somewhat more spirited cousins, the *Nation* and the *New Republic*, picked up and followed two stories that, for different reasons, rankled their liberal readerships. One involved an FBI fingerprint clerk, Thomas H. Carter, who sued J. Edgar Hoover when he was dismissed for "conduct unbecoming an employe of this bureau." The other, which reached into the highest political circles, concerned the far broader subject of wiretaps and other electronic surveillance devices used in FBI criminal investigations related to organized crime. The stories appeared in the liberal press in December 1965 and January 1966 but soon made their way into the pages of the mass circulation news weeklies and even the *Wall Street Journal*. Both stories continued to draw media attention for many months and provided a stream of negative publicity for the FBI.

The Carter incident first came to public attention in January 1966, when it was discussed in connection with a Senate investigation into invasion of employee privacy by government agencies.[25] The facts of the case were simple. Some anonymous person reported to the FBI that Carter had entertained a woman overnight in his room. His employer had confronted him with the accusation, ordered him to provide written details of what had transpired, and fired him without notice and with no possibility for appeal. But the repercussions were more complex. For the first time, the FBI's exemption from Civil Service regulations was questioned. More important, the public gained a rare glimpse into the personnel practices and employee surveillance system of the bureau.

---

able to restrain the writer and he came up with something that was totally unprecedented, then the FBI would refuse the script. Deke DeLoach was in charge of it for a long time, but it was Tolson who put the violence ban on us. . . . It was just when all the violence stuff was hitting the fan, and the story committee and all those people started to scream and point a couple of fingers at the FBI for having a show that, according to them, promoted violence. Tolson put out the order that there would be no more deaths—immortality. We didn't kill anybody, I think, the last two or three years" (Ovid Demaris, *The Director: An Oral Biography* [New York: Harper's Magazine Press, 1975], pp. 70–71).

25. The investigation was conducted by Senator Sam J. Ervin's Subcommittee on Constitutional Rights. The committee's printed proceedings noted: "An F.B.I. employe was queried extensively about his personal life, and then required to write a detailed statement of the hours spent [with a woman in his bedroom]. A week later, the employe was given a letter summarily discharging him as of the close of the working day, and was told he had no way of appealing the decision. Three other F.B.I. employes who shared an appartment with him reportedly were harassed by the agency for their continued association with him and finally resigned" (quoted in *New York Times*, April 21, 1966, p. 1).

The *New York Times* reported that the FBI was having difficulty keeping its employes in part because of a "puritanical surveillance" of their private lives. "Employes," it said, "are questioned in detail about their relations with members of the opposite sex, and they are required to report any indiscretions they discover about their fellow workers."[26] In the previous year, the FBI had lost 34.4 percent of its Washington staff, as compared with an overall government average loss for the capital area of 19.7 percent. Employees of the FBI were encouraged to live with other bureau staff in approved apartment buildings. They were admonished by a secret FBI employee handbook to report immediately "any occurrences or situations in which you or another employee are involved that might result in embarrassment to the bureau . . . [including] traffic and parking violations."[27]

Newsweek and *Time* poked fun at the FBI with columns headed "FBI: Bedtime Story" and "Sex & the Single FBI Man," respectively. The *Time* story, however, added some troublesome details. Carter had been "ordered to write a statement explaining why he had slept in the same room with a woman. . . . which had failed to satisfy his superiors." And in the end, all three of his roommates "were pressed to resign because none had reported Carter's original indiscretion."[28] But it was an editorial in the *Nation*, entitled "In Loco Parentis," that best explained why the Carter incident touched a raw liberal nerve. The editors suggested that "the colleges are going one way, J. Edgar Hoover's FBI the other." Tongue in cheek, they cited "a contrast between the high moral standards of the FBI and the permissiveness of the universities." Assistant Dean Ruth Darling at Cornell University reportedly stated, "We don't ask what they [the students] do and don't want to know." At Yale, Dean George S. May said, "We are not interested in the private lives of students as long as they remain private."[29]

The Carter incident tended to offend liberal sensibilities on at least three counts. First, it demonstrated that the bureau was rigidly out of step with prevailing social mores in the middle 1960s. If those bastions of conservatism known collectively as the Ivy League could abandon parietal rules, it was a sure sign that the society as a whole had moved

26.   Ibid., April 26, 1966, p. 50. The *Times* also quoted a bureau spokesman: "We have hundreds of young men and women coming to work for the F.B.I. in Washington. We must be sure their parents can be confident that they and their colleagues are living under exemplary standards" (ibid., p. 50).

27.   Ibid.

28.   *Time*, May 6, 1966, p. 23; *Newsweek*, May 2, 1966, p. 21.

29.   *Nation*, May 9, 1966, p. 542.

beyond institutional paternalism. But not the FBI. Second, liberals found themselves at odds with the bureau over the issue of personal privacy. The idea that one's colleagues and neighbors might snoop, at the direction of the police, on matters of private morality was repugnant to the liberal cast of mind. But not to the FBI. And, lastly, the FBI's code of conduct appeared to subordinate the civil liberties of individual employees to the larger institution, in this case, the state. Liberals sought to maximize personal freedom. The FBI, they felt certain, hoped to control its employees, to make them tools of the state, and to reduce their rights in the interests of the organization.

Perhaps the greatest controversy during this first stage in the disintegration of relations between the FBI and the liberal community centered on the issue of wiretapping and electronic eavesdropping in investigations of organized crime.[30] It was kicked off in December 1965, when Senator Edward V. Long indicated that his Subcommittee on Administrative Practice and Procedure might make a sustained inquiry into FBI wiretapping. Long had been reluctant to act on evidence that FBI agents had tapped the telephone lines of gambling casinos in Las Vegas that had surfaced earlier in his five-month-old investigation into government invasions of privacy. But when a lawsuit was filed against the FBI agents by a Las Vegas casino owner, Long was apparently moved to proceed. He told the *New York Times*, "We've had our men looking into F.B.I. wiretapping of gambling establishments out there. We have all the information we need for full hearings."[31]

If the senator's statement proved to be an empty threat, the litigation was not. Legal action continued to generate interest among liberals

30. In June 1965, President Johnson, acting on the advice of Attorney General Katzenbach, issued a confidential Executive Order effectively limiting wiretapping of telephone conversations to cases involving national security (Church, bk. 3, pp. 286–88). Its principal significance in the controversy that followed appears to have been that it enabled President Johnson to remain largely on the sidelines (*New York Times*, December 13, 1966, p. 39). The debate soon moved beyond the narrow confines of wiretapping to encompass the larger issue of electronic eavesdropping or surveillance generally.

31. *New York Times*, December 17, 1965, p. 17. Senator Long never acted on his threat. He was apparently persuaded not to hold hearings on the bureau by FBI Assistant Director Cartha Deloach. Deloach evaluated the situation several weeks later: "While we have neutralized the threat of being embarrassed by the Long Subcommittee, we have not yet eliminated certain dangers which might be created as a result of newspaper pressure on Long. We therefore must keep on top of this situation at all times" (C. D. Deloach to Tolson, January 21, 1966, quoted in Church, bk. 3, p. 310). The information on wiretapping was, of course, unavailable to the press and the liberal community generally until 1976.

and in the liberal press. One sydicated column, which appeared in the *Los Angeles Times*, the *Washington Post*, and elsewhere, suggested that the FBI had "illegally used electronic spying devices" on several occasions. "It was done in Las Vegas, it almost certainly happened in Kansas City, Mo., and it may have occurred elsewhere, including Los Angeles and Miami." According to the story, although the FBI was unwilling to supply any information, Justice Department officials had expressed concern that evidence tainted by FBI wiretaps might jeopardize important prosecutions then pending against organized crime figures.[32]

But such speculation was soon supplanted by hard fact when the solicitor general's office took action. The case involved the prosecution of Fred B. Black, Jr., who was charged with income tax evasion. Black had appealed, and the Supreme Court had refused to review his conviction on May 4. But in a remarkable turn of events, Solicitor General Thurgood Marshall advised the Court that "conversations between petitioner [Black] and other persons at about the time of petitioner's indictment had been overheard by government agents using a listening device installed in petitioner's hotel suite." During the prosecution, Justice Department attorneys involved in the case had been unaware that some of the evidence had been obtained through electronic surveillance. On May 21, Marshall told the Court:

> Under Departmental practice in effect for a period of years prior to 1963, and continuing into 1965, the Director of the Federal Bureau of Investigation was given authority to approve the installation of devices such as that in question for intelligence (and not evidentiary) purposes when required in the interest of internal security or national safety, including organized crime, kidnappings and matters wherein human life might be at stake. Acting on the basis of the aforementioned Departmental authorization, the Director approved the installation of the device involved in the instant case.[33]

The *Nation*'s assessment was blunt but not inaccurate: "Under Hoover's administration the FBI has assumed practically unlimited investigative powers. It can investigate almost anyone it wants to investigate, by almost any methods it sees fit."[34] Suddenly, the Las Vegas incident took on new significance, not only in liberal circles but for the

32. *Washington Post*, December 20, 1965, p. A6.
33. Quoted in *New Republic*, July 30, 1966.
34. *Nation*, July 11, 1966, p. 37.

readers of the nation's print news media. From the pages of *Time* and *Newsweek*, readers learned that the Henderson Novelty Company, an FBI front organization, had ordered twenty-five telephone lines from the local telephone company in 1961. Agents had "surreptitiously installed listening devices in the offices and homes of many of the town's top gambling-casino brass—and shipped recorded transcripts to FBI headquarters in Washington." The activity of these agents was presented as shady at best and possibly illegal. Nevada governor Grant Sawyer reportedly threatened to prosecute them. And Las Vegas district attorney Edward Marshall was quoted as saying, "I have no choice. They [FBI agent Dean Elson and his subordinates] must have known that eavesdropping is illegal in Nevada. We have to assume they took a calculated risk."[35]

One of the casino owners, Edward Levinson, who brought a $2 million damage suit against the FBI, was associated both with Black and with Bobby Baker. And Baker, a former Senate majority secretary and a close associate of President Johnson's, was then under indictment for conspiracy, tax evasion, and theft. All three men had conducted business meetings in Las Vegas that were monitored by electronic surveillance devices of questionable legal status.[36] All three cases were affected by the solicitor general's memorandum to the Court. *Newsweek* questioned "the scope of FBI bugging." It referred to the memo as "the first official admission that the FBI's long-rumored penchant for electronic snooping did indeed include the invasion of privacy outside the narrow area of national security."[37]

Throughout 1966, the wiretapping controversy continued to escalate, touching higher and higher political circles. The *New Republic* ran an in-depth article by Alan Barth that laid the blame squarely on J. Edgar Hoover.[38] It summarized recent wiretapping revelations and reviewed controlling legislation and case law such as the Federal Communications Act, the *Nardane* case in 1937, and the *Silverman* case in

---

35. *Newsweek*, July 18, 1966, p. 25.

36. In reference to the investigation of Fred Black, Alan Barth argued: "This is precisely the kind of penetration of private premises which the Supreme Court unanimously held to be an unlawful trespass and a breach of the Fourth Amendment in the *Silverman* case in 1959. Evidence obtained in this way is inadmissible in any American court" (*New Republic*, July 30, 1966, p. 19).

37. *Newsweek*, July 25, 1966.

38. Barth, like Tom Wicker, was a rare yet tenacious and responsible critic of the FBI. He had been an editorial writer for the *Washington Post* since 1943, and had published two books, *The Loyalty of Free Men* and *Government by Investigation*.

1959.[39] But most important, Barth—perhaps for the first time—trespassed on the hallowed ground of national security.[40] The article attacked Hoover's congressional testimony, which, year after year, claimed that wiretaps were strictly regulated and used only in exceptional cases involving the security of the United States. It argued that former attorney general Robert Kennedy had not authorized wiretaps in the Las Vegas cases and had said as much publicly on ABC's "Issues and Answers." "Now it is perfectly plain," Barth wrote, "that the eavesdropping in Las Vegas . . . did not involve internal security, kidnapping or extortion. And according to Senator Kennedy, it did not have authorization from him. . . . How, then, can the facts be squared with Mr. Hoover's strong disclaimer?"[41]

In the weeks that followed, concern over the question of electronic eavesdropping continued to expand, with the emphasis on the issue of tainted evidence in criminal prosecutions. In November, the Department of Justice informed the Supreme Court that it had "electronically monitored" conversations of crime figure Joseph F. Schipani, using a microphone that had been "installed by means of trespass." As a result, the Court set aside his conviction.[42] Acting Attorney General Ramsey Clark immediately ordered an extensive review of pending federal criminal cases. On November 3, he directed all United States attorneys to discontinue "any investigation or case which includes evidence illegally obtained . . . until such evidence and all of its fruits have been purged and we are in a position to assure ourselves and the court that there is no taint of unfairness."[43]

The FBI director was never one to take criticism lying down. In a letter to Representative H. R. Gross, Hoover wrote: "All wiretaps utilized by the F.B.I. have always been approved in writing, in advance by

39.   *Nardone v. United States*, 302 U.S. 338 (1939); *Silverman* (1959).

40.   The high deference that the claim of national security commanded was indicated when Attorney General Katzenbach testified during Senator Long's hearings on invasion of privacy by government agencies. At one point the attorney general was asked about national security wiretaps. Senator Long interrupted and said, "The committee, I am sure, wants in no way to interfere with your handling of security cases or to jeopardize anything where that would be involved in the course of the inquiry." Katzenbach responded, "I am sure of that" (U.S. Senate, Committee on the Judiciary, Subcommittee on Administrative Practice and Procedure, Hearings, *Invasions of Privacy (Government Agencies)*, S. Res. 39, pt. 3, 89th Cong., 1st sess., 1965, p. 1163).

41.   Alan Barth, "Lawless Lawmen," *New Republic*, July 30, 1966, p. 22.

42.   Quoted in *Wall Street Journal*, December 22, 1966, p. 10.

43.   Quoted in *New Republic*, December 24, 1966, p. 20.

the Attorney General." He charged that "Mr. Kennedy, during his term of office, exhibited great interest in pursuing such matters, and ... not only listened to the results of microphone surveillances but raised questions relative to obtaining better equipment." In addition, Hoover released documents, one signed by Kennedy, that addressed the subject of wiretapping, which Hoover argued proved that Kennedy had authorized FBI bugging operations against organized crime. In turn, Senator Kennedy produced a letter from former FBI Assistant Director Courtney Evans that exonerated the former attorney general. Evans had been present on all occasions when Robert Kennedy met with any representative of the FBI. According to Evans, Kennedy was unaware of FBI electronic surveillance in Las Vegas and elsewhere.[44]

On the following day, the director and the senator again traded charges. Hoover said it was "absolutely inconceivable" that Kennedy did not know about the eavesdropping. Kennedy responded that he first learned about it from press reports in connection with the Las Vegas investigation. He said, "I promptly ordered it ceased. It is curious that Mr. Hoover does not recall this."[45] A *New York Times* editorial entitled "Eavesdropping Unlimited" acknowledged confusion over the Kennedy-Hoover feud but noted "the apparent impossibility of putting effective restraints on invasions of privacy by electronic snoopers." It suggested that a court order ought to be required for any such activity.[46]

The conflict quickly expanded beyond the Las Vegas incident and the initial combatants. Senator Joseph F. Clark characterized the FBI as one of "three major threats to the successful survival of American democracy."[47] In a *New York Times* Op-Ed piece, James Reston paraphrased a remark by Representative Emanuel Celler, chairman of the House Jucidiary Committee: "Official wiretapping was so widespread that nobody in Washington could be sure his telephones were private." Reston questioned the accuracy of the national security claim. He wrote, "The definition of 'national security' is so vague that the F.B.I.

44.   *New York Times*, December 11, 1966, p. 1.

45.   Ibid., December 12, 1966, p. 33.

46.   Ibid., December 13, 1966, p. 46.

47.   Speaking on a radio talk show, "Reporters' Roundup," Clark also refered to "recent disclosures in the newspapers of the F.B.I. and the threat they pose to the privacy of the individual citizen and the further threat they pose by way of blackmail, direct or indirect, on anybody who has the effrontery to say anything unkind about Mr. J. Edgar Hoover" (quoted in ibid., December 19, 1966, p. 22).

has been able to interpret the term about as it liked." He also took the occasion to refer to unsubstantiated reports that the FBI had tapped the telephone of Martin Luther King, Jr., and that "information gathered in this manner was discussed with newspaper reporters by high officials of this Government."[48]

Diverse publications commented on the Kennedy-Hoover confrontation. The *Wall Street Journal* focused on the legal and moral complexities of the bugging issue: "Certainly some people—principally liberals in and out of Congress intensely concerned with individual rights—believe it's all wrong. But neither Congress nor the Supreme Court have taken that absolutist view."[49] After careful review of the controversy, one commentator questioned the significance of what he called the wiretap war: "Like all campaigns of psychological warfare, it risks one's own security as much as that of the enemy. Its infectious quality poisons the atmosphere in which leadership must continue to function."[50] Finally, the editors of the *Nation* came out swinging: "Everyone who knows Washington at all knows that Hoover has been his own boss, only nominally under the jurisdiction of the incumbent Attorney General." They quoted Justice Oliver Wendell Holmes, characterizing the whole episode as "a dirty business."[51]

By the spring of 1967, the wiretapping issue appeared to have run its course, perhaps because the Supreme Court took definitive action in the *Katz* case in reversing its holding in *Olmstead*, setting strict standards not only for wiretapping but also for electronic eavesdropping.[52] But this controversy was important to the liberal community in several respects. For the first time, a member of the liberal political elite had come to blows with the director of the FBI. Although the truth of the accusations could not definitely be established, the sordid episode reflected negatively on the FBI. To liberals, the evidence that Kennedy had authorized the bugging was circumstantial at best. But there was no doubt about the FBI; it had installed the surveillance devices, recorded the conversations, and provided the information to Justice De-

48.   Ibid., December 14, 1966, p. 46.

49.   *Wall Street Journal*, December 22, 1966, p. 10.

50.   Robert M. Cipes, "The Wiretap War," *New Republic*, December 24, 1966, p. 22.

51.   *Nation*, December 26, 1966, pp. 690–91.

52.   *Olmstead* v. *United States*, 277 U.S. 438 (1928), and *Katz* v. *United States*, 389 U.S. 347 (1967). *Olmstead* provided few restrictions on government eavesdropping, and although *Katz* required warrants in criminal cases, it specifically exempted national security cases.

partment attorneys. Liberals were not happy that Robert Kennedy had been implicated in what they regarded as improper and unsavory government conduct, but they could easily overlook the minor transgressions of the head of the nation's greatest liberal political family.

Additionally, the FBI appeared to act contrary to the law in an area not exempted by the dictates of national security. But liberals did not focus on this issue. They concentrated instead on the Fourth Amendment rights of criminals. Thurgood Marshall and Ramsey Clark did not attempt to limit invasion of privacy by the FBI. They acted, rather, to exorcise evidence from criminal prosecutions obtained by illegal electronic surveillance. It was a rear-guard action, aimed at eliminating only the consequences and not the source of questionable investigative techniques. The result was that the liberal community did not challenge the authority of the FBI to conduct electronic eavesdropping. The distinction between criminal and intelligence investigations shielded the FBI from liberal scrutiny. The former would be held to strict standards of due process, after the fact. With the latter, the tenuous right to privacy would be balanced against the superior claims of national security.

During this period, a steady trickle of negative publicity continued to irritate the FBI. There was an isolated report that FBI agents had made inquiries about radicals and antiwar protest at several college campuses.[53] Former FBI agent Norman Ollestad published *Inside the FBI*, which portrayed the bureau and its director in decidedly unflattering terms.[54] A federal judge indicated that former FBI clerk Thomas H. Carter might prevail in his lawsuit against J. Edgar Hoover.[55] The International Association of Chiefs of Police opposed expansion of the FBI training facilities at Quantico, arguing that centralizing "police training in the hands of the Director of the FBI could be the first step toward a national police."[56] And, finally, the American Trial Lawyers Association protested the use of FBI agents as claims adjusters in lawsuits against federal agencies, charging that their prestige gave the government an unfair advantage.[57]

If liberals gave the FBI guarded or reluctant support, they were still unwilling to question its authority in internal security matters. Indeed,

53.   James Ridgeway, "Patriots on Campus," *New Republic*, March 25, 1967, p. 12.

54.   *Saturday Review*, July 8, 1967, p. 6.

55.   *New York Times*, September 21, 1967, p. 27.

56.   Ibid., November 14, 1967, p. 34.

57.   Ibid., May 3, 1967, p. 37.

many retained an uncritical confidence in the FBI as an impartial and patriotic internal security institution, a view that had characterized the liberal position since World War II. This attitude was perhaps best reflected in a piece published in the *Atlantic*. Its author, Douglas Kiker, meandered back and forth on the subject of the FBI, presenting both praise and mild criticism. The problem with the bureau, he suggested, was only that J. Edgar Hoover had grown old. He reaffirmed traditional liberal faith in the bureau as the agency of internal security: "Despite all the criticism it has received in recent years, despite all the controversy, there really is little that is wrong with the Federal Bureau of Investigation."[58]

Stage II: Increasing Alienation

Beginning in the spring of 1968, however, a second phase in the disintegration of liberal entente with the FBI was initiated when presidential candidate Eugene McCarthy called for Hoover's dismissal.[59] In a televised interview on ABC's "Issues and Answers," McCarthy said that Hoover had been head of the FBI for so long that he had come to view it "as a kind of fief."[60] One month later, the Republican front-runner, Richard Nixon, took the opposite position. At a telethon question session during the Oregon primary, Nixon said that if he was elected, he would reappoint the FBI director. He added, "He's the kind of man I want to head the F.B.I., if I should have the opportunity to make that decision."[61]

The following day, McCarthy, who had advocated the resignation of J. Edgar Hoover on several occasions, broadened his attack. In a discussion of the issue of wiretapping, he recommended "a new look at the internal operations of the F.B.I. . . . [and its place] in the whole structure of the American Government." When asked by workers at a chain saw plant in Portland, Oregon, why he would replace Hoover, he replied, "Everybody knows that in a formal sense the F.B.I. is sub-

---

58. *Atlantic*, April 1967, p. 11.

59. The old issues did not go away. The *New York Times*, for example, continued to report on the Carter incident and, as late as October 1968, the *Atlantic* reviewed the entire Carter episode, saying that Hoover "is well on his way to qualifying as a leading authority on sexual behavior" (*New York Times*, July 27, 1968, p. 12; *Atlantic*, October 1968, p. 32).

60. *New York Times*, April 22, 1968, p. 18.

61. Ibid., May 27, 1968, p. 26.

ject to the Attorney General but [when] you allow someone to be built up like J. Edgar Hoover—it's as though he's not to be challenged."[62]

Hoover's allergy to criticism, by now legendary, flared up apparently in response to a statement by McCarthy that the bureau operated without adequate controls. In the preface to the FBI's widely circulated *Law Enforcement Bulletin*, the FBI director said that the candidate's statement "is not true, and it denotes either a contrived effort to mislead the public or a woeful lack of knowledge of our governmental system of checks and balances." Although Hoover did not name McCarthy, the report in the *New York Times* did in its headline, "Hoover Says McCarthy Tries to Mislead Public About F.B.I." The FBI director also issued a warning to the public: "All Americans should view with serious concern the announced intentions and threats by a political candidate, if elected, to take over and revamp the F.B.I. to suit his own personal whims and wishes."[63]

If some Democratic candidates hoped to fire J. Edgar Hoover, the Republicans embraced him. The *Wall Street Journal* reported that "the GOP is laying specific plans to enlist the FBI chief's image in its cause" during the final weeks of what would be a law-and-order campaign. Nixon had also attacked Attorney General Ramsey Clark in his acceptance speech at the Republican convention. One Nixon campaign strategist reportedly said, "There's a lot of Hoover's approach to law enforcement that happens to be the approach of the Republican Party. . . . We'll quote him. We'll say he has been saying it for years. We'll say the present Administration has been ignoring him for years and we won't ignore him."[64]

To many liberals, McCarthy's words put a fine point on their own

62. He added, "And if the Attorney General says that 'the head of the F.B.I. asked for it [wiretapping] and therefore I did it,' you have a complete inversion really of how the line of authority and responsibility should run" (*New York Times*, May 28, 1968, p. 9).

63. Hoover also wrote: "If there are those who disagree with the F.B.I. policy of vigorous enforcement of the law, protection of law-abiding citizens, preservation of the rights of all people, proper punishment for guilty law breakers, and the protection of our country from subversive elements and illegal forces, then let them admit this rather than make erroneous allegations which cannot be supported by facts" (ibid., June 29, 1968, p. 14).

64. The article, "Hoover Loses Immunity to Criticism Despite Law and Order Mood," also said that the FBI director was losing influence "in the inner circles of government and in his own law enforcement profession." It suggested that Hoover's decline was due in part to his failure to establish cordial relations with liberal Attorneys General Kennedy, Katzenbach, and Clark (*Wall Street Journal*, October 10, 1968, p. 1).

thoughts. To those in government, Hoover's attack on McCarthy represented an unwarranted and inexcusable incursion by a career bureaucrat into the politics of a presidential campaign. They knew that no other bureau chief could have done so with impunity. In liberal thinking, both the Nixon-Hoover alliance and the law-and-order campaign rhetoric were unfortunate responses to public disorder in the late 1960s. Mainstream liberals were more interested in government programs to eradicate social injustice toward blacks. Many backed the goals of the movement to end the war in Vietnam. Their support for the FBI weakened as it became evident that the bureau had redirected its official pronouncements, and possibly its resources, away from the Communist menace toward the arena of American dissent.

One public indication of a new security emphasis within the FBI was the increased use of the terms *extremism*, *New Left* and *black nationalist* to designate a wide variety of threats to the national security. The word *extremist* had entered the FBI security lexicon sometime in the late 1950s, when it was generally applied to such right-wing groups as the American Nazi party and the Ku Klux Klan.[65] But in April 1968, J. Edgar Hoover used it to describe unnamed sources that had criticized the FBI for failing to police local riots in the wake of the assassination of Martin Luther King, Jr. Hoover noted that "extremists" in "some highly vocal groups" had criticized the FBI and that there would be additional "unwarranted criticisms" in the future if more riots occurred.[66]

In his annual presentation to the House Appropriations Committee, Hoover also characterized New Left and black nationalist groups as "a distinct threat to the internal security of the nation." Seeking a budget increase of $11 million, he told the Congress that New Left groups constituted "a new type of subversive, and their danger is great." In addition, he named the Student Nonviolent Coordinating Committee (SNCC), the Black Muslims, and the Revolutionary Action Movement as militant black nationalist groups and expressed concern about reports that such organizations were building arsenals "for use against the white man."[67]

He argued that the Communist party sought to unite the forces of

---

65. At that time the term *subversive* was used to designate left-wing or communist-oriented groups.

66. Hoover's monthly message in the May issue of the FBI's *Law Enforcement Bulletin* was quoted in the *New York Times*, May 1, 1968, p. 26.

67. Hoover's testimony of February 2 was released on May 18 and quoted in the *New York Times*, May 19, 1968, p. 1.

civil rights and antiwar protest "to create one massive movement which they hope will ultimately change our government's policies, both foreign and domestic." And he explained to the funding subcommittee that the New Left had been infiltrated by Communists. "At the center of the [New Left] movement," he added, "is an almost passionate desire to destroy, to annihilate, to tear down. If anything definite can be said about the Students for a Democratic Society, it is that it can be called anarchistic."[68]

The liberal community soon learned that Hoover's warnings were apparently backed up by FBI countermeasures. In a remarkable lead article, the *Wall Street Journal* stated that the FBI had already become a national police force, conducting investigations relating to more than 170 laws and executive orders. But it went considerably farther: "Even now, the FBI is elite and secretive. If it isn't being used for suppression, it clearly is investigating dissent and potential insurrection. Its informers are infiltrating militant white groups, such as the Minutemen, militant black outfits, such as the Black Panthers, and even not-so-militant groups like the National Association for the Advancement of Colored People."[69]

Concern about the potential for political repression was heightened in June 1969, when the FBI raided the Black Panther party headquarters in Chicago without a search warrant.[70] In a predawn action, FBI agents entered the Panther offices and arrested eight persons, confiscating office equipment, some weapons, and papers including membership lists and petitions signed by nine thousand persons. The *Nation* carried the story, presenting it as a wider pattern of police action intended to "get the Panthers."[71]

The view of J. Edgar Hoover and his subordinates in these months was, however, quite different. They believed that the nation was experiencing "the progressive revolutionary steps of anarchy—coercion, intimidation, violence and unlawful takeover."[72] The FBI director la-

68.   Ibid.

69.   Louis M. Kohlmeier, "Focus on the FBI: Some Observers See Hoover Agency Turning into 'National Police,' " *Wall Street Journal*, October 15, 1968, p. 1.

70.   The agents did have an arrest warrant for George Sams, Jr., a Black Panther member wanted for murder in New Haven. Sams was not found on the premises. See L. F. Palmer, Jr., "Out to Get the Panthers," *Nation*, July 28, 1969, p. 79.

71.   Ibid., pp. 78–79.

72.   Hoover continued, "We are living in a day when defiance of authority is becoming the norm. We must establish a united resistance against the criminal forces

mented "an alarming increase in crime in all areas of the country, coupled with the mounting acts of violence by the new left and other extremists." He added, "But I have the utmost confidence that the cause of law and order will prevail."[73] These and similar reports evoked a strong response from within the liberal community. The editors of the *New York Times* wrote, "Under most Attorneys General, Mr. Hoover has been a law unto himself or very nearly so. A bureaucratic autocracy unchecked by Congress and unsupervised by the Executive has no place in a self-governing society."[74]

The views of the liberal editors resonated with the findings of the National Commission on the Causes and Prevention of Violence. In June 1969, the commission's Task Force on Demonstrations, Protests and Group Violence said that the nation's police had become "a self-conscious, independent political power," which often "rivals even duly elected officials in influence." According to the *New York Times* story, the commission blamed Hoover for promoting "the view among the police ranks that any kind of mass protest is due to a conspiracy promulgated by agitators, often Communists, 'who misdirect otherwise contented people.' " As a result, the commission's report said, "Police view students, the antiwar protesters and blacks as a danger to our political system, and racial prejudice pervades the police attitudes and actions."[75]

Stage III: "The Threat to Liberty"

A third stage in the gradual collapse of relations between the FBI and the liberal community was initiated abruptly in June 1969, when FBI agents acknowledged in open court that they had tapped the telephones of Elijah Muhammad and Martin Luther King, Jr.[76] This admission revived two contentious issues for the liberals. First, it con-

---

destroying the structure of our society . . . [or] we face chaos." These remarks were published in the May edition of the FBI's *Law Enforcement Bulletin* and quoted in the *New York Times*, April 1, 1969, p. 40.

73. *New York Times*, May 9, 1969, p. 93.

74. Ibid., May 4, 1969, sec. 4, p. 14. The *Times* had been building a case against Hoover for many months. When President Nixon announced in December 1968 that he would reappoint the FBI director, the *Times* had printed a negative editorial and two generally adverse Op-Ed pieces on Hoover and the FBI. See ibid., editorial, December 17, 1968, p. 46; Tom Wicker, "In the Nation: J. Edgar Forever," ibid., December 19, 1968, p. 46; ibid., December 22, 1968, sec. 4, p. 9.

75. Ibid., June 11, 1969, p. 1.

76. *Newsweek*, June 16, 1969, pp. 29–30.

firmed their suspicion that J. Edgar Hoover had not buried the hatchet back in 1964, when he and the late Martin Luther King, Jr., proclaimed an end to their feud. Instead, the FBI director had apparently pursued King, violated his privacy, and harassed him to the end.[77] Second, the old issue of wiretapping was resurrected with a passion. If liberals were uneasy about the recording of private conversations among suspected criminals, they were outraged by FBI efforts to undermine and snoop on the greatest civil rights leader, now martyred, to arise in American history.

As the details of the King wiretapping and electronic eavesdropping emerged, they helped to polarize the liberal political community on one side and the FBI and the Nixon administration on the other. Liberals were dismayed when they learned that the FBI had distributed summaries of the King wiretaps to a House Appropriations subcommittee, headed by Representative John J. Rooney, who had passed them on to the Speaker of the House.[78] These summaries made their way to other government officials, including Carl T. Rowan, when he was in charge of the United States Information Agency. Rowan reported that "for years the FBI has had a small army of agents and allies roaming the country whispering the dirt about Dr. King."[79]

As the controversy escalated, Hoover took the position that the late Robert Kennedy, then attorney general, had authorized the wiretaps on King and that Hoover had reluctantly gone along with the project.[80] Former attorneys general Ramsey Clark and Nicholas Katzenbach both categorically denied Hoover's account. Katzenbach said that the FBI director's statements were misleading. Clark suggested it was time for him to resign from the FBI. In an interview with CBS, Clark said, "Mr. Hoover repeatedly requested me to authorize F.B.I. wiretaps on Dr. King while I was Attorney General. The last of these requests, none

77.   Liberals suspected all along that the FBI had eavesdropped on King. As *Newsweek* put it: "For years it has been an open secret that the FBI maintained a tap on the telephone calls of Dr. Martin Luther King." But it remained only a rumor until two FBI agents admitted it in their testimony at the appeal of Muhamad Ali's conviction for violations of the Selective Service Act. Even after the agents testified, FBI headquarters in Washington refused to confirm that it had recorded King's conversations (ibid., June 16, 1969, pp. 29–30).

78.   *Congressional Record*, June 18, 1969, p. E-5056.

79.   *Nation*, July 7, 1969, p. 5. I. F. Stone put the matter more explicitly: "While the excuse for tapping King's phones was 'internal security' its chief result was to permit the FBI to spread stories about his sex life" (*I. F. Stone's Weekly*, June 30, 1969).

80.   Interview with Jeremiah O'Leary in *Washington Star*, June 20, 1969.

of which was granted, came two days before the murder of Dr. King."[81]

On the other side of the conflict, President Nixon defended J. Edgar Hoover in a news conference, saying that he had checked on the matter and found that it was former attorney general Robert Kennedy who had authorized the wiretaps on King.[82] And in the midst of charge and countercharge, the *Wall Street Journal*'s "Washington Wire" reported: "Hoover's relations with higher-ups improve sharply under the GOP regime. Nixon sees the FBI chief more often than LBJ did. Hoover cooperated fully with Mitchell's anti-crime crusade."[83]

This face-off between the liberal political community and J. Edgar Hoover over the King wiretaps represented a very deep conflict in American politics as the tumultuous decade of the 1960s drew to a close. Many liberals became increasingly antagonistic toward the FBI director and the law-and-order perspective of the incumbent administration. They viewed government efforts to crack down on radicals and dissent as a direct threat to the liberty of all Americans. At the same time, the Nixon administration embraced the FBI, and took steps to defend the society and government against anarchy and social disorder. The White House sided with the FBI director, who blamed social unrest on extremism, a new and powerful threat to the internal security of the United States.

With the change of administration in 1969, Hoover found his relationship with the Department of Justice far more congenial than it had been under successive liberal attorneys general during the preceding eight years. The department revealed in a legal brief, for example, that in Chicago it had used eavesdropping devices against antiwar leaders who were under indictment for inciting riots at the Democratic National Convention the previous summer.[84] Justice Department attorneys, however, now claimed legal authority to use electronic surveillance against members of any group that they believed might "attack and subvert the government by unlawful means." *Newsweek* concluded that "this serves notice that the Federal government feels legally free to eavesdrop on revolutionaries, black militants and other political activists."[85]

---

81.   *New York Times*, June 21, 1969, p. 11.

82.   Ibid., June 21, 1969.

83.   *Wall Street Journal*, June 20, 1969, p. 1.

84.   These leaders were the "Chicago 7." Their trial turned up evidence that two newsmen, Carl Gilman and Louis Slazberg, had acted as informants for the FBI (*Time*, November 14, 1969, p. 69).

85.   *Newsweek*, June 23, 1969, p. 37.

On Capitol Hill, Hoover received a warm reception from the House Appropriations subcommittee, responsible for the FBI budget. He testified in support of a supplemental authorization of $13.2 million to hire 525 new agents and 336 clerks. Hoover's request was one of the few budget increases backed by the Nixon administration.[86] Liberal journalists exhibited a greater willingness to attack the FBI but, curiously, not in the area of internal security.

In December 1969, for example, the *New York Times Magazine* published the most comprehensive and negative piece on the FBI to appear to that date. Tom Wicker wrote that Hoover's superb bureaucratic judgment had slipped, that FBI agents were consumed in paperwork, inflexible, and, therefore, inefficient in the areas of civil rights and organized crime. He argued that FBI training and crime laboratory techniques had fallen behind the times. Hoover's feuds with Kennedy and King, he suggested, had constituted a rift between the FBI and the liberal community generally. Wicker cited most of the adverse publicity the FBI had received in recent years and added some of his own. And he argued that the FBI director was not responsible to the attorney general because he had established a direct connection with the president.[87]

Wicker's article can only be construed as a liberal broadside against the FBI. But its real significance may be its demonstration that the liberal community had not yet gathered the information and other resources necessary to attack the FBI on internal security grounds. This is reflected in the Wicker piece in two respects. First, although it reviewed the King wiretaps and referred to electronic surveillance of the Black Panther party, it did not make a case concerning the FBI's activities against antiwar protests or the New Left. And, second, the article took Hoover and the FBI to task over dozens of specific items, but in the final analysis, it endorsed the job that J. Edgar Hoover had done: "With regrettable exceptions, he nevertheless appears to have maintained the integrity of those voluminous and dangerous files better than men of less will and character might have. . . . The real danger is that it [Hoover's office] might someday be filled by a man too weak to

---

86. *New York Times*, July 8, 1969, p. 24.

87. Wicker described the relationship between the FBI director and the president as follows: "At one end of that direct line of communication sat J. Edgar Hoover, presiding over a disciplined body of agents responsible to his slightest command, and over the huge bank of information residing in the dossiers he had collected, with ample means of collecting and disseminating more. At the other end sat the most powerful political official in the world" (*New York Times Magazine*, December 28, 1969, p. 29).

resist the pressures and temptations Hoover has largely scorned."[88] For the time being, the internal security aspects of FBI operations retained their status as the only sacred cow in American politics.

The liberal critique of authoritarianism and threats from government to individual privacy focused, at this time, not on the FBI but on law-and-order activities of the Nixon administration and on persistent reports that army intelligence agents had conducted extensive domestic surveillance of American citizens. Elements of the liberal community tended to take positions directly in opposition to those of the government. In one instance, a group of three hundred attorneys calling itself the Lawyers' Task Force on the November Moratorium contradicted the Nixon administration over the issue of whether a mass antiwar demonstration, conducted in Washington in November 1969, had been violent or peaceful. One administration advocate, J. Edgar Hoover, had charged that the groups that organized the demonstration were "strongly infiltrated by the Communists."[89]

The attorneys, who had worn light blue tags labeled "lawyer observer" during the demonstration, released a report based on their firsthand observations, stating in part that "after the event, and contrary to plain fact, official and unofficial spokesmen for the Administration sought to portray the weekend [of the mass demonstration] as one characterized generally by violence."[90] Former attorney general Ramsey Clark, who was a co-chairman of the group, chided the incumbent administration: "We need to recognize that dissent is the voice of powerless people, and the task of government is to provide ways to communicate effectively with these people."[91]

This was, of course, opposite to the approach favored by official Washington. At that time, the *New York Times* reported, "The Nixon Administration, alarmed by what it regards as a rising tide of radical extremism, is planning to step up surveillance of militant left wing groups and individuals." The plans were disclosed to reporters in a series of interviews by key White House officials who refused to be identified. According to the article, the plan to update and expand the

88.   Ibid.

89.   He added, "The Trotskyite Young Socialist Alliance is rapidly growing on the college level and played a key role in the November demonstration, especially through the Student Mobilization Committee, which can be found on a number of college campuses" (*New York Times*, December 28, 1969, p. 43).

90.   The report continued, "At the very least, this was a failure of leadership, of understanding. At worst, it was a calculated effort to mislead the public, to stifle dissent and to deny constitutional rights" (quoted in ibid., March 15, 1970, p. 32).

91.   Ibid.

nation's "domestic intelligence apparatus" had come from the president's more conservative aides because "liberal advisors have not provided him with alternatives. Indeed, the liberals do not appear to have any answers to the problem of American radicalism."[92]

The answer that liberals offered was an alternative construction of the problem, perhaps best articulated in a series of four editorials in the *New York Times* entitled "The Threat to Liberty." The first focused on recent government policies that, it warned, "tear at the fabric of a free, pluralistic society." It stated that "repressive administrative actions and retrogressive proposals and laws are directed from the very highest sources of Government against dissenters and nonconformists." It cited a contradiction between government statements affirming the right to dissent and "an epidemic of electronic eavesdropping [that] creates conditions approaching governmental lawlessness and moral disorder."[93] A second editorial lambasted intelligence techniques, including use of informants, wiretaps, electronic surveillance, and computerized intelligence dossiers. It argued that these were the telltale signs of a police state and added ominously, "It is happening here now."[94]

A third editorial referred to "a virus of electronic surveillance" but concentrated more on the language and rhetorical style of the Nixon White House, which it described as "the Administration's open exploitation of fear and discord."[95] And a fourth decried the violence of extremists, of both the Left and Right, but argued that neither the government nor dissidents could suspend the Bill of Rights "without being guilty of the ultimate and intolerable subversion of the American ideal and the democratic reality."[96] If the editors of the *New York Times* successfully articulated the liberal position on "the problem of Amer-

92.   Ibid., April 12, 1970, p. 1. One of the *Times*'s sources was probably Tom Charles Huston, whose efforts to expand and consolidate the nation's intelligence agencies later became known as the Huston Plan.

93.   Editorial, "The Threat to Liberty—I," *New York Times*, April 26, 1970, sec. 4, p. 12.

94.   Editorial, "The Threat to Liberty—II," *New York Times*, April 27, 1970, p. 32.

95.   The editors continued, "Verbal excesses and insinuations, apparently condoned by the President himself, have rendered suspect the Government's reaction to dissent and even to high-level disagreement on the part of the loyal opposition. Vice President Agnew not only rails against 'the whole damn zoo' of 'deserters, malcontents, radicals, incendiaries, the civil and uncivil disobedients,' but also hints darkly that Senator Muskie, in challenging the Administration's arms policies, 'is playing Russian roulette with U. S. security' " (editorial, "The Threat to Liberty—III," *New York Times*, April 28, 1970, p. 40).

96.   Editorial, "The Threat to Liberty—IV," *New York Times*, April 29, 1970, p. 40.

ican radicalism," they also failed to mention the dominant source of domestic intelligence activity directed against radicals and dissent—the FBI. The "Threat to Liberty" sequence demonstrated that by spring 1970 all that was left of the liberal entente with the FBI was an inhibition against attacking the nation's principal internal security agency by name.

For his part, J. Edgar Hoover remained unmoved by the liberal construction of the problem of American radicalism. Time and again the FBI director identified the Students for a Democractic Society and the Black Panther party as the twin nemeses of freedom and social harmony. The *FBI Annual Report* for fiscal year 1970 characterized the Panthers as the "most dangerous and violence-prone of all extremist groups."[97] The Weatherman faction of the SDS, it concluded, "was in the forefront of much of the activity deliberately calculated to provoke violent confrontations."[98]

President Nixon and his attorney general, John N. Mitchell, apparently agreed with the assessments of the FBI director. In September, Nixon reversed his previous position not to involve federal law enforcement in campus disorders. He asked Congress for one thousand additional FBI agents to investigate arson and bombings at the nation's colleges. In a three-hour conference at the White House, the president and attorney general outlined their plans to congressional leaders. In support of the appropriations request to fund the new agents, the FBI director "told the meeting [at the White House] that the Students for a Democratic Society was involved in 247 arson cases and 462 personal injury incidents in the past academic year."[99]

The *New York Times* suggested that Nixon had taken an extreme position on campus violence in an attempt "to blunt the impact of the report of the President's Commission on Campus Disorders," which was expected to place the blame for student uprisings largely on the government's failure to end the war in Vietnam.[100] The president was not without support in his position.[101] Law and order had again

---

97.   The report also said that: "Mr. Hoover deplored the fact that, despite its record of hate, violence, and subversion, the Black Panther party continues to receive substantial monetary contributions from prominent donors" (quoted in ibid., July 14, 1970, p. 21).

98.   Ibid.

99.   Ibid., September 23, 1970, pp. 1.

100. Ibid., p. 22.

101. One report said: "FBI chief Hoover cozies up still more to Nixon and Mitchell. He made a rare White House visit to brief GOP Congressional leaders on the

emerged as a central campaign issue in September 1970, and Congress raced to act on all of Nixon's key crime proposals, including the request for one thousand new FBI agents, before the mid-October election recess.[102] And in the politically charged preelection atmosphere, the White House proposed to link the FBI with state and local law enforcement agencies to prevent terrorist bombings and assaults against police and to create a new intelligence network for exchange of information on extremists.[103]

In the week following the midterm election of 1970, J. Edgar Hoover initiated a new public feud with his old adversary, the former attorney general Ramsey Clark. Clark had recently published a relatively mild criticism of the FBI in his book, *Crime in America*.[104] In a rare two-hour interview, the FBI director said Clark was "like a jellyfish . . . a softie." He added, "If ever there was a worse Attorney General [than Kennedy] it was Ramsey Clark. You never knew which way he was going to flop on an issue."[105] During the interview, Hoover also acknowledged that Kennedy was the first attorney general with whom he had had trouble and that he had not spoken to Kennedy during the last six months of his term as attorney general.[106]

Clark responded with the most forceful attack the liberal community had yet mounted against the FBI. He said Hoover was wrong in his assessment that the Black Panther party was the most dangerous group in America.[107] But more, he accused the FBI of deviating from accepted standards of impartial investigation. An investigator, he said, "has to be a disenthralled observer, a hard, hard pursuer of facts. He cannot be ideological. For reasons that are unfortunate, in my judge-

---

Administration's proposal to send FBI agents to troubled campuses. Hoover's appearance at a Mitchell-Volpe press conference on hijacking was his first TV performance in years" (*Wall Street Journal*, October 2, 1970, p. 1).

102. *New York Times*, September 24, 1970, p. 56.

103. Ibid., October 31, 1970, p. 1.

104. "In the book, 'Crime in America,' Mr. Clark assails what he termed Mr. Hoover's 'self-centered concern for his own reputation' and charged that the F.B.I. 'has so coveted personal credit that it will sacrifice even effective crime control before it will share the glory of its exploits' " (ibid., November 17, 1970, p. 39).

105. Hoover continued, "He [Clark] was worse then Bobby [Kennedy]. At least Kennedy stuck by his guns, even when he was wrong" (*Washington Post*, November 17, 1970, p. 1).

106. Ibid., p. 1.

107. Clark said, "That is patently absurd. I said it at the time and I'm still convinced of it. The FBI outnumbers the Black Panthers seven to one, and if they can't handle it, they should have stayed in bed" (ibid., November 18, 1980, p. A3).

ment, the FBI became ideological some time back. This has put scales over its eyes."[108] Clark made his remarks at a press conference called to announce the founding of the Committee for Public Justice, an organization established to counteract what it considered to be repressive tendencies in government.[109]

At this time, Hoover became remarkably outspoken in his condemnation of radicals. In the week following the dispute with Clark, he told a House Appropriations subcommittee that an "anarchist" group headed by Philip and Daniel Berrigan, the East Coast Conspiracy to Save Lives, was plotting to kidnap a high-ranking White House official.[110] In addition, he said, intelligence sources indicated that militant left-wing and black nationalist groups were turning to guerrilla tactics to achieve their ends. The Black Panthers, he reported, were heavily subsidized by Arab guerrillas and just had opened a new international office in Algiers under the direction of their fugitive leader, Eldridge Cleaver. He referred to "the ominous possibility that militants may seek to ape Arab tactics, including airplane hijackings, to gain release of jailed Panther members."[111]

Clark's use of "ideological" was, perhaps, a mild example of the

108. Ibid. An alternative version of Clark's statement is: "The F.B.I., for reasons I find unfortunate, became ideological sometime back and this put a scale over its eyes. It had an end before it and sought facts to fit that end" (*New York Times*, November 18, 1970, p. 48).

109. The Committee for Public Justice sponsored a conference on the FBI at Princeton University in October 1970, which was the first concerted attempt by the academic community to understand and publicize the operations of the FBI in the field of internal security. The proceedings of the conference were edited and collected in Watters and Gillers, eds., *Investigating the FBI*.

110. At a press conference, Attorney General Mitchell was asked repeatedly if he thought it was proper for the FBI director to attack former attorney general Ramsey Clark and to make public accusations against the Berrigans before formal charges had been brought against them. Mitchell responded: "Until he [Hoover] gets to the point, which he has not arrived at and I do not expect him to get to, where he is doing something that is improper within the confines of this department, he has a right to talk, just like anybody else. . . . From where I sit, he's doing a mighty fine job" (*New York Times*, December 19, 1970, p. 14).

111. Ibid., November 28, 1970, p. 1. On December 10, President Nixon was asked if he approved Hoover's recent public statements accusing the Berrigans of conspiracy before they had been formally charged with a crime, and a statement in which he continued "to call the late Martin Luther King a liar." Nixon praised Hoover and refused futher comment, except to say: "The Justice Department is looking into that testimony that Mr. Hoover has given [to the House Appropriations subcommittee] and will take appropriate action if the facts justify it" (ibid., December 11, 1970, p. 32).

exception that proves the rule. He did not explain what he meant by the term, but, rather, let the altercation die down. Mainstream liberals still refused to criticize the FBI specifically for civil liberties violations related to the national security. They concentrated instead on attacking the judgment of the FBI director. The press blasted Hoover, for example, for his decision to withdraw fifteen agents from the John Jay College of Criminal Justice because a professor had criticized the FBI in a seminar. The attention to this incident was sustained and intense, reflecting an increasingly negative attitude toward the FBI on the part of the liberal community.[112]

It was not a liberal, however, but rather a strict constitutionalist with impeccable conservative credentials, Senator Sam J. Ervin, who first moved to counter widespread domestic surveillance by government against citizens who had participated in political dissent or civil disorder.[113] In June 1970, Ervin made a series of speeches in which he alerted his Senate colleagues to the danger of what he called "a mass surveillance system unprecedented in American history." He warned that "the very existence of Government files on how people exercise First Amendment rights, how they think, speak, assemble and act in lawful pursuits, is a form of official psychological coercion to keep silent and to refrain from acting."[114] Ervin voiced his concerns at a time when Congress increasingly delegated to the executive broad grants of authority to prosecute crimes and conspiracies.[115]

112. Ibid., October 24, 1970, p. 1; ibid., editorial, October 30, 1970, p. 40; *Time*, November 30, 1970, p. 11; Fred J. Cook, "John Jay: College for Cops," *Nation*, November 30, 1970, pp. 555–58.

113. At the time, Ervin was described as follows: "The North Carolina Bourbon who has opposed virtually every civil-rights bill to come along, supported big business over organized labor, been a consistent hawk and daily infuriates the women's liberation movement has of late come out, in a number of ways on the side of poor blacks, the American Civil Liberties Union, despised left-wingers and those who oppose prayer in public schools" (*New York Times Magazine*, November 15, 1970, p. 51).

114. *New York Times*, June 28, 1970, p. 1. This article was based, in part, on "examination of some known data files and information supplied by the Senator [Ervin]." In addition, the article said that the Warren Commission's mandate for increased surveillance of " 'malcontents' and political assassins" was "widely cited in the Government as the authority for citizen surveillance."

115. At this time, the federal courts were still reluctant to act to curtail domestic intelligence activities. In April an ACLU lawsuit that would have prohibited domestic intelligence activities by the army was dismissed by a federal district judge in Chicago (ibid., April 23, 1970, p. 12). And two months later, the Supreme Court upheld the right of police to compile files on civil rights and other protes-

In the fall of 1970, Ervin pressed the attack, holding hearings before his Subcommittee on Constitutional Rights on the "computerized threat by the Government against Americans' constitutional freedoms."[116] He proposed the creation of an independent watchdog agency that would monitor government data banks and enforce the right of citizens to see and challenge adverse information. And in December, he charged that agents of the army's 113th Military Intelligence Group had collected information on Senator Adlai E. Stevenson, former Governor Otto Kerner, Representative Abner J. Mikva, and eight hundred other citizens of Illinois.[117] He said he would hold hearings and compel testimony from army agents in February.[118]

Ervin's sponsorship conferred credibility and authority on an earlier account of army surveillance by a former captain who claimed that the army's Conus Intelligence Branch operated three hundred domestic offices staffed by one thousand agents.[119] At that time he had written: "Today, the Army maintains files on the membership, ideology, programs, and practices of virtually every activist political group in the country."[120] In the wake of the Illinois case, the army, as before, denied the charges and "asserted that the 1,000 counter-intelligence agents in the continental United States had spent only 5 per cent of their time looking for potential civil disorders." Their purpose, the army said, was to conduct background checks on army personnel and to protect the security of domestic army installations.[121]

One measure of rising concern over the domestic intelligence activities of the government was indicated in a *Washington Post* survey, which found that "about one quarter of the members of Congress, lawyers, businessmen and journalists responding said they suspected or believed their phones were tapped or their offices bugged."[122] In the

---

ters, which had earlier been ordered destroyed by a lower court. The lawsuit had been brought by the ACLU against the the the state of New Jersey (ibid., June 2, 1970, p. 1, and June 7, 1970, sec. 4, p. 4).

116. Ibid., September 3, 1970, p. 23.

117. Ibid., December 17, 1970, p. 1.

118. Ervin's charge was backed up the following month in Federal District Court when John M. O'Brien, a former army intelligence officer, gave detailed testimony on his spying activities in Chicago that had targeted Jesse Jackson, Kerner, Stevenson, and Mikva, among others (ibid., January 3, 1971, p. 26).

119. CONUS is an abbreviation for continental United States.

120. Christopher H. Pyle, "CONUS Intelligence: The Army Watches Civilian Politics," *Washington Monthly* January, 1970, pp. 4–5.

121. *New York Times*, December 20, 1970, p. 27.

122. The survey was conducted in December 1970 and cited in the *Washington Post*, April 7, 1971.

first three months of 1971, the issue of army intelligence was much in the news.[123] In addition, the liberal community learned that the air force kept files on radicals, which it compiled from intelligence reports supplied by local police, the FBI, and various other intelligence agencies. This cooperation was made possible, it was revealed, through a "Delimitations Agreement," which was signed on July 2, 1969, "by members of the United States Counterintelligence Investigative Agencies, an association including the F.B.I. and Army, Navy and Air Force intelligence."[124] News reports also surfaced concerning local police intelligence units, including Bossi, later renamed the Security Investigation Section of the New York City Police.[125]

It is notable that most of the adverse publicity and criticism at this time failed to focus on the Domestic Intelligence Division of the FBI, from which emanated the great bulk of the government's domestic intelligence reports and programs. Liberals continued to restrict their criticisms of the FBI to other aspects of bureau operations.[126] The SCLC, for example, passed a resolution in 1970 attacking the FBI for "failure to meet [its] responsibility such as protecting civil rights leaders, stopping narcotics traffic and other organized crime."[127] T. R. Reid attacked the FBI policy of maintaining and distributing false criminal records.[128] And in February, Senator McGovern released an anonymous letter, reportedly written by ten FBI agents, which charged that the bureau had lost its effectiveness because its agents spent so much time worrying about and protecting the director's reputation.[129]

At this time, former FBI special agent John F. Shaw surfaced as the agent who wrote a letter to his professor at the John Jay College of Criminal Justice that was critical of the FBI. When a draft of the letter was discovered in the FBI typing pool, Shaw had been forced to tender

123. *New York Times*, January 6, 1971, p. 12, January 18, 1971, p. 1, January 19, 1971, p. 37, and February 24, 1971, p. 1.

124. Ibid., January 29, 1971, p. 10.

125. Ibid., March 8, 1971, p. 10.

126. One exception was an article by Richard T. Cooper of the *Los Angeles Times*. According to an editorial based on Cooper's reporting, an FBI informant had infiltrated the Weatherman faction of the Students for a Democratic Society, at times acting as an agent provocateur (*Nation*, January 25, 1971, p. 101).

127. *New York Times*, August 16, 1970, p. 56.

128. Judge Harry Tol Alexander had ordered that a false record be expunged. It was the first time any court had ever ordered a federal agency to expunge a record. See Thomas R. Reid III, "The Presumption of Guilt," *New Republic*, January 16, 1971, p. 15.

129. *New York Times*, March 1, 1971, p. 15.

his resignation, which was immediately accepted by Hoover "with prejudice." This meant that Shaw, an FBI veteran, would never again be able to find work within the law enforcement profession. Shaw quickly became a minor cause célèbre for the liberal community.[130]

But the criticisms contained in his confidential, academic letter did not focus on internal security matters. Shaw argued, instead, that Hoover had developed a "cult of personality," that advancement in the FBI depended on "adulation for the director" and that discipline was "swift and harsh . . . often quite arbitrary." In addition, he said that the FBI concentrated on crimes that could easily be solved "because these types of crime have produced high statistical success in the past."[131]

There were, however, two indications that the bureau's immunity to criticism in the area of internal security was coming to an end. The first, an excerpt from Victor Navasky's forthcoming book, *Kennedy Justice*, was published in the *Atlantic* in November 1970.[132] Navasky presented detailed information and analysis of the six-year FBI security investigation of King, including an evaluation of the roles played by Robert F. Kennedy and J. Edgar Hoover. The article served notice that internal security was no longer hallowed ground with respect to the case of Martin Luther King. Second, in February 1971, Professor H. H. Wilson of the Department of Politics at Princeton University called for comprehensive evaluation and reform of the FBI, including "adequate review of security measures and police activities by an independent and impartial authority."[133] Wilson concluded his article in the *Nation* with a proposal for a conference on the FBI, perhaps to be

130. On January 27, 1970, Shaw filed suit against J. Edgar Hoover, asking for reinstatement and back pay (ibid., January 28, 1971, p. 72). Shortly thereafter, presidential candidate Senator George McGovern wrote Attorney General Mitchell requesting an investigation of the incident, which was further promoted by the *Times*'s editors, who suggested that Hoover's "vindictive treatment [of Shaw] violates those liberties which the F.B.I. is supposed to protect" (ibid., February 1, 1971, p. 13, and editorial, February 8, 1971, p. 32). McGovern pressed his case further, saying that Hoover should be held in contempt of Congress for failure to provide information on the Shaw case (ibid., Feburary 11, 1971, p. 58). And, finally, the text of the letter was published in the *Nation* (February 8, 1971, pp. 172–77).

131. Quoted in *New York Times*, January 23, 1971, p. 27.

132. Victor S. Navasky, "The Government and Martin Luther King," *Atlantic Monthly*, November 1970, pp. 43–52.

133. H. H. Wilson, "The FBI Today: The Case for Effective Control," *Nation*, February 8, 1971, pp. 169–70.

sponsored by the Center for the Study of Democratic Institutions or the Committee for Public Justice.

Public support for the FBI was registered in a Gallup poll taken in August of 1970, in which 71 percent in a national survey gave a "highly favorable" rating to the FBI. The Gallup organization and news analyses treated this as a significant erosion of support for the FBI because in a previous poll, conducted in 1965, the bureau had received a "highly favorable" rating of 84 percent. The drop of thirteen percentage points must, however, be evaluated in relation to a general loss of public confidence in government at this time. For example, the Pentagon received a "highly favorable" rating for the same period from only 28 percent of those polled. These figures would tend to indicate that although the FBI had lost some support in the five years preceding 1970, it still enjoyed remarkable popularity at a time when government institutions were generally out of favor with the public.[134]

Dénouement

By 1971, the FBI had alienated much of the liberal constituency upon which it had relied for support over the past three decades. Liberals and the press they controlled openly and freely attacked the bureau in all areas except internal security. But following each volley of criticism, the FBI director, now seventy-six years old appeared able to rally supporters and ride out the storm. The FBI was still extremely resistant to political attack. It still exercised extraordinary autonomy in setting its own security agenda and in formulating its programs. Although there were suggestions now and again that Congress or the attorney general ought to supervise the FBI more closely, no one gave them serious consideration. The bureau remained highly insulated in its internal security operations—against investigative reporting, hostile former attorneys general, congressional oversight, executive regulation, pressure groups, and public inquiry generally.

On the face of it, then, the evidence does not appear to support the argument that the FBI could sustain hegemony over internal security policy only as long as it retained its liberal constituency. Indeed, the bureau did continue its domestic intelligence functions, for a short time, even after it had lost most of its liberal allies. The liberal community withheld its fire because it was still unable to focus on those aspects of FBI behavior which suggested the presence of an internal

134. *New York Times*, August 9, 1970, p. 66, and *Gallup Political Index*, Report no. 62, August 1970, p. 10.

security state in its midst. The reluctance of liberals to attack the bureau is remarkable because most Americans had become more sophisticated in their attitudes toward communism. The cold war consensus and the perception of a worldwide Communist conspiracy had weakened and had been largely replaced by movement toward a policy of détente with the Soviet Union.

But the argument, thus constructed, does not recognize inherent limitations that are built into the state maintenance functions of the agency of internal security in a constitutional republic. Just as liberalism is founded on contradictions, so too is the internal security apparatus. Liberalism can elevate individual freedom and rights above state interests only by refusing to recognize the coercive aspects of the modern state. Liberals wanted to venerate the civil and constitutional rights of individual citizens, but because they recognized the necessity to protect the state and to enforce public order, they also venerated the FBI. This tension is heightened when widespread social disorder or the threat of an ideological competitor forces the state to take action that constricts individual freedoms. But the liberal state is distinguished from its absolutist sister in that liberalism relegates the internal security function to the margins of acceptable state behavior, even refusing to recognize its existence. In contrast, the absolute state can eliminate these contradictions, but in so doing, it draws repression to its center, certifying it as a legitimate means of social control.

It may be that erosion of political support from liberals is insufficient to call into question established internal security procedures and institutions in an era of sustained and widespread public disorder. This leads to an explanation that is perhaps more refined: the internal security powers of the FBI, its hegemony over domestic security policy, could be sustained with or without the support of liberals only when the agency directed its security and intelligence activities against generally acknowledged ideological enemies of the state such as Nazi saboteurs and Communists.[135] But when the internal security function reaches beyond this point, it begins to constitute a power, or state form, that is fundamentally incompatible with those constitutional requirements which define the limits and authority of the larger state.

After the middle 1960s, the FBI focused its counterintelligence activ-

135. As demonstrated in chapter 3, the internal security powers of the liberal state can also be applied against groups such as the Ku Klux Klan that would deny the legitimate rights of other citizens. But even against the Klan, application required significant modifications of liberal theory in relation to the internal security powers.

ities against hundreds of individuals and groups that were not acknowledged ideological enemies of the state. The terms *New Left* and *Black Nationalist*, it should be recalled, were never specifically defined. Sometimes they referred to groups such as the SDS and the Black Panther party, which were ideologically opposed to the American state. But, more often, they designated organizations or individuals who protested against the war in Vietnam or participated in civil rights demonstrations. In this situation, FBI hegemony in domestic intelligence matters depended on the ability of the agency to conceal its activities from the natural enemies of extraordinary internal security powers, that is, liberals and their allies with strict constitutionalist convictions.

In this context, the argument concerning liberal support can perhaps be evaluated in relation to another point—that continued FBI dominance depended on control of the files, especially those that documented the ongoing activities of the bureau. In this regard, the FBI was unique among all domestic agencies of the United States government. First, its files were restricted as a matter of routine procedure. Nothing could be released except on the authority of the director, who had more then once proven his ability to withhold information from the Congress. But secrecy must be distinguished from insularity because, in fact, tens of thousands of FBI documents were circulated outside the bureau, to the White House, to the Internal Revenue Service, to state and local police, and to a host of intelligence units located in the great bureaucracies throughout government.[136]

The FBI was able to insulate itself from inquiry and criticism generally. Secrecy of the files is clearly not a sufficient condition to achieving insularity of operations and, in certain respects, neither is it a prerequisite. Files varied considerably in their degree of sensitivity and accessibility in the intelligence community and even within the FBI. It is one of the more remarkable circumstances in American politics that thousands of FBI clerks and agents possessed full knowledge of the Cointelpro operations for more than a decade and a half, and not one among them leaked a single document or otherwise revealed their existence. That these and other programs could be established without

---

136.   For example, the Justice Department's Interdivisional Intelligence Unit (IDIU) gleaned most of its information from the FBI: "The [IDIU] analysts and attorneys during the year 1968 reviewed more than 32,000 FBI investigative reports, teletypes, army intelligence reports and other material concerning individuals and organizations involved primarily in the area of racial agitation" (Assistant Attorney General J. Walter Yeagley to Deputy Attorney General Richard G. Kleindienst, February 6, 1969, quoted in Church, bk. 3, p. 500).

specific congressional or executive authorization indicates a complete absence of pluralistic influences, both from within government and the society at large.

Although secrecy and control of the files helped to preserve the insularity of FBI operations throughout the 1960s, secrecy is too fragile to be considered the dominant element in an explanation of FBI power. Many secrets were not well kept; there was little need, because liberals and the mass media they controlled in the 1960s were apparently not interested in penetrating FBI insularity in the area of internal security. Insularity perhaps depended more on the willingness of liberals and strict constitutionalists to make national security exceptions to the Bill of Rights and due process, which permitted the emergence of a sacred cow in their midst.

If liberal journalists, politicians, and academics in the main avoided attacking the FBI on security grounds, it was perhaps because they did not wish to confront the complexities, tensions, and contradictions implicit in the exercise of state security powers in a liberal polity. It was, after all, possible to construe the extraordinary libertarian dimensions of the Warren Court and the advances in equal protection and civil rights in this period as representative of the true character of the American state.

When the liberals confronted communism in the United States in the decade following World War II, they found themselves face to face with all the tensions of their own ideology. But rather than acknowledging them, they stowed them away in a central agency of internal security, believing they would be dissolved through a process of administration. In this way, liberals helped to insulate the agency from attack and from view, hiding some of the more coercive aspects of the American state behind an ideological curtain that could not be probed or questioned because its function was nothing less than the defense of the American way of life.[137]

The FBI became vulnerable to attack after the liberal community had disengaged its support and was no longer willing to participate in a general ideologically oriented effort to insulate the agency. But it was not liberals alone who raised the curtain on the FBI. It was, instead, a mainstream politician, House Majority Leader Hale Boggs; a strict

137. Even today political scientists and other educators have largely failed to incorporate the security operations of the FBI into their orienting paradigms. Academic disinterest in sustained study of the FBI, an agency about the size of the Department of State in budget and staff, paralleled the inability of liberals to penetrate FBI insularity in the 1960s, as well as the willingness of the agents to conduct domestic counterintelligence operations in silence.

constitutionalist, Senator Sam Ervin; and an extremely well-timed accident of history. This accident, the theft and selective distribution of more than a thousand FBI documents by the self-styled Citizens Commission to Investigate the FBI, showed the fragility of secrecy and initiated a series of events that shed considerable light on the process by which the FBI finally lost its immunity to political attack in the area of internal security.

In the month following the theft of the FBI files at the resident office in Media, Pennsylvania, on March 8, 1971, the secrecy of FBI internal security operations was, for the first time, thoroughly and publicly compromised. The Citizens Commission to Investigate the FBI, which claimed credit for the break-in at Media, sent copies of selected intelligence reports to Senator George McGovern and Congressman Parren J. Mitchell. Both members of Congress turned their packets over to the FBI, but not without comment. Mitchell was more outspoken, calling the burglary and the FBI intelligence activities that were revealed "equally criminal."[138]

The following day the *Washington Post* received a copy of the same materials from the Citizens Commission. The *Post* reporter quoted extensively from the fourteen documents, which largely described FBI surveillance of anitwar groups, black student organizations, professors, college campuses, the Black Panther party, and the National Black Economic Development Conference, among others. For the first time, actual FBI files documented the existence of widespread domestic intelligence activities aimed at containing dissent. The mass audience learned about acronyms like SI and PSI, which reportedly stood for "student informant" and "paid student informant." What liberals had often whispered among themselves in private, that the FBI had infiltrated the antiwar and civil rights movements, was proved to be true.[139]

The reaction was swift and unequivocal. Though refusing to discuss the documents specifically, McGovern charged that the FBI was a "separate law unto itself, and beyond the reach of the Attorney General or even the President." He renewed his demand for a full congressional

---

138. *Washington Post*, March 23, 1971, p. A3.

139. The *Post* also published and completely ignored Attorney General Mitchell's warning that the stolen documents contained information "relating to the national defense" that could "injure the United States," including his request that the paper not circulate or publish the materials (ibid., March 24, 1971, pp. A1, A11). Mitchell also said that "disclosure of this information could endanger the lives or cause other serious harm to persons engaged in investigative activities on behalf of the United States" (ibid., March 25, 1971, p. A1).

investigation of the agency.[140] But his reaction was mild compared with that of Majority Leader Boggs. Without informing Speaker Carl Albert in advance, Boggs delivered a one-minute speech that was characterized as "the harshest criticism of Hoover ever heard in the House." He said, "When the FBI taps the telephones of Members of this body and of Members of the Senate, when the FBI stations agents on college campuses to infiltrate college organizations, when the FBI adopts the tactics of the Soviet Union and Hitler's Gestapo, then it is time—it is way past time, Mr. Speaker—that the present Director thereof no longer be the Director."[141]

This was the first time that the leadership of the House or the Senate had called for the resignation of J. Edgar Hoover. The majority leader's comments caused a furor, particularly because they could not be dismissed as just another partisan criticism. Boggs was no liberal and had, in fact, only recently denounced a move by his own party caucus to put the Democrats on record as favoring withdrawal of American troops from Vietnam by the end of the year.[142]

On the same day that Boggs spoke against J. Edgar Hoover in the House, the Citizens Commission sent a second batch of FBI materials to the *Washington Post* and other liberal newspapers. Eleven new documents described, among other procedures, FBI surveillance of New Left groups on college campuses, development of an extensive informant network throughout black neighborhoods in Philadelphia, and the opening of investigations on black student organizations at ten Pennsylvania colleges and universities.[143] The following day, director Hoover released a statement through the office of Senate Majority Leader Hugh Scott that denied the Boggs charge: "I want to make a positive assertion that there has never been a wiretap of a senator's phone or the phone of a member of Congress since I became director in 1924, nor has any member of the Congress or the Senate been under surveillance by the FBI."[144]

140. Ibid., March 24, 1971, p. A1.

141. *New York Times*, April 6, 1971, p. 1; *Washington Post*, April 6, 1971, p. A1; *Congressional Record*, April 5, 1971, p. 9470.

142. "Boggs's statement [denouncing the resolution to work toward withdrawal of U.S. forces from Vietnam], accompanied by praise for President Nixon's 'outstanding' achievements in foreign policy, gave evidence of a sharp split in the opposition party leadership over how to handle the Vietnam issue in the months leading up to the 1972 election" (*Washington Post*, March 13, 1971, p. A6).

143. Ibid., April 6, 1971, p. A1.

144. Ibid., April 7, 1971, p. A1. Boggs countered in a broadcast interview that "the

But this time, the director's statement did not put the matter to rest. In a letter to Attorney General Mitchell, the chairman of the Senate Constitutional Rights Subcommittee, Sam J. Ervin, "requested documents involving surveillance guidelines, criteria for intelligence gathering and specific information on FBI activities in this field."[145] That same day, Judge Damon J. Keith of the United States Court of Appeals in Cincinnati ruled that domestic intelligence wiretapping without a court order was prohibited by the Constitution, specifically in "domestic subversion" cases. The defense, the court said, was entitled to review the records of such FBI surveillance in a case involving the White Panther party.[146] And in the following week, the *New York Times*, the *Boston Globe*, and other newspapers received additional FBI intelligence documents from the Citizens Commission.[147] Suddenly, the liberal press, a powerful Senate subcommittee, and the federal courts all sought to penetrate FBI insularity, specifically in the area of domestic security intelligence operations.

In the next two weeks several members of Congress and the liberal press called for formal investigations of the FBI. Senator Edward Muskie disclosed that FBI agents had infiltrated Earth Day activities across the country in April 1970. He argued for establishment of a domestic intelligence review board.[148] Senator Nelson introduced S. 1550, the Constitutional Rights and Civil Liberties Act of 1971, to establish a twenty-four member commission to investigate domestic intelligence activities. And Representative Ogden R. Reid called for congressional hearings to look into the domestic activities of intelligence agencies.[149]

The editors of the *Washington Post* hoped to draft Senator Sam Ervin for the job. They argued that both Congress and the public had "a right to know the reach of the FBI's surveillance, the kinds of information it is compiling in its limitless dossiers, the extent to which it is

---

FBI had me under surveillance, my personal life." He said that "numerous members of Congress" had told him of "their firm conviction that their telephone conversations and activities are the subject of surveillance by the FBI." He added that several members of Congress "have made available to me detailed information confirming my own experience . . . and it is my intention to make proper use of it in the near future" (ibid., p. A1).

145. Ibid., April 9, 1971, p. A1.
146. Ibid.
147. *New York Times*, April 8, 10, 12, 13, 1971.
148. *Congressional Quarterly Weekly*, 1971, p. 840.
149. Ibid., p. 941.

invading the privacy of Americans for the sake of protecting them from themselves."[150] At the *New York Times*, the editors were disappointed at the reluctance of Senator Ervin's subcommittee "to look into the FBI's work." They cited a "growing public awareness that for decades, most Attorneys General have feared Mr. Hoover's political influence and have negotiated with him as a sovereign entity, instead of supervising him as a subordinate."[151]

When Hale Boggs charged that the FBI had wiretapped the telephones of members of Congress, he heightened the controversy that had been initiated and sustained by the continuous and strategically timed disclosure of documents stolen from the FBI office at Media, Pennsylvania.[152] Although Boggs failed to substantiate the specific charge of wiretapping, his sponsorship lent credibility to the stream of revelations concerning FBI surveillance of antiwar and civil rights activists, among others, then appearing in the pages of the mass circulation newspapers. Although the editors of the *Washington Post* conceded "Boggs' transparent failure to back up his specific charge," they took the opportunity to question why Congress had failed to exercise its oversight powers in relation to the FBI and to suggest, once again, that Sam Ervin was just the man for the job.[153]

For its part, the FBI launched a massive investigation of the burglary, designated by the term *Medburg*, which failed to produce any indictments but did pile up more than thirty-three thousand pages of investigative reports.[154] Over a period of four months following the break-

150. *Washington Post*, April 12, 1971, p. A18.

151. The editorial continued: "The effusive endorsements of Mr. Hoover in recent days by President Nixon and Attorney General Mitchell suggest that top-level supervision within the executive is no firmer under this Administration" (*New York Times*, April 21, 1971, p. 46).

152. The purloined documents continued to flow into the mass media. On May 12, 16, and 18, 1971, the *New York Times* published additional accounts of FBI domestic intelligence activities, which were based on a sixth batch of materials, bringing the total to sixty documents in all.

153. "But the outstanding senator to head a thoroughgoing investigation of the FBI— of the whole range of domestic intelligence and criminal investigating activity by the federal government—is, in our judgement, Sam Ervin of North Carolina. Tough, fair-minded and with a profound commitment to American constitutional liberties, Senator Ervin has pioneered in the study of incursions into privacy. It would offer reassurance to the whole country if he would now indicate a willingness to take on this difficult and important assignment" (*Washington Post*, April 28, 1971, p. A22).

154. The Medburg files are available in the FOIA/PA reading room at the J. Edgar Hoover Building in Washington, D.C. See "Conducting Research In FBI Rec-

in, the FBI closed 103 of its 538 resident agencies.[155] But Hoover's most significant action of this period was to terminate all of the FBI domestic counterintelligence programs or Cointelpros on April 28, 1971.[156] Although no official explanation was offered, it is likely that the master bureaucrat sought to cut his losses because he knew that FBI insularity had finally been penetrated.

ords," Research Unit, Office of Congressional and Public Affairs, Federal Bureau of Investigation, 1988, p. 34.

155. *New York Times*, March 18, 1971; Ungar, *FBI*, pp. 484–86.

156. Director, FBI, to SAC, Albany, "Counterintelligence programs (Cointelpros) Internal Security—Racial Matters," April 29, 1971. In an earlier draft of this memorandum, C. D. Brennan wrote: "To afford additional security to our sensitive techniques and operations, it is recommended the Cointelpros operated by the Domestic Intelligence Division be discontinued" (C. D. Brennan to W. C. Sullivan, "Counterintelligence programs (Cointelpros)/ Internal Security–Racial Matters," April 27, 1971).

CHAPTER FIVE

Rise of a Domestic Intelligence State

THE FOREGOING chapters have analyzed the contribution of the liberal political community to internal security policy in the twenty-five years following World War II, as well as the demise of the FBI's liberal constituency in the late 1960s. Support from liberals helped the FBI achieve policy autonomy and insulate its programs from outside review for more than a quarter of a century. By the middle 1960s, the bureau had assumed powers and initiated projects, such as the White Hate Groups Cointelpro, that could not be reconciled with constitutional norms and other legal requirements of the American political system.

This chapter examines the institution in which the liberal community vested its support. It analyzes FBI domestic intelligence programs that were conducted during the 1960s and addresses the hypothesis that in the two decades following 1950, the FBI transformed itself from a bureau of internal security with delimited functions into an agency resembling more a political police and an independent security state within the state. The project here is to document specific changes in the nature of FBI domestic security intelligence programming in terms of (1) an overall increase in aggressive and counterintelligence activity, (2) enhanced autonomy of policy formation, and (3) a higher degree of insularity in operations.

The FBI contained elements of all three models of the agency of internal security in a liberal polity. Although this was true to a limited extent almost from the outset of FBI domestic intelligence operations,[1] an unmistakable trend emerged during the middle 1960s. It consisted of the addition of new programs that designated an increasing number

---

1. Even in the 1940s, the FBI conducted hostile investigations and other intelligence operations against the Communist party that preceded the establishment of any formal Cointelpro or domestic counterintelligence programs. As the chief of the FBI Domestic Intelligence Division testified, "We were engaged in Cointelpro tactics, to divide, confuse, weaken, in diverse ways, an organization. We were engaged in that when I entered the Bureau in 1941" (Testimony of William C. Sullivan, Assistant Director for the Domestic Intelligence Division [1961–1970] and Assistant to the Director [1970–1971], 11/1/75, pp. 42–43, quoted in Church, bk. 2, p. 66).

of persons for intensive investigation, and potential summary detention, and involved the infiltration and disruption of their political and
organizational activities. Such programs indicated that the FBI had
built up its domestic intelligence capacities far beyond the minimum
standard necessary to maintain the security interests of the United
States.

The White Hate Cointelpro, for example, suggests the presence of
an agency after 1964 with elements that resemble closely the characteristics of an internal security state within the larger liberal polity.
Neither the executive nor the Congress exercised ministerial controls
over the White Hate program. Although the goal of the program, to
disrupt and eradicate the southern Klan groups, was supported by liberal elites, no outside authority, not even the attorney general, was
officially advised of its existence. Its budget was carved out of general-
purpose funds allocated at the discretion of the FBI director with no
external process of approval or oversight. The covert methods and tactics directed against the Klan were designed so that they circumvented
due process requirements of the Constitution and could not be brought
to the attention of the courts.

At the same time, and at the opposite extreme, other security arrangements of the FBI corresponded more nearly with those of a domestic intelligence bureau. These were programs thought to be essential to the national security. They included passive investigations of
Communist, extremist, and terrorist groups, for example, and operations publicly ordered by the president that probed the causes of civil
disturbances. In the early phases of FBI domestic security activity, the
bureau had even conducted investigations of Communists pursuant to
specific statutes, including the 1949 Smith Act prosecutions of Eugene
Dennis and ten coconspirators.[2] But there was, from the outset, a tendency for FBI intelligence programs to verge toward the model of a
political police and beyond. That trend accelerated dramatically in the
1960s.

When J. Edgar Hoover authorized an aggressive campaign to disrupt
the Klan in 1964, he placed his agency deeply at odds with the liberal
tradition, even though more than one liberal president had spoken out
against the Klan. As the number of bureau programs and intelligence
investigations focusing on indigenous groups expanded in the 1960s,
it became increasingly more difficult to explain them in terms of a lib-

2.   For a comprehensive account of FBI activity in relation to the Smith Act convic-
      tions, see Kevin J. O'Brien, "*Dennis v. U.S.*: The Cold War, the Communist
      Conspiracy, and the F.B.I." (Ph.D. diss., Cornell University, 1979).

Table 5.1

Three Models of FBI Domestic Security Intelligence Operations

Type of Internal Security Apparatus	Mode of Intelligence Operations	Autonomy of Policy Formation	Insularity of Program Implementation
1. Bureau of Domestic Intelligence	Passive. Collects and analyzes information	Low. Subject to democratic policy process	Low (ministerial). Responsive to legislature, courts, and higher executive authority
2. Political Police	Aggressive. Adds hostile intelligence techniques to above	Moderate. Policies and goals in common with political elite	Moderate (mixed). Penetrated by political elites and selected others with shared goals
3. Internal Security State	Disruptive. Operates covert and formal domestic counterintelligence programs	High. Independent security policies may or may not coincide with goals of other state actors	High (discretionary). Records, methods, and programs known only to security personnel

eral theory of internal security or to reconcile them with liberalism itself. The alternative to explanation is of course secrecy, and the FBI reached a pinnacle in the late 1960s, if only because it conducted a greater number of disruptive Cointelpros and aggressive intelligence investigations that could not withstand open scrutiny.

Table 5.1 displays three different models of FBI domestic security intelligence activity against three characteristics, or variables, that help to define the agency of internal security in a liberal state. There is a definite direction of variation for each characteristic when models 1, 2, and 3 are considered in sequence. Note, for instance, that autonomy of policy formation tends to increase as ministerial control over agency programs decreases. As agency operations become more insulated from democratic institutions and from public debate, the type of security apparatus shifts toward that of the third model, an independent security state. And the severity of intelligence techniques increases and becomes less consistent with established legal procedure as the agency deviates from the model of a bureau of domestic intelligence.

Each conception of the FBI is intended to represent an extreme or very pure form of an empirical phenomenon. These categories are not intended to be logically exhaustive or mutually exclusive. They do, however, indicate the range of possibilities within the overall structure of a constitutional republic, with the understanding, of course, that any of the extraordinary powers associated with internal security functions push against the limits and define the scope of constitutional forms. It should accordingly be possible to establish an empirical relationship between each particular program or series of like programs that the FBI operated in the 1960s and the security model that it most closely exemplifies. Variation in the form of FBI domestic security intelligence programming over time indicates alterations in the type of internal security apparatus for the period in question.

In the 1960s, domestic intelligence activities of the FBI became far-flung and intensive, touching the lives of hundreds of thousands, if not millions, of American citizens.[3] In 1963, the number, scope, and variety of FBI programs proliferated dramatically. The bureau initiated more than forty domestic security intelligence programs from 1960 through 1970. In six years (1958 through 1963) the FBI developed six programs, and in the next six years, it implemented twenty-eight. (These programs are listed in Table 5.2 on p. 161.) The effort to count and assess the domestic intelligence programs of the FBI, however, presents several difficulties. First, some of the larger programs contain smaller ones or areas of concentration within them. The designation Cominfil (Communist Infiltration), for example, refers both to a kind of investigation and to a theory about the way in which Communists operate in the United States.[4]

Briefly stated, the theory behind Cominfil is that Communist party members seek to infiltrate or join the ranks of legitimate organizations, rise to positions of leadership, establish effective control of the organization, and ultimately convert it into a vehicle for mass communist

3.   "FBI headquarters alone had developed over 500,000 domestic intelligence files, and these have been augmented by additional files at FBI Field Offices [where the bulk of FBI files are located]. The FBI opened 65,000 of these domestic intelligence files in 1972 alone. In fact, substantially more individuals and groups are subject to intelligence scrutiny than the number of files would appear to indicate, since typically, each domestic intelligence file contains information on more than one individual or group, and this information is readily retrievable through the FBI General Name Index" (Church, bk. 2, p. 6).

4.   The theory of Communist infiltration formed part of the initial impetus for gathering domestic intelligence in the late 1930s and remained an essential element of its justification thereafter (Church, bk. 3, pp. 412–13).

revolution.[5] Cominfil investigations were therefore opened on groups that were thought to be influenced or infiltrated by Communists. Within Cominfil operations there were specific intensified efforts over the years that were directed at certain types of groups. Two examples are the targeting of student groups and the development of the CIRM program in 1965 and 1964, respectively.[6]

The need to distinguish discrete but smaller programs within larger program designations is also encountered when considering the domestic counterintelligence programs, or Cointelpros, of the 1960s. By most counts, the FBI established and conducted seven formal domestic Cointelpros. Some of them, however, spawned smaller programs when orders were issued by the director to intensify activity against certain groups such as the Black Panther party in 1968 and the Students for a Democratic Society in 1969. In addition, several operations, such as the Key Black Extremist program, were used to direct Cointelpro actions against specific persons. They thus merit consideration as distinct programs under the larger Cointelpro caption.

In the abstract, Cointelpro operations can be distinguished from Cominfil investigations because the intent of the former was to go beyond investigation and to disrupt the investigatory subject (usually an individual or a group, but sometimes even a social movement). In practice, however, the difference was not hard and fast. Some standard Cominfil investigative techniques such as twenty-four-hour surveillance or interviews with the subject could be taken as harassment and could disrupt the activities of the person or group under investigation. Similarly, a Cointelpro operation, such as breaking into the headquarters of an organization and photocopying its membership lists, could yield intelligence that was useful in the context of a Cominfil investigation. When information collected in a Cominfil investigation was used to inform and target a Cointelpro operation, and the same agents were involved in both activities, it is easy to see how the distinction between the two tended to break down.[7]

---

5.   In his 1964 formal statement before a House Appropriations subcommittee, FBI director J. Edgar Hoover argued that " 'Communist influence' in the 'Negro movement' was 'vitally important' because 'it can be the means through which large masses are caused to . . . succumb to the party's propaganda lures.' The number of Negroes recruited by the Communists was 'not the important thing.' Rather, Director Hoover said it was 'an old Communist principle' that: 'Communism must be built with non-Communist hands' " (Church, bk. 3, p. 480).

6.   CIRM stands for Communist Influence in Racial Matters. It was part of a broader FBI effort to gather intelligence on civil rights and other black organizations in 1964.

7.   In addition, intensive investigations and Cointelpro activities were sometimes

A further difficulty involves interpreting the program designations themselves. The first two Cointelpros, for example, were directed specifically against the Communist party and the Socialist Workers party. But as counterintelligence techniques gained acceptance within the Domestic Intelligence Division of the FBI and in the field, the programs expanded and the targets became less well defined. In the originating memorandum of the White Hate Groups Cointelpro, for instance, seventeen Klan and nine fascist organizations are enumerated and listed by name.

But in subsequent programs, such as the New Left Cointelpro, responsibility for designating groups and individuals for disruption fell largely to agents in the field. The meaning and application of the term *New Left* remained nebulous. As the program supervisor testified, "It is my impression that the characterization of New Left groups rather than being defined at any specific time by document, . . . more or less grew. . . . It has never been strictly defined, as far as I know. . . . It is more or less an attitude, I would think."[8] In addition to being vague, several important terms, including *Black Nationalist* and *New Left*, cut across larger program categories such as Cominfil and Cointelpro, and were used to indicate investigative subject areas by themselves.

The problem of distinguishing different FBI domestic security intelligence programs is further complicated because, in some cases, existing programs were renamed and given a different emphasis, while others were significantly expanded. Programs involving index cards or computerized lists, for example, evolved in character and function over a twenty-five-year period. The initial Custodial Detention List was renamed the Security Index in 1943. Later the FBI added a Communist Index, which was restructured and retitled the Reserve Index in 1960. And in 1968, the standards upon which the Security Index was based were substantially revised. The general purpose of these index programs was to designate certain dangerous individuals for ongoing intensive investigation and potential detention in the event of an internal security emergency.

---

administratively integrated by FBI headquarters. For example, the authorizing memorandum for the White Hate Groups Cointelpro states: "Counterintelligence action directed at these [Klan] groups is intended to complement and stimulate our accelerated intelligence investigations. Each investigative Agent has a responsibility to call to the attention of the counterintelligence coordinator suggestions and possibilities for implementintg the [White Hate Groups] program" (Director, FBI, to SAC, Atlanta, "Counterintelligence Program/Internal Security/Disruption of Hate Groups," September 2, 1964, p. 4, reprinted in Church, vol. 6, pp. 378–82).

8.   Church, bk. 3, p. 23, n. 99.

In this analysis, various intensifications, redirections, and significant smaller programs within existing program designations will be considered as distinct. Each of the programs is described in the Church Committee reports. This procedure does not guarantee that every program initiated during this period will be considered. But it is probable that a very large percentage of FBI domestic intelligence efforts are represented because the Church investigation sought to be as comprehensive as possible. For every program listed in table 5.2, the FBI director issued a new set of specific written instructions to the special agents in charge of the field offices that were expected to carry out the program.

Investigation, Infiltration, and Disruption

New operations of the FBI tended to develop from those already in existence, so that if a program was considered successful, it often gave rise to a series of like efforts modeled on the original idea. When it was found, for example, that the CPUSA Cointelpro was an effective means of damaging the Communist party, similar programs were directed first against the Trotskyite Socialist Workers party and later against a variety of other targets. This tendency created a functional differentiation among the various programs based principally on the purposes of the programs and to some extent on the intelligence techniques that were employed. Table 5.2 divides the FBI domestic intelligence programs initiated from 1960 through 1970 into seven different types according to the purpose or function of each.

Each program type can also be distinguished in historical and descriptive terms. Type 1 programs are closely associated with the threat of communism and the fear of subversion prevalent in the late 1940s and early 1950s. To a large extent, they can be explained as the result of the tenacity and persistence of the anti-Communist consensus established in that period. Such programs also reflected the ideology and personal beliefs of J. Edgar Hoover, whose powerful personality dominated FBI activities—from the instigation of new programs at headquarters in Washington to administration and operations in the field.

As these programs evolved during the 1960s, the specific relationship to the threat of Communist subversion became increasingly indirect. In the Investigation of Cuban Activities (Program 1), the actions of persons and groups both against and for the Castro regime were investigated because of "the close ties between the Castro government of Cuba and the Soviet bloc."[9] Investigations of persons or groups op-

9.   Interdepartmental Intelligence Conference Report, "Status of U.S. Internal Secu-

Table 5.2
Typology of FBI Domestic Security Intelligence Programs
(Implemented 1960–1970)

Type 1. Investigation of Communist-infiltrated and Communist-related Groups and In-
    dividuals (subversive activity):

    1. Investigation of Cuban Activities (1961)
    2. CIRM (Communist Influence in Racial Matters) (1964)
    3. SDS Investigations (1965)
    4. Student Groups Investigations (1965)

Type 2. Investigations Related to Possible or Actual Civil Disturbances:

    5. General Racial Matters (1965)
    6. Racial Conditions Reporting (1966)
    7. Civil Disturbance Investigations (1966)
    8. IDIU (Interdivisional Intelligence Unit) (1967)[a]
    9. VIDEM (Vietnam Demonstrations) (1968)

Type 3. Lists Designating Persons for Intensive Investigation, Possible Apprehension,
    and/or Detention:

    10. Reserve Index (1960)
    11. Cuban Section of Security Index (1962)
    12. Security Index Revision (1968)
    13. Key Activist Program (1968)
    14. Black Nationalist Photograph Album (1968)
    15. Priority Apprehension Program (1968)
    16. Key Activist Program Intensification (1969)
    17. Key Activist Photograph Album (1969)

Type 4. Investigation and/or Penetration of Extremist, Violent, or Militant Groups and
    Individuals:

    18. Klan Intelligence (1964)
    19. Ghetto Informant Program (1967)
    20. Black Nationalist Groups TOPLEV Informant Program (1967)
    21. Black Nationalist Organizations Investigation (1968)
    22. New Left Investigations (1968)
    23. Stag (Student Agitation) (1968)
    24. Investigation of SDS Field Office Staff (1969)

[a] IDIU was a Department of Justice operation not specifically under the control of the
FBI. It is included here because a substantial proportion of its intelligence base on civil
disturbances was generated from FBI reports.

Table 5.2 (*cont.*)

---

25. Investigation of Black Student Unions (1970)
26. Investigation of Marxist-oriented Communes (1970)
27. Investigation of New Left Terrorists (1970)
28. Terrorist Informants (1970)

Type 5. Lists Designating Persons for Intensive Investigation and Counterintelligence Action:

29. Rabble-Rouser Index (1967)
30. Agitator Index (1968)
31. Key Black Extremist Program (1970)

Type 6. Counterintelligence Programs to Disrupt or Neutralize Individuals and Groups:

32. CPUSA (Communist Party, USA) Cointelpro (1960)
33. Socialist Workers Party Cointelpro (1961)
34. Puerto Rican Nationalist Counterintelligence (1962)
35. White Hate Groups Cointelpro (1964)
36. Operation Hoodwink Cointelpro (1964)
37. Black Nationalist–Hate Groups Cointelpro (1966)
38. New Left Cointelpro (1968)
39. Black Panther Party Cointelpro Intensification (1968)

Type 7. Intelligence Activity for the President:

40. Investigation of Urban Ghetto Riots (1964)
41. Democratic National Convention Coverage (1964)
42. INLET (Intelligence Letter) (1969)

---

posing the Cuban Communists would, accordingly, be at least two steps removed from internal subversion, first because these persons did not promote communism in the United States and, second, because they worked against a foreign Communist power.

The bureau also conducted programs to investigate persons and groups in relation to possible or actual civil disturbances. These focused on civil rights activities, riot situations, and demonstrations against the war in Vietnam. Type 2 programs were largely uncon-

---

rity Programs, July 1, 1960 through June 30, 1961," quoted in Church, bk. 3, p. 466.

cerned with communism or the anti-Communist consensus of the 1950s, except in one respect. Hoover usually assumed—and insisted that his subordinates agree—that communists had instigated, or were, at the very least, involved in, any given social movement, demonstration, or other civil disturbance. These programs address directly the threat of internal disorder. Some Type 2 programs were broad and nebulous, such as Racial Conditions Reporting (Program 6), which sought to determine the liklihood of violence in urban neighborhoods. Others were far more coherent and specific, such as Videm (Program 9), through which intelligence on demonstrations against the war in Vietnam was gathered and teletyped to the White House.

Lists designating persons for intensive investigation and detention in an internal security emergency form a third type of FBI domestic intelligence program. They reach back past the Custodial Detention List of World War II to 1919, when the first chief of the General Intelligence Division of the Bureau of Investigation, J. Edgar Hoover, supervised the compilation of an index containing the names of 100,000 "radically inclined individuals."[10] Attorney General Francis Biddle ordered such lists to be discontinued in 1943, but instead they were surreptitiously maintained and, finally, sanctioned in part by the Emergency Detention Act of 1950. In 1960, a highly secret Communist Index was renamed the Reserve Index (Program 10) and expanded to include groups and individuals, other than Communists, who were considered to be dangerous. Type 3 programs trace their origins to wartime contingencies, were nurtured by the anti-Communist consensus of the 1950s, and were modified to address additional domestic threats throughout the 1960s.

The notion that extremists are dangerous to internal security goes back at least to the early 1950s, when certain Klan groups were placed on the first Attorney General's List of subversive organizations. But the FBI did not undertake significant numbers of extremist investigations until 1959 or 1960.[11] Type 4 programs, which use informants to penetrate and report on extreme or violence-prone groups and individuals, are largely an invention of the 1960s. Their proliferation parallels the growth of the civil rights, anti–Vietnam War, and black power move-

10.   In a few months, Hoover's system expanded to include index cards on 200,000 radicals, and grew in one year to contain the names of 450,000 persons (Max Lowenthal, *The Federal Bureau of Investigation* [New York: William Sloane Associates, 1950], p. 91).

11.   The number of extremist investigative matters received by the FBI climbed from about five hundred in the year 1959 to over twenty-five thousand in 1971 (Church, vol. 6, p. 350).

ments. Type 4 programs are by far the most numerous, accounting for over 25 percent of the domestic intelligence programs initiated by the FBI in the 1960s.

A second kind of list in this period designated persons for intensive investigation and counterintelligence action. Although persons on these lists probably would have been detained in an internal security emergency, Type 5 programs are distinguished from Type 3 because the intent of the former was to neutralize the investigatory subject in the absence of such an emergency. Type 5 programs focus on the prevention of social disorder. The Rabble-Rouser Index (Program 29), for example, was intended to disrupt the activities of persons who were thought to have a "propensity for fomenting racial discord."[12] It was renamed the Agitator Index (Program 30) in 1968, and its composition was expanded to include persons who were thought likely to foment disorder of any kind, specifically including antigovernment demonstrations related to the war in Vietnam.

The FBI Cointelpros form a sixth kind of domestic security intelligence program. They are related to Type 5 programs in that the latter were used largely to select individuals for concentrated counterintelligence attention. Type 6 programs can be distinguished from other FBI efforts because they employed aggressive and intrusive intelligence techniques for the purpose of disorganizing, harassing, disrupting, and diminishing the influence of individuals and groups. Standard Cointelpro operations included anonymous communications, use of fictitious organizations, forwarding financial data to the IRS, character assassination, confrontation of employers, friends, and relatives, electronic surveillance, providing confidential or fabricated information to reporters, constant interviewing of the subject, disinformation, innuendo, overwhelming and aggressive informant penetration, twenty-four-hour stakeouts, and "other means too numerous to mention."[13]

Although the FBI employed isolated counterintelligence techniques probably as early as the late 1940s,[14] the first formal Cointelpro was directed exclusively against the Communist party in 1956. Like several of the other categories, Type 6 programs arose specifically out of the anti-Communist consensus of the 1950s, but were broadened to in-

12.   C. D. Brennan to W. C. Sullivan, August 3, 1967 quoted in Church, bk. 3, pp. 510–11.

13.   Director, FBI (157-9-4), to SAC, Birmingham (157-833), "Counterintelligence Program/Internal Security/Disruption of Hate Groups/(United Klans of America National Klonvocation)," June 27, 1966, p. 2.

14.   See note 1 above.

clude an ever-wider circle of domestic groups and citizens throughout the 1960s. By 1964, the White Hate Groups Cointelpro (Program 35) could claim no relationship to the threat of communism. Type 6 programs represent instead an effort on the part of the FBI to direct state powers against individuals and groups without reference to the legal system.

Finally, certain domestic intelligence operations were ordered by the president or his close associates. Some, like the Investigation of Urban Ghetto Riots (Program 40), generated significant publicity and even fanfare. Others involved special arrangements between the White House and obliging bureaucrats at the bureau. The Democratic National Convention Coverage (Program 41) is an example. In this highly secret operation, presidential aides Bill Moyers and Walter Jenkins directed the FBI to establish a special squad to gather civil disturbance and political intelligence relating to the 1964 convention in Atlantic City.[15] Type 7 programs had little to do with subversion and Communist threats to internal security and much to do with the time-honored tradition of close relations between the chief executive and the FBI director.

The individual domestic intelligence programs within each type exhibit certain obvious historical and functional similarities. In addition, programs within a given type also bear a strong analytical resemblance to one another when examined with respect to three characteristics: autonomy in policy formation, insularity of operations, and severity of intelligence methods. Table 5.3 presents a brief description of each of the forty-two domestic security intelligence programs considered in this analysis, together with an assessment of their associated characteristics.

For every category of program, there is striking empirical consistency in all three characteristics. For example, within Type 6 programs (domestic counterintelligence) and Type 5 programs (Cointelpro targeting lists), the mode of intelligence was always disruptive. Strictly speaking, the term *counterintelligence* refers to the measures that security forces of one nation undertake to disable the intelligence operations of another, especially against the agents of hostile foreign powers and in time of war. In this situation, a state of emergency is presumed, and such operations have historically taken place within or near a theater of military conflict. The FBI domestic Cointelpros adapted and redirected foreign counterintelligence methods in an ef-

15.   Church, bk. 2, pp. 117–19; Church, vol. 6, pp. 175, 623–37.

Table 5.3
Characteristics of FBI Domestic Security Intelligence Programs
(Programs Implemented 1960–1970)

Program/ Date	Description	Intelligence Mode	Autonomy	Insularity

Type 1. Investigation of Communist-infiltrated and Communist-related Groups and Individuals:

Program/ Date	Description	Intelligence Mode	Autonomy	Insularity
(1) Investigation of Cuban activities (intensification, 1961) 3:467[a]	Expanded coverage of pro-Cuban groups and individuals	Largely passive. Some informant penetration of pro- and anti-Castro groups	Low to moderate. Directly related to Bay of Pigs operation	Moderate. Known to IIC (Interdepartmental Intelligence Conference) and WH (White House) (Bundy). President JFK advised by Hoover
(2) CIRM (Communist Influence in Racial Matters) (Cominfil expansion, 1964) 3:479–83; 6:609	Investigated/ reported Communist influence in civil rights movement	Largely passive. Extensive use of informants to gather information on civil rights groups	Low to moderate. Ordered by Hoover, even against advice from subordinates	Low. JEH statements to public and Congress. Wide dissemination of intelligence
(3) SDS Investigations (Cominfil intensification, 1965) 3:484	Effort to penetrate SDS with informants and intensify investigations	Largely passive. But aggressive effort to penetrate SDS with informants	Low to moderate. LBJ concerned over Communist role in antiwar demonstrations	Low. President and WH informed. Hoover attacks SDS publicly, to LBJ, in Congress

[a] Indicates the source or sources and page references on which each program entry is based: the letter *G* refers to a GAO Report (GGD-76-50) entitled "FBI Domestic Intelligence Operations—Their Purpose and Scope: Issues that need to be Resolved," February 24, 1976; numbers 2, 3, and 6 refer to Church Committee reports, bk. 2, bk. 3, and vol. 6, respectively. This reference is to Church, bk. 3, p. 467.

Table 5.3 (*cont.*)

Program/ Date	Description	Intelligence Mode	Autonomy	Insularity
(4) Student Groups Investigations (intensification, 1965) 3:485	Assessed subversive/Communist infiltration of student groups	Passive. Some use of informants	Low to moderate. LBJ, others, believed Communists were behind campus demonstrations	Moderate. FBI informed WH of efforts to track Communist influence in student groups

Type 2. Investigations Related to Possible or Actual Civil Disturbances:

(5) General Racial Matters (expansion, 1965) 3:475	Reporting and investigation of riots, racial violence, and demonstrations	Passive	Low. Program implemented in close cooperation with DOJ Civil Rights Div.	Low. JEH tells H. Appro. Com. FBI is following the "racial situation from an intelligence viewpoint"
(6) Racial Conditions Reporting (1966) 2:71; 3:476	Investigation/ detection of possible racial violence in urban areas	Passive	Low. 1963:AG asked FBI to cooperate in survey of racial conditions	Low to moderate. DOJ, WH received intelligence product
(7) Civil Disturbance Investigations (1966) 3:490, 492	Advance detection of protests against war in Vietnam	Passive	Low to moderate. Pursuant to demand for intelligence	Low to moderate. Intelligence fed to DOJ and state, local, and other authorities
(8) IDIU (Interdivisional Intelligence Unit) (1967) 3:495; 6:533	DOJ unit that used FBI reports, among others, to evaluate civil disturbances	Passive	Low to moderate. Set up in DOJ by J. Doar. Used tens of thousands of FBI reports	Moderate. Known to executive branch and within intelligence community

Table 5.3 (*cont.*)

Program/ Date	Description	Intelligence Mode	Autonomy	Insularity
(9) VIDEM (Vietnam Demonstra- tions) (1968) 2:72; 3:488; 6:683	Gathered in- telligence on demonstra- tions against the war in Vietnam	Passive	Moderate. In- telligence on antiwar pro- tests immedi- ately tele- typed to WH	Low to mod- erate. Rou- tine dissemi- nation to WH and intelli- gence and other inter- ested agencies

Type 3. Lists Designating Persons for Intensive Investigation, Possible Apprehension, and/or Detention:

Program/ Date	Description	Intelligence Mode	Autonomy	Insularity
(10) Reserve Index (exten- sion of Com- munist Index, 1960) G:69; 3:468	Targeted per- sons danger- ous to IS (in- ternal security) for investigation, possible de- tention	Aggressive/ passive. Per- sons on list subject to in- tensive FBI investigations	Moderate. Emergency Detention Act still in force	High. DOJ (Department of Justice) of- ficials under Kennedy ad- min. not in- formed of ex- istence of Reserve In- dex
(11) Cuban Section of Se- curity Index (intensifica- tion, 1962) 3:467	New section established to target pro- Cuban indi- viduals	Aggressive/ passive	Moderate. Directly re- lated to Cu- ban missile crisis	Moderate. Probably known by WH and DOJ officials
(12) Security Index (revi- sion, 1968) 3:515	Targeted per- sons for in- vestigation, possible emergency detention	Aggressive/ passive	Moderate. Revision ap- proved by DOJ, Office of Legal Council	Moderate. Known in FBI, DOJ, WH, and intelli- gence com- munity
(13) Key Ac- tivist Pro- gram (1968) G:74; 3:516	Targeted SDS members and antiwar pro- test leaders for intensive investigation	Aggressive/ passive	Moderate. Developed within FBI as a refinement of Security and Agitator indexes	Moderate to high. Known only in FBI, but intelli- gence prod- uct probably circulated

Table 5.3 (*cont.*)

Program/ Date	Description	Intelligence Mode	Autonomy	Insularity
(14) Black Nationalist Photograph Album (1968) 3:517	Identified and continuously located Black Nationalist leaders	Aggressive/ passive	Moderate. Developed from conference of FBI agents from 42 field offices	High. Known within FBI only
(15) Priority Apprehension Program (1968) G:68; 3:515	Targeted individuals for ongoing investigation and priority apprehension in an emergency	Aggressive/ passive	Moderate. DOJ studied standards pursuant to "Review of Presidential Emergency Action Documents" ordered by LBJ	Moderate. Known to WH and to DOJ officials
(16) Key Activist Program Intensification (1969) 3:518	Targeted protest leaders for intensive investigation and potential prosecution	Aggressive/ passive	Moderate. Intensified by FBI administrators. See program 13 above	Moderate to high. Known only in FBI, but intelligence product probably circulated
(17) Key Activist Photograph Album (intensification, 1969) 3:518	Identified and continuously located persons designated as key activists	Aggressive/ passive	Moderate. See programs 13 and 16 above	Same as above

Type 4. Investigation and/or Penetration of Extremist, Violent, or Militant Groups and Individuals:

(18) Klan Intelligence (intensification, 1964) 3:470	Investigation of Klan groups and Klan violence in South	Passive/aggressive. Informant penetration of Klan organizations	Low to moderate. Ordered by AG Robert Kennedy and president	Low. Wide publicity

Table 5.3 (*cont.*)

Program/ Date	Description	Intelligence Mode	Autonomy	Insularity
(19) Ghetto Informant Program (1967) 3:252, 493	Infiltration of black nationalist and urban ghetto organizations	Passive/aggressive. Over 7,000 informants operated	Moderate. AG Ramsey Clark ordered FBI to infiltrate SNCC, etc. Grew out of Kerner Com.	Moderate. Known to AG. LBJ quite vocal. But not clear if specific program known outside FBI
(20) Black Nationalist Groups TO PLEV Informant Program (intensification, 1967) 3:494	Obtained information about terrorists who might be planning guerrilla warfare during urban riots	Passive/aggressive. Informant penetration of black groups	Moderate. Developed in response to orders from AG Clark. Same order as above	Same as above
(21) Black Nationalist Organizations Investigation (expansion, 1968) 3:506	Investigations related to student disorder at Columbia and other colleges	Passive/aggressive	Moderate. Developed by FBI administrators but consistent with orders from AG Clark	Moderate to high. Known in FBI only, but reports distributed to WH, AG, intelligence community
(22) New Left Investigations (expansion, 1968) G:88; 2:72, 90; 3:506	Expanded investigation related to SDS activity at Columbia and other colleges	Passive/aggressive	Moderate. Same as above	Moderate to high. Same as above
(23) Stag (Student Agitation) (1968) 2:72; 3:505; 6:683	Gathered intelligence on and targeted student agitators for investigation	Passive/aggressive	Moderate to high. Developed by FBI administrators	Moderate to high. Known only within FBI, but intelligence product circulated

Table 5.3 (*cont.*)

Program/Date	Description	Intelligence Mode	Autonomy	Insularity
(24) Investigation of SDS Field Office Staff (intensification, 1969) 3:518	Effort to determine if SDS members should be targeted as key activists	Aggressive. All SDS regional staff subject to intensive investigation	Moderate to high. Program expanded by FBI administrators	Moderate. FBI public statements against SDS continued
(25) Investigation of Black Student Unions (1970) 2:75; 3:528; 6:709	Prelim. investigations of about 4,000 groups to determine their goals, leaders	Passive/aggressive	High. Developed following FBI Executives' Conference	Moderate to high. Intelligence product circulated
(26) Investigation of Marxist-oriented Communes (1970) 3:509	Identified, investigated, Marxist-oriented communes	Aggressive. Infiltration of communal living situation	High. Developed internally following explosion of Weatherman bomb factory in N.Y. City	High. Intelligence product probably circulated
(27) Investigation of New Left Terrorists (intensification, 1970) 3:510	Intensive investigation of all New Left/Weatherman–type groups, activities	Aggressive	High. Developed internally following 1969 campus disorders. Initially 450, then 741, new agents requested	High. Same as above
(28) Terrorist Informants (intensification, 1970) 3:525	Directed field offices to develop informants who could penetrate terrorist groups	Aggressive	High. Same as above	High. Same as above

Table 5.3 (*cont.*)

Program/ Date	Description	Intelligence Mode	Autonomy	Insularity

Type 5. Lists Designating Persons for Intensive Investigation and Counterintelligence Action:

Program/ Date	Description	Intelligence Mode	Autonomy	Insularity
(29) Rabble-Rouser Index (1967) G:73; 2:89; 3:492, 510	Cointelpro actions against persons with propensity for fomenting racial disorder	Disruptive	High. Developed in response to Pres. Com. on Civ. Disorder. Counterintelligence is strictly FBI	High. Intelligence product probably circulated, but Cointelpro aspect restricted to FBI only
(30) Agitator Index (expansion of Rabble-Rouser Index, 1968) 3:517, 512	Cointelpro actions against persons thought likely to foment disorder of any kind	Disruptive	High. Developed in relation to LBJ review of Pres. Emergency Action Documents. Counterintelligence was strictly FBI	Perhaps known to DOJ and WH, but Cointelpro targeting function restricted to FBI only
(31) Key Black Extremist Program (1970) G:74; 2:91; 3:530	Cointelpro operations against key black activists who were thought to be violence prone	Disruptive	Very high. Developed following FBI Executives' Conference. No outside inputs	Known only within FBI

Type 6. Counterintelligence Programs to Disrupt or Neutralize Individuals and Groups:

Program/ Date	Description	Intelligence Mode	Autonomy	Insularity
(32) CPUSA Cointelpro (expansion, 1960) 3:17	Counterintelligence program to disrupt Communist infiltration of mass organizations	Disruptive	High. Decision to target mass organizations made by FBI administrators	Very high. Known only within FBI

Table 5.3 (*cont.*)

Program/ Date	Description	Intelligence Mode	Autonomy	Insularity
(33) Socialist Workers Party Cointelpro (1961) G:84; 3:17; 6:377	Counterintelligence program to disrupt Socialist Workers party	Disruptive	High. Decision to target SWP made by FBI administrators	Very high. Known only within FBI
(34) Puerto Rican Nationalist Counterintelligence (1962) G:84	Limited counterintelligence program to disrupt radical Puerto Rican groups in U.S.	Disruptive	High. Decision to target PR groups made by FBI administrators	Very high. Known only within FBI
(35) White Hate Groups Cointelpro (1964) G:84; 6:378	Counterintelligence program to disrupt Klan and Nazi groups	Disruptive	High. Decision to target Klans made by FBI administrators	Very high. Known only within FBI
(36) Operation Hoodwink Cointelpro (1964) G:84	Counterintelligence to create conflict between CPUSA and organized crime	Disruptive	Very high. Conceived by FBI administrators	Very high. Known only within FBI
(37) Black Nationalist– Hate Groups Cointelpro (1966) G:84; 6:383	Counterintelligence program to disrupt radical black and civil rights groups/leaders	Disruptive	Very high. Decision to target black groups made by FBI administrators	Very high. Known only within FBI

Table 5.3 (*cont.*)

Program/ Date	Description	Intelligence Mode	Autonomy	Insularity
(38) New Left Cointelpro (1968) G:84; 6:395	Counterintelligence program to disrupt protesting groups and individuals	Disruptive	Very high. Developed by FBI administrators	Very high. Known only within FBI
(39) Black Panther Party (BNHG Cointelpro intensification, 1968) 3:22	Counterintelligence activity to disrupt Black Panther party, which also affected United Slaves, SDS, etc.	Disruptive	Very high. Developed by FBI administrators	Very high. Known only within FBI
Type 7. Intelligence Activity for the President:				
(40) Investigation of Urban Ghetto Riots (1964) 3:475	Investigation of riots in 9 cities, summer 1964	Passive	Ordered by President Johnson	Low. LBJ made investigation public at press conference
(41) Democratic Nat. Convention Coverage (1964) 2:117	Protected and provided political intelligence for the president	Passive	Requested by WH	Highly secret. Need-to-know basis only
(42) INLET (Intelligence Letter) (1969) 6:368	Furnished high-level intelligence data to AG and president	Passive	Developed by FBI administrators, origin of idea unknown	Known to AG, WH, and probably to others

fort to contain the Communist party and stem the tide of public disorder at home.

The FBI domestic Cointelpros were created and conducted with a uniformily high degree of autonomy. No piece of legislation, regulation, executive order, or cabinet-level administrative directive has come to light that recognizes the existence of any of the Cointelpros or the targeting lists related to them. In every case, bureau administrators recommended the establishment of such a program to the FBI director. Without exception, each Cointelpro was implemented solely on the authority of an internal memorandum initiated by J. Edgar Hoover. Although many Cointelpro targets such as the Klan, the Students for a Democratic Society, and the Black Panther party were unpopular in government circles, no one outside the FBI advocated covert actions to undermine them.

And, finally, Type 5 and 6 programs were clearly the most highly insulated domestic programs, not only in the FBI but perhaps within the entire government. No evidence has come to light that indicates that any attorney general, president, or Congress was informed of the bureau's intention to establish any particular domestic Cointelpro. There was no congressional oversight, authorization, or specific appropriation for any of the Cointelpros. Extraordinary precautions were taken to ensure that these programs would remain unknown to persons not employed by the FBI. Most internal communications, for example, carried an admonition such as: "You are cautioned that the nature of this new endeavor is such that under no circumstances should the existence of the program be made known outside the bureau and appropriate within-office security should be afforded this sensitive operation."[16] Type 5 and 6 programs were completely insulated from all other state and nonstate actors for more than fifteen years.

Dramatic yet systematic variation can be observed between the different categories of programs. For example, when compared with the Cointelpros, Type 1 programs (investigations related to domestic communism) and Type 2 programs (investigations of civil disturbances) rated at the opposite end of the scale for all three characteristics. Autonomy of policy formation was low or low to moderate for every program. In the investigation of General Racial Matters (Program 5), the FBI worked in close association with the Civil Rights Division of the Department of Justice. Two years later, the department set up its own

16.   Director, FBI, to SAC Albany, "Counterintelligence Program/Internal Security/ Disruption of the New Left," May 10, 1968, pp. 2–3.

group to monitor civil disturbances known as the Interdivisional Intelligence Unit, or IDIU (Program 8). It was authorized by Attorney General Ramsey Clark and set up by Assistant Attorney General John Doar.

Type 1 and 2 programs were often based on policies developed in conjunction with the White House and the Department of Justice. Cominfil investigations of the SDS (Program 3) and of student groups (Program 4) were holdovers from the anti-Communist consensus established in the early 1950s. This amounted to a general policy orientation that Communist activity in the United States would not be tolerated. The Congress had made its will known in the McCarran Act in 1950 and in the Communist Control Act of 1954. Successive presidents had endorsed the anti-Communist policies, and President Johnson approved FBI investigations of antiwar and student groups because "there was no doubt in his mind that they [Communists] were behind the disturbances [demonstrations against the war in Vietnam] that have already occurred."[17]

With respect to insularity, several of the Type 1 and 2 programs collected intelligence for the purpose of broad dissemination. Reports from the Civil Disturbance Investigations (Program 7) were routinely fed to the Department of Justice, the White House, the wider intelligence community, and state and local authorities. Intelligence from the Videm investigations of antiwar demonstrations (Program 9) was available to most interested federal, state, and local agencies. And in the case of investigations of General Racial Matters (Program 5), J. Edgar Hoover specifically informed the House Appropriations Committee that the FBI was following the "racial situation from an intelligence viewpoint."[18] In general, these programs reflected acute, widespread concern in official Washington and elsewhere over what appeared to be an accelerating pace of urban riots, mass demonstrations, and other forms of social unrest in the middle to late 1960s.

The mode of intelligence employed in these investigative programs was generally passive. A large portion of FBI activity in this regard involved collecting public information on a group or other investigative subject and then analyzing and classifying the information for possible future reference. But most Type 1 and 2 programs went further,

17.   Memorandum by J. Edgar Hoover, 4/28/65. According to Hoover's account of the meeting: "He [President Johnson] stated he would like me to take prompt and immediate steps to brief at least two Senators and two Congressmen, preferably one of each Party, on the demonstrations in this country of the anti-Vietnam groups so that they might in turn not only make speeches upon the floors of Congress but also publicly" (substantially reprinted in Church, bk. 3, p. 485).

18.   Quoted in Church, bk. 3, p. 476.

using informant penetration as a technique for collecting intelligence.[19] In most cases, it appears that the way in which informants were used in Type 1 and 2 programs was largely passive. But the extensive use of informants in this regard raises empirical problems. It is often impossible to determine what effect, if any, informant coverage exerted on an individual or group under investigation. Without question, informants can be employed as a hostile or aggressive intelligence technique, as with the Klan, in which case overwhelming informant penetration disrupted and sometimes redirected Klan activity.[20]

But the use of informants is of analytical interest as well because it raises questions concerning the status of many FBI programs in relation to the larger state. The use of informants in FBI investigations was ubiquitous, and their deployment was solely at the discretion of the agent concerned and the agency he served. Informants were recruited, paid, and directed in the field by individual FBI agents. The guidelines that regulated informant activity were internal and unavailable outside the FBI. The numbers of informants, their names, their pay, and their record of performance for the FBI were classified and available only within the bureau. First Amendment questions regarding informants did not come before the courts because informants were rarely exposed, and the information they gathered was used for intelligence purposes, almost always unrelated to criminal prosecutions.[21]

The control of informants, then, even for Type 1 and 2 programs, was largely discretionary in nature. Accordingly, there can be no presumption that the mode of intelligence was definitely passive. When considered in relation to the three models of the agency of internal security,[22] this provides some empirical validation for the view that security arrangements that combine passive modes of intelligence with

19. "The paid and directed informant is the most extensively used technique in FBI domestic intelligence investigations. Informants were used in 85 percent of the domestic intelligence investigations analyzed in a recent study by the General Accounting Office. By comparison, electronic surveillance was used in only 5 percent of the cases studied. The FBI places strong emphasis on informant coverage in intelligence investigations, instructing agents to 'develop reliable informants at all levels and in all segments' of groups under investigation" (Church, bk. 3, p. 228).

20. Attorney General Katzenbach testified, "It is true that these techniques [the FBI informant program] did in fact disrupt Klan activities, sowed deep mistrust . among the Klan members, and made Klan members aware of the extensive informant system of the FBI and the fact that they were under constant observation" (quoted in Church, bk. 3, p. 240).

21. Church, bk. 3, p. 231.

22. See Table 1.

a lack of ministerial controls are inherently unstable. When an agency employs intelligence techniques that are not publicly circumscribed by institutional or legal instruments, it tends to move away from a model of a bureau of domestic intelligence toward that of a political police or beyond to an internal security state.

It is, however, still possible to make rough distinctions regarding the use of informants, and these can be related to the purpose of the program in which penetration techniques were employed. With the White Hate Groups Cointelpro (Program 35) the purpose of overwhelming informant penetration was to misdirect and confuse Klansmen and to encourage suspicion and distrust within the organization. With the related Klan Intelligence investigations (Program 18) the initial purpose of informant coverage of the Klan was to gather intelligence on the activities of members that could be used to detect Klan violence in advance. It is, nevertheless, extremely difficult to classify the mode of intelligence when large numbers of informants are used in a program.

For this reason, many Type 4 programs (penetration of extremist or militant groups) are classified "passive/aggressive," indicating that extensive use of informants most likely exerted a disorienting effect on the group involved, but that the activity of informants stopped short of disrupting organizational activity. In addition, Type 3 programs (intensive investigation/detention lists) are rated "aggressive/passive," suggesting that such investigations usually harassed the subject but employed passive techniques as well. In general, Type 3 and 4 programs occupy a middle ground between the Cointelpros and the Type 1 and 2 investigatory programs for all three characteristics, suggesting an agency most closely resembling the model of a political police.

With respect to insularity of operations, Type 3 and 4 programs rated moderate to high in every case but two. In the first, intensification of Klan Intelligence investigations (Program 18), the issue of Klan violence became politically charged against the backdrop of the presidential election and the Civil Rights Act of 1964. President Johnson made it a major national issue, even giving details of the program in nationally televised news conferences.[23] In the second, the Reserve Index (Program 10), there is no evidence that the existence of the program was made known to Justice Department officials or to the White House during the Kennedy administration. This may be because certain index programs had historically been hidden by the FBI director from the attorney general, after Francis Biddle had ordered the wartime Custodial Detention List destroyed in 1943.

23. *New York Times*, August 9, 1964, p. 1.

This middle tier of programs (Types 3 and 4) also exibited generally middle range autonomy in policy formation. For example, Type 3 programs (intensive investigation/detention lists) could claim some relation to legislative sanction because the concept of emergency detention had been codified in the Emergency Detention Act of 1950. But this connection must not be overrated because none of the lists conformed to the requirements of the act, and some directly flaunted it. Because the act was on the books, however, the FBI usually sought guidance from the Department of Justice in developing standards for the programs, especially when they diverged significantly from those mandated by the act. Accordingly, the revision of the Security Index (Program 12) was approved by the Justice Department's Office of Legal Counsel, and the Priority Apprehension index (Program 15) was studied by the department in relation to a review of presidential emergency action documents ordered by President Johnson.

And finally, Type 4 programs (investigation/penetration of extremist and militant groups) exibited medium-to-high autonomy in goal formation, with a definite trend emerging toward greater policymaking autonomy after 1968. Prior to that year, Type 4 programs reflected the sanction of higher executive authorities.[24] The intensification of Klan intelligence, for example, was directly and publicly ordered by the attorney general and the president. In addition, the Ghetto Informant and the Black Nationalist Toplev Informant operations (Programs 19 and 20) were a direct result of specific written orders from Attorney General Ramsey Clark. Moreover, the expansion of Black Nationalist and New Left investigations (Programs 21 and 22), though initiated by FBI administrators, were also consistent with the orders from the attorney general.

Following 1968, however, the FBI appeared to take the bit in its mouth when implementing Type 4 programs, expanding such operations more in response to current events than to direction from higher executive authorities. For example, the Investigation of SDS Field Office Staff (Program 24) appears to have been undertaken on the initiative of FBI administrators. And the Investigation of Black Student Unions (Program 25) originated at the FBI Executives Conference in 1970. That year, the FBI undertook Investigation of Marxist-oriented

24.   Type 4 programs clustered around 1967, the year in which President Johnson created the National Advisory Commission of Civil Disorders. It was charged with investigating "the origins of the recent major civil disorders in our cities" and with making recommendations for "the development of methods and techniques for averting or controlling such disorders" (quoted in Church, bk. 3, p. 491).

Communes (Program 26) immediately following the explosion of a Weatherman bomb factory in New York City. The campus disorders at Columbia University and elsewhere in 1969 resulted in the Investigation of New Left Terrorists (Program 27) and a Terrorist Informants operation (Program 28).

Each pair of program types can be distinguished both empirically and analytically from the others, because each suggests the presence and activity of a different kind of agency of internal security in a liberal polity. For example, Type 1 and 2 investigatory programs and Type 5 and 6 counterintelligence programs can be defined empirically as near opposites in terms of the autonomy, insularity, and mode of intelligence associated with them. But each also conforms analytically to what might have been expected. Absence of autonomous policy formation, relative permeability, and passive intelligence methods all describe an agency acting in tandem with the liberal state. In investigating, compiling, and disseminating intelligence on civil disorders, the wishes and goals of the FBI director cannot easily be distinguished from those of the attorney general, the Congress, most judges, the president, and a host of other officials at all levels of government. Here is the FBI acting as a balance wheel to mass democracy, to liberalism, and to persons voting with their feet.

At the other end of a continuum, the capacity to formulate highly autonomous policies in the absence of legal sanction and total insularity of operations combined with disruptive intelligence tactics describes a kind of sovereignty usually associated with independent states. With respect to Type 5 and 6 domestic counterintelligence programs, the FBI most closely resembles a state within the state capable of conducting coercive actions against individuals and groups on its own authority. These are the goals of an administrative elite whose ideas about existing social and political structures in the United States may or may not conform to public opinion, the Constitution, or the preferences of the elected representatives in an era of social and political dislocation.

Toward an Independent Security State

Table 5.4 summarizes the characteristics of the various types of FBI domestic security intelligence programs in the 1960s. Each pair of program types is associated with a single conception of the FBI as an agency of internal security. But notice that the characteristics of FBI programs and the security arrangements they describe only approximate the models of a domestic intelligence bureau, a political police,

Table 5.4
Attributes of FBI Programs by Kind of Security Agency
(1960–1970)

Kind of Security Agency	Type of Intelligence Program	Mode of Intelligence Activity	Autonomy of Policy Formation	Insularity of Operations
Domestic Intelligence Bureau	1: Investigations related to domestic communism	Largely passive	Low to moderate	Low to moderate
	2: Investigation of civil disturbances	Largely passive	Low to moderate	Low to moderate
Political Police	3: Intensive investigation/detention lists	Aggressive/passive	Moderate	Moderate to high
	4: Investigation/penetration of extremist groups/individuals	Passive/aggressive	Moderate to high	Moderate to high
Independent Security State	5: Counterintelligence target lists	Disruptive	Very high	Very high
	6: Domestic Cointelpros	Disruptive	Very high	Very high

and an independent security state as defined in chapter 1. There is a definite shading toward the increasingly autonomous and insulated programming that employs aggressive or disruptive modes of intelligence activity.

From the outset, for example, Type 1 and 2 programs used informants as a standard investigative technique. Because it is not possible to assess accurately the effect such informant penetration exerted on the individuals and groups under investigation, there can be no assumption that the mode of intelligence was entirely passive. It is probable that Type 1 Cominfil investigations altered the behavior of organizations like the SCLC and the NAACP because the leaders and staffs of these groups became aware that they were subject to informant, wiretap, and microphone surveillance. Although the FBI was never as benign as the pure model of a bureau of domestic intelligence would suggest, Type 1 and 2 intelligence techniques were generally more passive than aggressive.

At times, Type 1 and 2 investigatory programs exceeded the degree of policy autonomy and insularity of operations strictly associated with a pure model of a bureau of domestic intelligence, but they stopped short of that of a political police. They can be distinguished from program Types 3 and 4 across all three characteristics, but there is still a tendency for Type 1 and 2 programs to verge toward the second model. Similarly, there is also a movement in Type 3 and 4 intensive investigations toward the model of an independent security state within the state. Some Type 4 programs were characterized by aggressive intelligence activity with correspondingly higher levels of autonomy and insularity. But most of these stopped short of outright disruption, and the existence of such programs was usually—but not always—made known to superior officials in the Justice Department.

In contrast, Type 5 and 6 domestic counterintelligence programs conform precisely to what would be expected from the model of an independent security state. Both policy autonomy and insularity of operations are extreme by any standard connected with a democratic republic. And the mode of intelligence is unambiguously disruptive in every case. Although these data begin to suggest an overall movement within FBI programming in the direction of the model of an independent security state, there are two anomalies that require explanation. First, no program type clearly represents the concept of the FBI as a national police force. And yet it was certainly the case that, during this period, the bureau assumed many police functions in relation to a growing body of federal statutes that specifically required FBI intervention. Second, an apparent internal movement within Type 4 after the year 1968 presents a strong contrast with the continuity associated with the other program types over time.

Because liberals had delegated the function of internal security policymaking to the FBI in the early 1950s, few specific laws were passed that governed the programs the bureau might undertake. Although the FBI functioned increasingly as a national law-enforcement agency throughout the 1960s, it did so in accordance with criminal statutes unrelated to internal security matters. In general, domestic intelligence activity was not conducted pursuant to specific statutory authority, and intelligence investigations did not generate prosecutions.[25]

The FBI could not function as a national police force in the area of domestic security because the legal structure required to support such activity did not exist. The liberal state failed to generate an enduring statutory structure for a national internal security police perhaps because the contradictions were too weighty to be contained within the legal system. Even a national police force that enforced federal statutes unrelated to internal security required a kind of repudiation of federalism. In a sense, it was part and parcel of the emergence of the positive liberal state in the early 1960s. As the liberal state piled up regulatory and social welfare policies, it added a new set of national controls to the traditional police powers of state and local government.[26]

These events helped to generate a countervailing movement in liberalism characterized by the Warren Court's attacks on state and local police powers in the areas of criminal procedure, civil rights, abortion, privacy rights, and obscenity, among others. Whereas the Court had been unable or unwilling to stem the flow of national criminal statutes and the advance of social welfare and regulatory policy, it chose to draw the line against formal and legal powers of internal security. Authority for domestic security intelligence programs therefore continued to be vague and executive in nature and was not codified in a body of written law that could be openly enforced by a national internal security police force.

A second anomaly, that Type 4 programs related to the investigation of extremists increasingly suggested the presence of a security state

25. In a study of FBI domestic intelligence programs, the GAO specifically addressed the subject of prosecutions and convictions: "The cases we reviewed resulted in few prosecutions or convictions or even in referrals by the FBI—to appropriate authorities—for prosecution. Of the 797 cases sampled in which the subject was an individual, only 24 cases (about 3 percent) resulted in referrals by the FBI to a local U.S. attorney or to local authorities for possible prosecution. All of these were for violations of various criminal statutes which perhaps could have been investigated as criminal matters. None involved any of the internal security statutes under which the subject was being investigated. Twenty-four cases were referred for prosecution; 10 were prosecuted and 8 were convicted" (General Accounting Office, FBI Domestic Intelligence Operations—Their Purpose and Scope: Issues That Need to Be Resolved [Washington, D.C.: GAO (GGD-76-50), February 24, 1976], p. 138).

26. Theodore J. Lowi, "Europeanization of America? From United States to United State," in Theodore J. Lowi and Alan Stone, eds., Nationalizing Government: Public Policies in America (Beverly Hills, Calif.: Sage Publications, 1978), pp. 15–29.

within the state after 1968, can perhaps also be explained in terms of the liberal tradition. Up to and including that year, Type 4 programs were clearly associated with the model of a political police (Programs 18 through 22). These programs, to investigate the Klan, Black Nationalists, and the New Left, for example, exhibited only moderate autonomy and insularity because they were known to the attorney general or because they produced an intelligence product widely circulated in the executive branch. While they did employ informants and other aggressive intelligence techniques, they stopped short of disrupting the investigative subject. They indicate the presence of an agency of internal security acting in opposition to widespread public disorder.

In this respect, the bureau's relationship to the liberal tradition could be characterized as one of shared contradictions. Liberal presidents and attorneys general like Lyndon Johnson and Ramsey Clark were not prepared to tolerate the activities of individuals who would break the rules of the game and deny to others the rights and privileges guaranteed by the Constitution. For this reason, they authorized a series of initiatives in the middle 1960s to investigate and follow the activities of persons and groups such as the Klan (Program 18), black militants (Programs 19, 20, and 21) and radicals on the Left (Program 22).[27]

Following 1968, when liberals conceded control of the government to the Nixon administration, Type 4 programs to investigate extremists and infiltrate their organizations became increasingly aggressive, autonomous, and isolated from other units of government. The three programs implemented in 1970—Investigation of Marxist-oriented Communes (Program 26), Investigation of New Left Terrorists (Program 27), and Terrorist Informants (Program 28)—were probably unknown to any official outside the FBI. They were intended to disrupt the activities of the target groups and individuals. For these reasons, they are most closely allied with the model of the independent security state. An obvious explanation points to the absence of liberals at the helm of the state. But any account will also have to explain a wider, yet still systematic, change among FBI domestic security intelligence programs that occurred after the middle 1960s.

Table 5.5 displays the various programs according to the kind of internal security agency they suggest on a simple time line. The vast majority, about 85 percent of the programs, were implemented in 1964 and after. Of the eleven programs that associate the FBI with the

27.   These formal distinctions should not obscure the fact that programs to investigate the Klan and keep track of antiwar protest complemented the policy goals of the Johnson administration.

Table 5.5
Distribution of FBI Programs by Kind of Security Agency
(1960–1970)

Kind of Security Agency	Year Program Implemented										
	1960	1961	1962	1963	1964	1965	1966	1967	1968	1969	1970
Domestic Intelligence Bureau:		[2]			[1] [40]	[3] [4] [5]	[6] [7]	[8]	[9]	[42]	
Political Police:	[10]		[11]		[18] [41]			[19] [20]	[12] [13] [14] [15] [21] [22] [23]	[16] [17] [24]	[25]
Independent Security State:	[32]	[33]	[34]		[35] [36]			[29] [37]	[30] [38] [39]		[26] [27] [28] [31]

Note: Numbers in brackets refer to individual FBI domestic security intelligence programs as described in Table 5.3.

model of a bureau of domestic intelligence, ten cluster in the period 1964 through 1969. But there was variation in the form of the FBI that was much broader than Type 4 programs alone would suggest. In 1967, and after, a second significant trend can be observed relating to the seventeen programs that indicate that the FBI also resembled an American version of a political police. Thirteen of these programs were implemented in the four-year period 1967 through 1970.

These data indicate that the FBI changed from an agency of internal security largely compatible with the liberal state and its democratic institutions to one more closely tied to the secret machinations of a political elite. This trend can also be stated in terms of a shift within domestic intelligence programming toward increasing autonomy of goals, greater insularity of operations, and more aggressive modes of intelligence, with a definite break occurring in 1968.

Domestic counterintelligence programs, which suggest the presence of an independent security state within the state, appear to be somewhat more evenly distributed across the decade of the 1960s. Seven of the fourteen were implemented before 1967. But closer examination of the individual programs in this category reveals a separate movement that nevertheless reinforces the larger trend. Counterintelligence activity against the Communist party was first formalized as a Cointelpro in 1956. Four years later, the CPUSA Cointelpro was expanded to disrupt the activities of known Communists who were thought to have infiltrated larger organizations (Program 32). Although the program inevitably harassed legitimate groups, such as the NAACP, its primary focus was against members of the Communist party.[28] In 1961, a second Cointelpro (Program 33) focused exclusively on Socialist Workers party, a rival faction that had split from the Communist party and that followed the teachings of Trotsky. These programs clearly exhibit a very high degree of insularity and disruptive intelligence, but their goals may have been more widely shared because they were directed against Communists and the Communist party.

In 1964, the White Hate Groups Cointelpro (Program 35) first significantly expanded the concept of domestic counterintelligence programming. It specifically targeted twenty-six different organizations, ranging from highly related Klan groups in the South to a variety of Nazi and fascist-leaning groups in the Midwest. The White Hate Groups Cointelpro constituted a break with the past because it was the first attempt to disrupt and undermine indigenous groups that were neither communistic nor under the influence of a foreign power. It was also unique because of the large number of groups specifically slated for counterintelligence activity. As such, the development of the White Hate Groups Cointelpro antedates the expansion after 1964 of programs that suggest the presence of an FBI that resembled both the model of a domestic intelligence bureau and that of a political police.

But more, this program presaged a dramatic increase in counterintelligence activity—in terms of the volume of actions undertaken, the number of programs implemented, and the range of groups and individuals targeted for disruption by the state. The language used in 1967 to authorize the Black Nationalist–Hate Groups Cointelpro (Program 37), for example, suggests the broadened scope of activity contemplated. Agents were instructed "to expose, disrupt, misdirect,

---

28.   Church, bk. 3, p. 17.

discredit, or otherwise neutralize the activities of black nationalist, hate-type organizations and groupings, their leadership, spokesmen, membership, and supporters, and to counter their propensity for violence and civil disorder."[29] The authorizing memorandum specified that "intensified attention" should be directed at such groups as the Southern Christian Leadership Conference, the Student Nonviolent Coordinating Committee, the Revolutionary Action Movement, the Deacons for Defense and Justice, the Congress of Racial Equality, and the Nation of Islam. The memorandum also specifically directed counterintelligence action against Stokely Carmichael, H. "Rap" Brown, Elijah Muhammed, and Maxwell Stanford.[30]

The original program involved only twenty-three field offices, but was extended to forty-one offices in March of 1968. One of the goals of the expanded effort was to "prevent the rise of a 'messiah' who could unify, and electrify, the militant black nationalist movement." Martin Luther King, Jr., Stokely Carmichael, and Elijah Muhammed were named as likely candidates.[31] The term *Black Nationalist–Hate Groups* was not well-defined, and it did not have a specific meaning within the bureau. From the list of organizations and leaders initially targeted, it is clear that the program was intended to extend to groups such as the SCLC that could not be considered either black nationalist or hate-oriented. Under this program, the bureau cast its net more widely into the society, and it did so acting in the capacity of an independent state within the state.

By 1967, the bureau had established its Rabble-Rouser Index (Program 29) to direct counterintelligence resources more effectively against black leaders. This index represented an integration of heretofore largely independent tracking and counterintelligence systems. Two additional domestic Cointelpros were added in 1968. One was an intensification of the Black Nationalist–Hate Groups operation (Program 37), which directed the field offices to "submit imaginative and hard-hitting counterintelligence measures aimed at crippling the BPP [Black Panther party]."[32] The other was the New Left Cointelpro

29.   Director, FBI, to SAC, Albany, "Counterintelligence Program/ Black Nationalist–Hate Groups/Internal Security," August 25, 1967, p. 1.

30.   Ibid., p. 2.

31.   Director, FBI, to SAC Albany, "Counterintelligence Program/Black Nationalist–Hate Groups/Racial Intelligence," March 4, 1968, p. 3.

32.   Director, FBI, to SAC, Baltimore, "Counterintelligence Program/Black Nationalist–Hate Groups/Black Panther Party," November 25, 1968, quoted in Church, bk. 3, p. 22.

(Program 38), established in May and directed against "the New Left movement and its Key Activists." The documents that set up the New Left Cointelpro contain much of the same language as previous counterintelligence authorizations, but nowhere is the term *New Left* defined, and no organization or individual is named.[33] A cover memorandum that accompanied the authorization also fails to define the New Left or to provide examples of New Left organizations or Key Activists. It does, however, specify the reasons why the FBI established the New Left Cointelpro.[34]

Immediately after the New Left Cointelpro was instituted, the FBI director ordered all field offices to prepare in-depth reports "suitable for dissemination, for each college and/or university in their respective territories where organized New Left groups are in existence or where there have been campus disturbances during the past year."[35] These instructions resulted in hundreds of detailed analyses of activists and organizations at the nation's institutions of higher learning. At each field office, the special agent in charge selected, at his discretion, which New Left groups and activists to report. In most cases, field offices had already initiated domestic security investigations of protest groups. In addition, all offices were instructed to prepare analyses of potential counterintelligence operations against the New Left. One typical analysis, from the Chicago field office, identified the Students for a Democratic Society, the Student Mobilization Committee, the National Mobilization Committee to End the War in Vietnam, and the Chicago Area Draft Resisters as targets under the new counterintelligence program.[36]

The New Left Cointelpro represented a culmination of programs through which the FBI resembled the model of a security state within the state. It was open-ended and undefined with respect to tactics and targets. It was implemented in 1968, when the bureau significantly expanded its domestic security programs most closely associated with the

33.   Director, FBI, to SAC, Albany, "Counterintelligence Program/Internal Security/ Disruption of the New Left," May 10, 1968.

34.   "Our nation is undergoing an era of disruption and violence caused to a large extent by various individuals generally connected with the New Left. Some of these activists urge revolution in America and call for the defeat of the United States in Vietnam" (C. D. Brennan to W. C. Sullivan, "Counterintelligence Program/ Internal Security/Disruption of the New Left," May 9, 1968, p. 1).

35.   Director, FBI, to SAC, Albany, "Counterintelligence Program/Internal Security/ Disruption of the New Left," May 28, 1968, p. 1.

36.   SAC, Chicago, to Director, FBI, "Counterintelligence Program/Internal Security/ Disruption of the New Left," 5/[illegible]/68, p. 1.

model of a political police. It thus symbolized an overall shift in the middle and late 1960s from protection of the liberal state toward the creation of a political police and ultimately an independent security state.

It heralded a head-on collision between the FBI and the liberal tradition in the United States. The domestic security policies adopted by the bureau after 1964 were increasingly hostile to the spirit of liberalism. They persisted only because the FBI had developed secrecy and administrative controls to a fine point, sufficient to insulate its activities from the courts, the Congress, and the public. But by this time the causes of liberal political community had become the object of state disruption at the hands of the FBI. Liberals only waited for an opening through which to attack the bureau and assert constitutional controls. Within the liberal state, the FBI had in effect set up its own competing shop. The larger state would soon move to enforce its more enduring sovereignty.

CHAPTER SIX

Conclusion

THE STUDY of domestic security intelligence policy presents unique obstacles and unusual opportunities. Before 1975, a paucity of research materials precluded serious consideration of this subject by the scholarly community. Except for a few years in the early 1950s, internal security policy left little impression on the public record because it evolved within the executive branch and largely within the institutional walls of the FBI. Social scientists and historians failed to generate a literature of the bureau and the programs it operated, even though the staff and budget of the FBI approached the size of those of the State Department.

The bureau and internal security policy did not fit the standard paradigms applied by most scholars in the 1950s and 1960s. The FBI's passion for secrecy helped to disable students of public administration. In addition, strict observance of hierarchy and patriarchal forms of authority within the bureau, as well as persistent internal control of budgeting, personnel, and accounting functions, contrasted with major administrative trends of the period. With respect to policy, internal security powers circumvented the legal system and the system of interest intermediation. This meant that any analysis of security policy based on the social or political organization of interest groups and their relation to the government was bound to fail.

This book has proceeded from the understanding that the state reveals itself most clearly when confronted with a threat to its survival. Highly centralized powers and autonomous actions of the American polity are invoked time and again when U.S. military or territorial integrity is challenged. In this capacity, even the liberal state is a structure of domination and coercion. Because the highest and most compelling state interest is self-preservation, the state also acts against the sympathizers and agents of hostile foreign powers, as well as indigenous organizations that seek to overthrow the government by force and violence.

In the United States, the threat of subversion, espionage, sabotage, extremism, and terrorism has functioned historically as the domestic and moral equivalent of war. In time of war, niceties of civil liberty are suspended because government must protect the nation from conquest and invasion by an alien force. In an internal security emergency, there is likewise an inalienable state interest in detecting and controlling the agents of a foreign enemy or ideology that would place the state at risk. But internal security arrangements, like military preparations, do not depend on the actual outbreak of hostilities. The cold war military buildup to deter future conflict is analogous to the domestic security intelligence buildup to prevent potential subversion, sabotage, civil unrest, and even revolution. In both spheres, the liberal polity demonstrates its stateness.

Two lines of argument inform this book. One focuses on the internal structure of the FBI, and the other concerns the relationship of the bureau to the liberal political community in the 1950s and 1960s. The first suggests that after 1950, the FBI transformed itself from a bureau of internal security with delimited functions into an agency resembling more a political police and an independent security state within the state. This transformation is indicated by dramatic variation in the character of FBI programming, particularly after 1964, when the FBI first operated domestic counterintelligence programs aimed at indigenous groups in the South that were neither supported by foreign powers nor influenced by communist or fascist ideologies.

To evaluate the first argument, three models of an agency of internal security in a liberal state have been distinguished: a bureau of domestic intelligence, a political police, and an independent security state within the state. An agency that resembles the first model exhibits low autonomy in the formation of intelligence policy. In general, it is not well insulated from other units of government, the press, or public opinion. It employs passive intelligence techniques only. With the second and third models, the degree of autonomous goal formation, the ability to insulate operations from outsiders, and the agressiveness of intelligence techniques all increase.

The data, which are presented in chapter 5, indicate alteration in the form of the agency of internal security across all three dimensions. First, FBI policies became increasingly autonomous, beginning in the late 1950s, and this process accelerated in the middle and late 1960s. In 1956 and 1961, the bureau established formal domestic counterintelligence programs, with the goal of disrupting and neutralizing the efforts of the Communist party and the Socialist Workers party. These programs were not specifically authorized by legislation or by higher executive direction. In 1964 and after, the FBI director initiated additional domestic Cointelpros, which affected an expanding number and wider range of persons and groups.

Second, FBI operations became progressively more insulated from other units of government, from the press, and from the public after the middle 1950s. Following the Smith Act trials of Communist leaders in 1949, everyone knew that the FBI worked against communism. But by the middle 1960s, the bureau had achieved sufficient insularity of operations to enable it to investigate any individual or group at will and without the knowledge or interference of interested parties, the Congress, or the courts. Martin Luther King, leaders of the Ku Klux Klan, New Left groups, antiwar demonstrators, civil rights groups, fraternal organizations in black neighborhoods, and the nation's institutions of higher education all fell under the watchful eyes of the bureau.

Third, although the FBI employed isolated aggressive intelligence techniques against the Communist party as early as the late 1930s, the regular use of aggressive and disruptive modes of intelligence activity to neutralize non-Communist groups did not commence until the middle 1960s. The data show a sharp rise in penetration by informants into protest and civil rights organizations, especially after 1967.[1] In the next three years, the bureau targeted many new categories of groups and persons for intensive investigation and counterintelligence disruption. In general, increasing aggressiveness in the mode of intelligence activity kept pace with expanded policy autonomy and greater insularity in FBI domestic security intelligence operations.

These observations constitute strong support for the first argument because after 1964, FBI programming indicated the growing presence of an agency that closely resembled the model of a security state within the state. But the historical reality was actually more complex. Elements of all three models of the agency of internal security coexisted within the bureau. A larger trend toward expanded domestic security intelligence activity of all kinds emerged, but with a strong emphasis in the direction of the models of a political police and independent security state within the state after the middle 1960s. This development might have been anticipated because the intelligence product generated by lower-level intelligence operations feeds into and informs other activities, such as intensive investigation and counterintelligence, which are contemplated by the more intrusive security models.

These tendencies are best explained in conjunction with the second argument—that the consistent support of a liberal constituency was necessary for the tranformation of the FBI. Accordingly, this book has concentrated on establishing the contribution of the liberal political

---

1.   This trend is not restricted to protest groups. Communes, black student unions, and the SDS, among others, were included.

community to internal security policy in the 1950s and 1960s. The historical evidence suggests that liberal leaders from Franklin Roosevelt in the 1930s to Hubert Humphrey in the 1950s delegated internal security powers to J. Edgar Hoover and the FBI. Liberals loosened ministerial controls over the agency early on and were unable or unwilling to impose them again until 1975.

The liberal approach to internal security was founded in part on calculations of political advantage. President Roosevelt needed a way to deal with the wartime contingencies of probable Nazi sabotage and communist subversion. In the autocratic executive environment of the early 1940s, internal security was merely another presidential function to be executed without public debate in the national interest. In the 1950s, liberals sought a way to remove the issue of Communist subversion from the political arena; it had become an electoral liability for them in the context of sustained cold war. They threw their support behind the bureau, believing the issue of internal security would go away if it could be transformed into a set of routine administrative practices within the FBI.

In the context of the anti-Communist consensus of the 1950s, there could be little doubt about the job of the FBI. The liberal senators assumed that the FBI would pick up all the dangerous Communists in the event of an emergency, and they sought to give the bureau policy direction when they framed the Emergency Detention Act of 1950. They even hoped to crush the Communist party once and for all by passing the Communist Control Act of 1954. But beyond these two legislative enactments, the liberals left the field of domestic security intelligence policy to the discretion of the FBI director. In effect, they substituted broad-based public consensus for specific policy guidance.

J. Edgar Hoover was, accordingly, able to authorize extremely disruptive intelligence techniques against American citizens. At the same time, he could sustain the confidence of successive presidents and attorneys general largely because he and his subordinates instigated the specific policies of the FBI and could control the information that reached their superiors. The liberal political community, which might otherwise have functioned as a counterbalance to a repressive internal security apparatus, continued to support the bureau. No one told the liberals what programs and policies the bureau had implemented, and, for whatever reasons, they failed to question the authority of the FBI director.

After 1960, liberals discovered the political value of an effective security police, even though it required a reformulation of their theories about the nature of the threat and the role of internal security powers in a constitutional republic. Attorneys General Kennedy and Katzenbach pressed the FBI to enter the struggle to extend civil and voting rights to blacks in the South. They hoped to use the FBI to break up the unlawful activities of the southern Klan because state and local police refused to enforce the law. The Kennedy and Johnson administrations needed to show progress in civil rights, and solving a string of brutal Klan murders in 1963 and 1964 was a first step. At this time, liberal leaders altered their basic approach to internal security to enable their political police to reach and contain Klan violence in the South. They defined extremism as a threat to the national security and the activities of the Klan as subversive of the Constitution and laws of the United States.

Perhaps the bureau pushed its anti-Klan activities farther than liberal leaders might have expected or countenanced. In any event, by 1965 FBI officials had developed administrative controls that enabled them to operate a domestic counterintelligence program against the Klan without informing their superiors in the Justice Department, the White House, or the Congress. For the balance of the 1960s, the FBI continued to conduct intelligence programs that could not have withstood challenges in the legal system or in the court of public opinion. But to the very end of the decade, the liberal political community failed to mount a significant charge against the FBI or its aging director.

Instead, relations between the FBI and liberals deteriorated slowly, perhaps beginning in 1964 when J. Edgar Hoover referred publicly to Martin Luther King as a "notorious liar." Thereafter, often unsubstantiated bits and pieces of improper or questionable FBI activity seeped into the mass media. When cumulated, this information suggested that the FBI was engaged in a variety of activities that offended liberal values and even attacked their causes, including the civil rights and antiwar movements. In the summer of 1969, FBI agents testified under oath that they had tapped the telephone of Martin Luther King. But most liberals withheld their fire. The agency still retained its status as a sacred cow in American politics, even if many liberals found the statements and actions of its director more and more distasteful.

It was not until March 1971, when the Citizens Commission to Investigate the FBI stole more than a thousand intelligence documents from an FBI office in Media, Pennsylvania, that liberal entente with the bureau finally collapsed. The self-appointed commission released documents to the major newspapers that, for the first time, made the domestic intelligence activities of the FBI a part of the public record. Even though the publicized materials did not reveal the existence of FBI domestic counterintelligence operations, Congress, the press, and the public were outraged. A process was set in motion that led, in 1975, to a full-scale congressional investigation of all FBI intelligence activities. Exposure of these internal FBI communications prompted Hoover to terminate all of the bureau's Cointelpros in April 1971.

These events suggest the second argument, that liberal support was necessary to the transformation of the FBI, but that insularity of FBI operations was required if the bureau was to retain its liberal constituency. It was after FBI insularity was compromised in the spring and summer of 1971 that the liberal community, and the mass media that shared its perspective, turned against the bureau. The FBI could employ disruptive intelligence techniques against liberal causes only because liberals were willing to delegate internal security policymaking and programming to the FBI director and his subordinates.

Political expediency explains only a portion of the liberals' relationship to the FBI. It is true that Franklin Roosevelt welcomed political intelligence that the FBI provided. Liberals of the early 1950s did seek to diminish their political and electoral losses by removing the issue of communism from the committees of Congress and installing internal security powers in the FBI as a set of administrative procedures. Liberal presidents pressured the FBI to support their civil rights policies in the South, primarily by forcing a reluctant agency to infiltrate the Klan and solve major crimes in the early 1960s. But their support for the FBI was grounded in a deeper logic than calculations of short-run political expediency could supply.

It stemmed, in part, from tensions and contradictions central to the logic of the liberal state. In the *Federalist* papers James Madison had set the parameters of the problem: "You must first enable the government to control the governed; and in the next place oblige it to control itself." He and his colleagues had proposed a solution, and their Constitution proved to be sufficient for ordinary times. But threats to the sovereignty of the liberal state generated extraordinary conditions in the decades immediately following World War II—the threats of communism and cold war in the 1950s, and the public disorder in the 1960s that was manifested on both sides of the struggle over civil rights as well as in the organization of New Left groups and antiwar protest.

The American experience with internal security suggests implications for liberalism, for the FBI, and for the liberal state. As an ideology, liberalism possesses inherent limitations, especially when applied as a ruling philosophy of governance. In the United States it presents a shining face of the moon, extending civil and political rights to the masses in a conscious strategy to diffuse the powers of government. But precisely because it contemplates a weak state structure, liberal government also generates and even encourages challenges to the existing social and political order.

To cope with these challenges, liberals delegated extensive, concentrated, and unknown powers to the agency of internal security, hiding them away within the FBI as if they did not exist. This is the dark side of the moon where liberalism confronts an authoritarian adversary using authoritarian tactics as a means of dispatching it. In so doing, liberals risked the creation of a second threat, a state within the state, which would not be bound by the constraints of the constitutional order at the foundation of the liberal enterprise.

Democratic governments and peoples naturally fear the emergence of an independent security state, particularly in the United States, where police powers have traditionally been decentralized and vested in state and local authorities.[2] Conversely, Americans also fear subversion of their way of life and government, even at times when the nation has enjoyed hegemonic economic and military might in the international state system. They are accordingly reluctant to strip the agency of internal security of many of its quasi-legal functions. They are apt to grant higher autonomy and insularity to government when they feel that a palpable threat to the national security exists.

There is perhaps a tendency for internal security arrangements in a liberal state to converge on the model of a political police. As this book has demonstrated, such a drift is not uncharacteristic of the modern American polity. Indeed, the political police concept has, at times, supplied the kind of internal security with which American politics has been most comfortable. To be sure, disruptive intelligence techniques associated with an independent security state encounter demands for reform as soon as they are exposed. But at the other extreme, there is a natural pressure to increase the autonomy and insularity of a domestic intelligence bureau on the ground that it cannot otherwise adequately protect the security of the nation.

The political police is, accordingly, situated in a kind of legal or constitutional limbo. But this is more than mere analytical ambiguity because the experience of other states tends to confirm it. In Britain, for example, a former Military Intelligence (MI5) officer revealed in 1985 that "organisations such as trade unions, peace movements, and the National Council for Civil Liberties were regarded as subversive and were subject to infiltration and surveillance."[3] And in 1981, the inter-

2.   See Theodore J. Lowi, "Why Is There No Socialism in the United States?" *International Political Science Review* 5, no. 4 (1984): 375–76.

3.   *Manchester Guardian Weekly*, March 3, 1985, p. 5. The officer, Cathy Massi-

nal security section of the Royal Canadian Mounted Police (RCMP) faced similar disclosures: "The perception of threats to security and the concept of subversion were gradually extended [by the RCMP] to encompass a wide spectrum of groups associated with radical dissent, political, social and constitutional change."[4]

The existence of political police may not be acceptable to liberals and to liberalism under ordinary conditions. But when a threat is perceived, there is a readiness to engage the domestic intelligence powers. This expansion is propelled, stepwise, by the logic of promoting the national security. A tangible threat is identified and steps are taken to meet it; when a second threat arises, additional measures are taken, and so on. But because domestic intelligence is largely preventive in nature, there can never really be enough of it, especially in a world where armed conflict, ideological competition, and nuclear deterrence define operating conditions. There is, accordingly, a propensity for the agency of internal security to move into the zone of a political police and then to go beyond. But here, going beyond means building a domestic intelligence state within the state, but also, beyond the very tolerant limits of liberalism. And liberalism will go very far to accommodate the national security requirements of the state.

In the 1970s, the Church Committee and the Congress sought to decrease substantially the level of domestic intelligence activity and to establish institutional controls over security operations in the future. These took the form of standing intelligence committees in both houses of the Congress, a proposed legislative charter for the FBI, intelligence laws, and new guidelines for the conduct of domestic intelligence investigations, among others. These efforts brought the domestic intelligence community back in line with the ideology and legal structure of the Republic. Now that more than a decade has elapsed since reform of the FBI, it seems fair to question if that equilibrium still holds espe-

---

ter, charged that for fifteen years, MI5 had been "illegally wiretapping British union officials as well as human-rights and political activists" (*Time*, March 18, 1985, p. 32).

4.   McDonald Royal Commission, quoted in *Manchester Guardian Weekly*, March 3, 1985, p. 10. The commission concluded, "Security service surveillance was not directed by any explicit government policy or guidelines. Nor was there explicit authorisation for a number of the investigative and countering activities developed over the years by the RCMP" (ibid.). In South Australia, in 1977, a judicial inquiry of the state Special Branch found that the intelligence unit had not revealed its operations to the state government and that its files were based on "the unreasoned assumption that any persons who thought or acted less conservatively than suited the security force were likely to be potential dangers to the security of the state" (quoted in ibid.).

cially in the light of recently released FBI documents which indicate that the bureau "conducted extensive surveillance of hundreds of American citizens and groups opposed to the Reagan Administration's policies in Central America."[5]

Social disorder will come again. Domestic and ideological threats will arise. It is even possible that intelligence officials will perceive an internal enemy and act against it, irrespective of the nature and actual magnitude of the threat. The problem with national security is that when excesses are revealed, if indeed they are, it is too late to do anything about the cases in point. This argues that liberals should err on the side of safety. The domestic intelligence capacities that were dismantled in the middle 1970s could easily and quickly be reconstructed. There are, today, many more highly trained intelligence officers with more sophisticated means of collecting and analyzing information than ever before in American history.

The combined foreign and domestic intelligence budget increased by a factor of 3 in ten years to reach $25 billion in 1985.[6] This enormous commitment to intelligence activity in multiple centers of government is striking on its face. But when it is combined with new technologies for tracking and observing the movements, speech, communications, associations, and habits of masses of individuals, the potential is ominous indeed. It was possible to compile information on tens and perhaps hundreds of thousands of persons in the 1950s and 1960s, but the technologies—both administrative and electronic—now exist to collect, monitor, and analyze intelligence on millions and perhaps tens of millions of citizens. Employing such a capacity and learning to control it taxes the limits of political will and democratic resolve. This is especially true when juxtaposed with the rise of new and ever more deadly threats to the national security.

As the twentieth century draws to an end, the United States is confronted with the apparently intractable threat of random terrorist violence, both from indigenous sources and from fanatical sects and governments across the globe. Meeting the threat of terrorism, however, poses special challenges to the guardians of internal security. Catching a terrorist is, after all, something like trying to find a needle in a haystack; the problem is that to locate the needle, one must first line up all the straws. The question is not whether the nation now possesses the capability to track and peer electronically into the lives of citizens. If it

5.   *New York Times*, January 28, 1988, p. 1. See also *Washington Post*, January 28, 1988, p. A6, and January 30, 1988, p. A18.

6.   *New York Times*, July 7, 1986, p. 1.

is not already a fait accompli, it will be in the not too distant future. The question reverts, instead, to the issue of the limits of liberal tolerance pushed outward by the security requirements of the state. It is a dilemma that may ultimately redefine the nature of the state and the meaning of individual freedom.

Selected Bibliography

Books and Articles

American Bar Association. Special Committee to Study Federal Law Enforcement Agencies. *Preventing Improper Influence on Federal Law Enforcement Agencies.* Washington, D.C.: ABA, 1976.

Association of the Bar of the City of New York. *The Federal Loyalty-Security Program.* New York: Dodd, Mead & Co., 1950.

Bales, James D., ed. *J. Edgar Hoover Speaks Concerning Communism.* Washington, D.C.: Capitol Hill Press, 1970.

Barth, Alan. *The Loyalty of Free Men.* New York: Viking Press, 1951.

————. *Government by Investigation.* New York: Viking Press, 1955.

Belknap, Michael R. *Cold War Political Justice: The Smith Act, the Communist Party, and American Civil Liberties.* Westport, Conn.: Greenwood, 1977.

Bendiner, Robert. "Civil Liberties and the Communists: Checking Subversion without Harm to Democratic Rights." *Commentary* 5 (1948): 423–31.

————. "Has Anti-Communism Wrecked Our Liberties? The Liberals' Role in the Fight Against Subversion." *Commentary* 12 (1951): 10–16.

Berman, Jerry J., and Halperin, Morton H. *The Abuses of the Intelligence Agencies.* Washington, D.C.: Center for National Security Studies, 1975.

Biddle, Francis. *In Brief Authority.* New York: Doubleday, 1962.

Blackstock, Nelson. *Cointelpro: The FBI's Secret War on Political Freedom.* New York: Vintage Books, 1976.

Blackstock, Paul W., and Schaf, Frank L. *Intelligence, Espionage, Counterespionage, and Covert Operations: A Guide to Information Sources.* Detroit: Gale Research Company, 1978.

201

Blum, Richard H., ed. *Surveillance and Espionage in a Free Society: A Report by the Planning Group on Intelligence and Security to the Policy Council of the Democratic National Committee.* New York: Praeger, 1972.

Bontecou, Eleanor. *The Federal Loyalty-Security Program.* Ithaca: Cornell University Press, 1953.

Bouza, Anthony J. *Police Intelligence: The Operations of an Investigative Unit.* New York: AMS Press, 1976.

Brock, Clifton. *Americans for Democratic Action: Its Role in National Politics.* Washington, D.C.: Public Affairs Press, 1962.

Caute, David. *The Great Fear: The Anti-Communist Purge Under Truman and Eisenhower.* New York: Simon and Schuster, 1978.

Center for National Security Studies. *Report No. 103: A Report Comparing the Proposed FBI Charter Act of 1979 with Attorney General Levi's Domestic Security Guidelines, The Recommendations of the Church Committee, and Other Proposals to Regulate FBI Investigative Activities.* Washington, D.C.: Center for National Security Studies, 1979.

Chafee, Zechariah. *Free Speech in the United States.* Cambridge, Mass.: Harvard University Press, 1941.

Clark, Ramsey. *Crime in America.* New York: Simon and Schuster, 1970.

Coben, Stanley. *A. Mitchell Palmer: Politician.* New York: Columbia University Press, 1963.

Columbia Human Rights Law Review Staff, eds. *Surveillance, Dataveillance, and Personal Freedoms: Use and Abuse of Information Technology.* Fair Lawn, N.J.: R. E. Burdick, 1973.

Cook, Fred J. *The FBI Nobody Knows.* New York: Pyramid, 1965.

———. *The Nightmare Decade: The Life and Times of Senator Joe McCarthy.* New York: Random House, 1971.

Costello, Mary. "FBI in Transition." Editorial Research Reports. Washington, D.C.: Congressional Quarterly, Inc., 1977, pp. 723–44.

Cowan, Paul, et al. *State Secrets: Police Surveillance in America.* New York: Holt, Rinehart and Winston, 1974.

Craig, Gordon A. *The Politics of the Prussian Army, 1640–1945.* Oxford: Clarendon Press, 1955.

Demaris, Ovid. *The Director: An Oral Biography*. New York: Harper's Magazine Press, 1975.

Donner, Frank J. "How J. Edgar Hoover Created His Intelligence Powers." *Civil Liberties Review* 3 (February–March 1977): 34–51.

———. *The Age of Surveillance: The Aims and Methods of America's Political Intelligence System*. New York: Alfred A. Knopf, 1980.

Dorsen, Norman, and Gillers, Stephen, eds. *None of Your Business: Government Secrecy in America*. New York: Viking Press, 1974.

Douglas, Paul H. *In the Fullness of Time: The Memoirs of Paul H. Douglas*. New York: Harcourt Brace Jovanovich, 1971.

Elliff, John T. *Crime, Dissent, and the Attorney General: The Justice Department in the 1960's*. Beverly Hills, Calif.: Sage Publications, 1971.

———. *The Reform of FBI Intelligence Operations*. Princeton: Princeton University Press, 1979.

Epstein, Edward J. *Agency of Fear*. New York: G. P. Putnam's Sons, 1977.

Felt, W. Mark. *The FBI Pyramid from the Inside*. New York: G. P. Putnam's Sons, 1979.

Finegold, Kenneth, and Skocpol, Theda. "State Capacity and Economic Intervention in the Early New Deal." *Political Science Quarterly* 97 (1982).

Freeland, Richard M. *The Truman Doctrine and the Origins of McCarthyism*. New York: Schocken Books, 1974.

Fried, Richard M. *Men Against McCarthy*. New York: Columbia University Press, 1976.

Garrow, David J. *Bearing the Cross: Martin Luther King Jr., and the Southern Christian Leadership Conference*. New York: William Morrow, 1976.

———. *The FBI and Martin Luther King, Jr*. New York: Penguin Books, 1981.

Gerth, H. H., and Mills, C. Wright, eds. *From Max Weber: Essays in Sociology*. New York: Oxford University Press, 1980.

Goldstein, Robert J. *Political Repression in Modern America*. Cambridge, Mass.: Schenkman, 1978.

Goodell, Charles. *Political Prisoners in the United States*. New York: Random House, 1973.

Gorman, Joseph Bruce. *Kefauver: A Political Biography*. New York: Oxford University Press, 1971.

Griffith, Robert. *The Politics of Fear*. Lexington: University Press of Kentucky, 1970.

Griffith, Robert et al. *The Spector: Original Essays on the Cold War and the Origins of McCarthyism*. New York: New Viewpoints, 1974.

Halperin, Morton H. et al. *The Lawless State: The Crimes of the U.S. Intelligence Agencies*. New York: Penguin Books, 1976.

Halperin, Morton H., and Hoffman, Daniel N. *Top Secret: National Security and the Right to Know*. Washington, D.C.: New Republic Books, 1977.

Hamby, Alonzo L. *Beyond the New Deal: Harry S. Truman and American Liberalism*. New York: Columbia University Press, 1976.

Hamilton, James. *The Power to Probe: A Study of Congressional Investigations*. New York: Random House, 1976.

Hartz, Louis. *The Liberal Tradition in America*. New York: Harcourt Brace Jovanovich, 1955.

Harvard University. Institute of Politics. *Report of the Study Group on Intelligence Activities*. Boston: Institute of Politics, 1976.

Haynes, John Earle. *Dubious Alliance The Making of Minnesotas's DFL Party*. Minneapolis: University of Minnesota Press, 1984.

Hook Sidney. *Heresy, Yes—Conspiracy, No*. New York: John Day, 1953.

———. *Political Power and Personal Freedom*. New York: Criterion, 1959.

Jensen, Joan M. *The Price of Vigilance*. Chicago: Rand McNally, 1968.

Johnson, Loch K. *A Season of Inquiry: The Senate Intelligence Investigation*. Lexington: University Press of Kentucky, 1985.

Katzenstein, Peter J., ed. *Between Power and Plenty*. Madison: University of Wisconsin Press, 1978.

Kaufman, Herbert. *The Forest Ranger: A Study in Administrative Behavior*. Baltimore: Johns Hopkins University Press, 1967.

Kelly, Alfred H. et al. *The American Constitution: Its Origins and Development*. 6th ed. New York: W. W. Norton, 1983.

Key, V. O. *Politics, Parties, and Pressure Groups.* 2d ed. New York: Thomas Y. Crowell, 1947.

Kirchheimer, Otto. *Political Justice: The Use of Legal Procedure for Political Ends.* Princeton: Princeton University Press, 1961.

———. *Politics, Law, and Social Change.* New York: Columbia University Press, 1969.

Kirkpatrick, Lyman B. *The U.S. Intelligence Community: Foreign Policy and Domestic Activities.* New York: Hill and Wang, 1973.

Krasner, Stephen D. *Defending the National Interest.* Princeton: Princeton University Press, 1978.

Kristol, Irving. " 'Civil Liberties,' 1952—A Study in Confusion." *Commentary* 13, no. 3 (1952): 228–36.

Latham, Earl. *The Communist Controversy in Washington: From the New Deal to McCarthy.* Cambridge, Mass.: Harvard University Press, 1966.

Lewin, Kurt. *Resolving Social Conflicts: Selected Papers on Group Dynamics.* New York: Harper and Brothers, 1948.

Lewis, Eugene. *Public Entrepreneurship: Toward a Theory of Bureaucratic Political Power.* Bloomington: Indiana University Press, 1984.

Lowenthal, Max. *The Federal Bureau of Investigation.* New York: William Sloane Associates, 1950.

Lowi, Theodore J. *The Politics of Disorder.* New York: W. W. Norton, 1971.

———. *The End of Liberalism: The Second Republic of the United States.* 2d ed. New York: W. W. Norton, 2d ed., 1979.

———. *The Personal President.* Ithaca: Cornell University Press, 1985.

Lowi, Theodore J., and Stone, Alan, eds. *Nationalizing Government: Public Policies in America.* Beverly Hills, Calif.: Sage Publications, 1978.

Lukas, J. Anthony. *Nightmare: The Underside of the Nixon Years.* New York: Viking Press, 1976.

McAuliffe, Mary Sperling. *Crisis on the Left: Cold War Politics and American Liberals.* Amherst: University of Massachusetts Press, 1978.

Martin, David. "Investigating the FBI." *Policy Review* 18 (Fall 1981): 113–32.

Mitford, Jessica. *The Trial of Dr. Spock*. New York: Vintage Books, 1973.

Morgan, Richard E. *Domestic Intelligence: Monitoring Dissent in America*. Austin: University of Texas Press, 1980.

Murphy, Walter F. *Congress and the Court: A Case Study in the American Political Process*. Chicago: University of Chicago Press, 1962.

Murray, Robert K. *Red Scare*. Minneapolis: University of Minnesota Press, 1955.

Navasky, Victor S. *Kennedy Justice*. New York: Atheneum, 1971.

Niebuhr, Reinhold. *The Irony of American History*. New York: Charles Scribner's Sons, 1952.

———. *Christian Realism and Political Problems*. New York: Charles Scribner's Sons, 1953.

Nordlinger, Eric A. *On the Autonomy of the Democratic State*. Cambridge, Mass.: Harvard University Press, 1981.

O'Brian, John Lord. *National Security and Individual Freedom*. Cambridge, Mass.: Harvard University Press, 1955.

O'Reilly, Kenneth. *Hoover and the UnAmericans: The FBI, HUAC, and the Red Menace*. Philadelphia, Pa.: Temple University Press, 1983.

———. "The FBI and the Origins of McCarthyism." *Historian* 45 (May 1983): 372–93.

Pells, Richard H. *Radical Visions and American Dreams: Culture and Social Thought in the Depression Years*. New York: Harper & Row, 1973.

———. *The Liberal Mind in a Conservative Age: American Intellectuals in the 1940s and 1950s*. New York: Harper & Row, 1985.

Powers, Richard Gid. *Secrecy and Power: The Life of J. Edgar Hoover*. New York: Free Press, 1987

Preston, William. *Aliens and Dissenters*. Cambridge, Mass.: Harvard University Press, 1963.

Ransom, Harry Howe. *The Intelligence Establishment*. Cambridge, Mass.: Harvard University Press, 1970.

Reeves, Thomas C. *Freedom and the Foundation: The Fund for the Republic in the Era of McCarthyism*. New York: Knopf, 1969.

———. *The Life and Times of Joe McCarthy: A Biography*. New York: Stein and Day, 1982.

Roche, John P. *Shadow and Substance: Essays on the Theory and Structure of Politics*. New York: Macmillian, 1964.

Rogin, Michael P. *McCarthy and the Intellectuals: The Radical Spector*. Cambridge, Mass.: MIT Press, 1967.

Ross, Caroline, and Lawrence, Ken. "J. Edgar Hoover's Detention Plan: The Politics of Repression in the United States, 1939–1976." Jackson, Miss.: American Friends Service Committee, 1978.

Rossiter, Clinton L. *Constitutional Dictatorship: Crisis Government in the Modern Democracies*. Princeton: Princeton University Press, 1948.

Rourke, Francis E., ed. *Bureaucratic Power in National Politics*. 2d ed. Boston: Little, Brown and Company, 1972.

Rovere, Richard H. "Communists in a Free Society." *Partisan Review*, 19, no. 3 (1952), 339–46.

———. *Senator Joe McCarthy*. New York: Harper and Row, 1973.

Salisbury, Harrison E. "The Strange Correspondence of Morris Ernst and John Edgar Hoover, 1939–1964." *Nation*, December 1, 1984, pp. 575–89.

Schlesinger, Arthur M., Jr. *The Vital Center: The Politics of Freedom*. Boston: Houghton Mifflin, 1949.

———. *Robert F. Kennedy and His Time*. Boston: Houghton Mifflin, 1978.

Shannon, David, A. *The Decline of American Communism: A History of the Communist Party of the United States since 1945*. Chatham, N.J.: The Chatham Bookseller, 1959

Simon, Herbert A. et al. *Public Administration*. New York: Alfred A. Knopf, 1950.

Skocpol, Theda et al. *Bringing the State Back In*. Cambridge: Cambridge University Press, 1985.

Skowronek, Stephen. *Building a New American State*. Cambridge: Cambridge University Press, 1982.

Smith, James Morton. *Freedom's Fetters: The Alien and Sedition Laws and American Civil Liberties*. Ithaca: Cornell University Press, 1956.

Sorrentino, Frank M. *Ideological Warfare: The FBI's Path Toward Power*. Port Washington, N.Y.: Associated Faculty Press, 1985.

Starobin, Joseph, R. *American Communism in Crisis, 1943–1957.* Cambridge, Mass.: Harvard University Press, 1972

Sullivan, William C., with Brown, Bill. *The Bureau: My Thirty Years in Hoover's FBI.* New York: W. W. Norton, 1979.

Tanner, William Randolph. "The Passage of the Internal Security Act of 1950." Ph. D. diss., University of Kansas, 1971.

Theoharis, Athan G., and Meyer, Elizabeth. "The 'National Security' Justification for Electronic Eavesdropping: An Elusive Exception." *Wayne Law Review* 14 (1968).

Theoharis, Athan G. *Spying on Americans: Political Surveillance from Hoover to the Huston Plan.* Philadelphia, Pa.: Temple University Press, 1978.

———. ed. *Beyond the Hiss Case: The FBI, Congress, and the Cold War.* Philadelphia, Pa.: Temple University Press, 1982.

Trilling, Diana. "A Memorandum on the Hiss Case." *Partisan Review* 17, no. 5 (1950): 484–500.

Turner, William W. *Hoover's FBI: The Men and the Myth.* Los Angeles: Sherbourne Press, 1970.

Unger, Sanford J. *FBI.* Boston: Little, Brown, 1975.

Watters, Pat, and Gillers, Stephen, eds. *Investigating the FBI.* New York: Doubleday 1973.

Weaver, Suzanne. *Decision to Prosecute: Organization and Public Policy in the Antitrust Division.* Cambridge, Mass.: MIT Press, 1977.

Weber, Max. *Economy and Society.* Edited by Guenther Roth and Claus Wittich. Berkeley and Los Angeles: University of California Press, 1978.

Westin, Alan F. "Our Freedom—and the Rights of Communists: A Reply to Irving Kristol." *Commentary,* 14, no. 1 (1952): 33–40.

———. "Libertarian Precepts and Subversive Realities: Some Lessons Learned in the School of Experience." *Commentary,* 19 (1955): 1–9.

Whitehead, Don. *The FBI Story.* New York: Random House, 1956.

———. *Attack on Terror: The FBI against the Ku Klux Klan in Mississippi.* New York: Funk & Wagnalls, 1970.

Wilson, James Q. *The Investigators: Managing FBI and Narcotics Agents.* New York: Basic Books, 1978.

Wise, David. *The Politics of Lying: Government Deception, Secrecy, and Power*. New York: Random House, 1973.

———. *The American Police State: The Government against the People*. New York: Random House, 1976.

Yarmolinsky, Adam. *The Military Establishment: Its Impacts on American Society*. New York: Random House, 1976.

Yergin, Daniel. *Shattered Peace: The Origins of the Cold War and the National Security State*. Boston: Houghton Mifflin, 1977.

Congressional Publications

United States House of Representatives

Committee on Government Operations. *Inquiry into the Destruction of Former FBI Director J. Edgar Hoover's Files and FBI Recordkeeping*. 94th Cong., 1st sess., 1975.

———. *Secret Service and Internal Revenue Service Surveillance and Record Policies*. 94th Cong., 1st sess., 1975.

———. *Hearings: Notification to Victims of Improper Intelligence Activities*. 94th Cong., 2d sess., 1976.

———. Government Information and Individual Rights Subcommittee. *Hearings: FBI Compliance with the Freedom of Information Act*. 95th Cong., 2d sess., 1978.

———. *Report: FBI Undercover Operations*. 98th Cong., 2d sess., 1984.

Committee on Internal Security. *Hearings: Domestic Intelligence Operations for Internal Security Purposes*. Pt. 1. 93d Cong., 2d sess., 1974.

———. *Terrorism*. Pts. 1–4. 93d Cong., 2d sess., 1974.

Committee on the Judiciary. Subcommittee on Civil and Constitutional Rights. *Hearings: FBI Counterintelligence Programs*. Serial No. 55. 93d Cong., 2d sess., 1974.

———. *Hearings: FBI Oversight*. Serial No. 2, pts. 1–3. 94th Cong., 1st and 2d sess., 1975.

———. *Hearings: FBI Oversight*. Serial No. 33, pts. 1 and 2. 95th Cong., 1st and 2d sess., 1978.

———. *Hearings: FBI Oversight*. Serial No. 46. 96th Cong., 1st and 2d sess., 1980.

Committee on the Judiciary. *Hearings: Legislative Charter for the FBI*. Serial No. 52. 96th Cong., 1st and 2d sess., 1980.

———. *Hearings: Use of Classified Information in Federal Criminal Cases*. Serial No. 54. 96th Cong., 2d sess., 1980.

———. *Hearings: FBI Undercover Guidelines*. Serial No. 18. 97th Cong., 1st sess., 1981.

———. *Hearings: Intelligence Identities Protection Act*. Serial No. 92. 96th Cong., 2d sess., 1981.

———. *Hearings: Prepublication Review and Secrecy Requirements Imposed upon Federal Employees*. Serial No. 90. 96th Cong., 2d sess., 1981.

———. *Hearings: FBI Undercover Operations*. Serial No. 76. 97th Cong., 2d sess., 1983.

———. Joint Hearings with Subcommittee on Crime of the Committee on the Judiciary. *Hearings: Merger of the FBI and the DEA*. Serial No. 103. 97th Cong., 2d sess., 1983.

Committee on the Judiciary. Subcommittee on Courts, Civil Liberties, and the Administration of Justice. *Hearings: Wiretapping and Electronic Surveillance*. Serial No. 41. 93d Cong., 2d sess., 1974.

———. *Surveillance*. Serial No. 26. Pts. 1 and 2. 94th Cong., 1st sess., 1975.

———. *Foreign Intelligence Surveillance Act*. Serial No. 65. 94th Cong., 2d sess., 1977.

Committee on the Judiciary. Subcommittee on Crime. *New Directions for Federal Involvement in Crime Control*. 95th Cong., 1st sess., 1977.

Permanent Select Committee on Intelligence. *Disclosure of Funds for Intelligence Activities*. 95th Cong., 2d sess., 1978.

———. *H.R. 7308: Foreign Intelligence Surveillance Act of 1978*. Report No. 95-1283. 95th Cong., 2d sess., 1978.

———. *Compiliation of Intelligence Laws and Related Laws and Executive Orders of Interest to the National Intelligence Community*. [As Amended through 1 March 1983.] 98th Cong., 1st sess., 1983.

Select Committee on Intelligence ["Pike Committee"]. *Hearings: U.S. Intelligence Agencies and Activities: Domestic Intelligence Programs*. 94th Cong., 1st sess., 1975.

————. *U.S. Intelligence Agencies and Activities.* Pts. 1–6. 94th Cong., 1st and 2d sess., 1975 and 1976.

United States Senate

Committee on the Judiciary. Subcommittee on Administrative Practice and Procedure. *Hearings: Warrantless Wiretapping.* 92d Cong., 1st sess., 1975.

Committee on the Judiciary. Subcommittee on Administrative Procedure and the Subcommittee on Constitutional Rights. Joint Hearings with the Committee on Foreign Relations, Subcommittee on Surveillance. *Warrantless Wiretapping and Electronic Surveillance.* 93d Cong., 2d sess., 1974.

Committee on the Judiciary. Subcommittee on Constitutional Rights. *Federal Data Banks and Constitutional Rights: A Study of Data Systems on Individuals Maintained by Agencies of the United States Government.* Vols. 1 and 2. 93d Cong., 2d sess., 1974.

————. *Staff Report: Surveillance Technology—1976.* 94th Cong., 2d sess., 1976.

Committee on the Judiciary. Subcommittee on Internal Security. *Hearing: The Nationwide Drive against Law Enforcement Intelligence Operations.* 94th Cong., 1st sess., 1975.

————. *Terroristic Activity: Hostage Defense Measures.* Pt. 5. 94th Cong., 1st sess., 1975.

Committee on the Judiciary. Subcommittee on Security and Terrorism. *Hearings: Terrorism: Origins, Direction, and Support.* Serial No. J-97-17. 97th Cong., 1st sess., 1981.

————. *Hearings: Oversight of the Drug Enforcement Administration.* Serial No. J-97-10. 97th Cong., 1st sess., 1981.

————. *Hearings: Government Files: Retention or Destruction.* Serial No. J-97-64. 97th Cong., 1st sess., 1982.

————. *Hearings: Domestic Security (Levi) Guidelines.* Serial No. J-97-124. 97th Cong., 2d sess., 1983.

Committee on the Judiciary. Subcommittees on Criminal Laws and Procedures and Constitutional Rights. *Joint Hearings: Electronic Surveillance for National Security Purposes.* 93d Cong., 2d sess., 1974.

Select Committee on Intelligence. Joint Hearings with the Committee on Human Resources, Subcommittee on Health and Scientific

Research. *Project MKULTRA, the CIA's Program of Research in Behavioral Modification.* 95th Cong., 1st sess., 1977.

———. *National Intelligence Reorganization and Reform Act of 1978.* 95th Cong., 2d sess., 1978.

———. Subcommittee on Secrecy and Disclosure. *The Use of Classified Information in Litigation.* 95th Cong., 2d sess., 1978.

Select Committee to Study Undercover Activities of Components of the Department of Justice. *Final Report.* 97th Cong., 2d sess., 1982.

Senate Committee to Study Governmental Operations with Respect to Intelligence Activities ["Church Committee"]. *Hearings.* Vols. 1–7. 94th Cong., 1st sess., 1975.

———. *Final Report.* Bks. 1–6 and Interim Reports. 94th Cong., 1st and 2d sess., 1975.

Other Government Publications

Canada. Commission of Inquiry Concerning Certain Activities of the Royal Canadian Mounted Police. *Freedom and Security under the Law.* August 1981.

Commission on CIA Activities in the United States ["Rockefeller Commission"]. *Report to the President.* Washington, D.C.: Government Printing Office, Stock No. 041-015-00074-8, June 1975.

General Accounting Office. Report to the House Committee on the Judiciary by the Comptroller General of the United States. *FBI Domestic Intelligence Operations—Their Purpose and Scope: Issues That Need to be Resolved.* GAO No. GGD-76-50. February 24, 1976.

———. *FBI Domestic Intelligence Operations: An Uncertain Future.* GAO No. GGD-78-10. November 9, 1977.

National Advisory Commission on Criminal Justice Standards and Goals. Task Force on Disorders and Terrorism. *Report: Disorders and Terrorism.* Washington, D.C.: Law Enforcement Assistance Administration, February 1977.

United States Department of Justice. *Guidelines for Domestic Security Investigations.* Washington, D.C.: Department of Justice, 1976.

Index

Albert, Carl, 150
American Civil Liberties Union, 39; anti-Communist credentials of, 48; Ernst defense of FBI, 5–51; and internal security legislation, 40; support of FBI, 49–51
Americans for Democratic Action, 28–29; and internal security legislation, 40
anti-Communist consensus, 6, 160, 163–64, 193; effects/consequences of, 36, 55, 69–70; liberal contribution to, 28, 35–36
autonomy, 19–23; and the FBI, 71, 145; and security state operations, 18

Benton, William, 30
Berrigan, Phillip and Daniel, 140
Biddle, Francis, 61
Black Nationalist-Hate Groups Cointelpro, 12
Black Panther party, 5, 117, 131, 135, 138–40, 147, 149, 158, 175, 187
Boggs, Hale, 148, 150, 152
Bossi, 143

Chaney, James, 99
Charmichael, Stokely, 187
Church, Frank, 114
Church Committee, 86, 160, 197
Citizens Commission to Investigate the FBI, 115–16, 149–51, 194
Clark, Ramsey, 91, 124, 127, 133, 136, 139, 176, 179, 184
Clark, Tom C., 62
Cointelpro(s), 4, 144, 147; authority for, 175; autonomy of, 175; distinguished from Cominfil, 158; termination of, 153
cold war, 8, 10, 29, 148, 191
Cominfil, 175–59; investigation of Martin Luther King, 109
Communist Control Act of 1954, 6, 65–67, 176, 193
Communist party (U.S.), 30, 37, 67–68, 71, 72, 75, 101, 157, 160, 164, 186
Congress of Racial Equality, 187

Conus Intelligence Branch (U.S. Army), 142
counterintelligence, 11, 75; defined, 165

Deacons for Defense and Justice, 187
delegation: of security powers, 15, 17, 29, 49, 58, 69–70, 91, 195; threat to liberalism, 90
Democratic Farmer-Labor party, 29
discretion: and FBI agents, 177, 188; of FBI director, 110, 111, 155; and security state activity, 18
domestic security intelligence programs: authority for, 183; description and characteristics of, 166–74; typology of, 160–65; variation in form of, 175, 185, 191
Douglas, Paul, 30, 32; support of emergency detention legislation, 41–43
due process: and the Emergency Detention Act, 31; and FBI programs, 11; security exceptions to, 7, 148, 155
Dulles, Allen, 101

East Coast Conspiracy to Save Lives, 140
EDA. *See* Emergency Detention Act of 1950
Emergency Detention Act of 1950: administrative logic of, 56; and constitutional requirements, 31; liberal alternative to McCarran Act, 32; motivation of liberal sponsors, 43; origins of, 42; public policy v. secret administration of, 63; support from liberal press, 53–55
emergency detention plan, 62
Ervin, Sam J., 115, 141, 142, 149, 151
extremism, 130

Federal Bureau of Investigation: budget authority, 27, 111, 135; code of conduct, 26; disruption of groups, 6; disruption of Ku Klux Klan, 75–85; liberal constituency/support of, 7, 13, 23, 27, 33, 45, 72, 128; liberal opposition to, 135; and local law enforcement, 94; role in civil rights, 92–95; secrecy and,